The Krio of West Africa

NEW AFRICAN HISTORIES SERIES

SERIES EDITORS: JEAN ALLMAN AND ALLEN ISAACMAN

Books in this series are published with support from the Ohio University National Resource Center for African Studies.

David William Cohen and E. S. Atieno Odhiambo, *The Risks of Knowledge: Investigations into the Death of the Hon. Minister John Robert Ouko in Kenya,* 1990

Belinda Bozzoli, *Theatres of Struggle and the End of Apartheid*

Gary Kynoch, *We Are Fighting the World: A History of Marashea Gangs in South Africa, 1947–1999*

Stephanie Newell, *The Forger's Tale: The Search for Odeziaku*

Jacob A. Tropp, *Natures of Colonial Change: Environmental Relations in the Making of the Transkei*

Jan Bender Shetler, *Imagining Serengeti: A History of Landscape Memory in Tanzania from Earliest Times to the Present*

Cheikh Anta Babou, *Fighting the Greater Jihad: Amadu Bamba and the Founding of the Muridiyya in Senegal, 1853–1913*

Marc Epprecht, *Heterosexual Africa? The History of an Idea from the Age of Exploration to the Age of AIDS*

Marissa J. Moorman, *Intonations: A Social History of Music and Nation in Luanda, Angola, from 1945 to Recent Times*

Karen E. Flint, *Healing Traditions: African Medicine, Cultural Exchange, and Competition in South Africa, 1820–1948*

Derek R. Peterson and Giacomo Macola, editors, *Recasting the Past: History Writing and Political Work in Modern Africa*

Moses Ochonu, *Colonial Meltdown: Northern Nigeria in the Great Depression*

Emily Burrill, Richard Roberts, and Elizabeth Thornberry, editors, *Domestic Violence and the Law in Colonial and Postcolonial Africa*

Daniel R. Magaziner, *The Law and the Prophets: Black Consciousness in South Africa, 1968–1977*

Emily Lynn Osborn, *Our New Husbands Are Here: Households, Gender, and Politics in a West African State from the Slave Trade to Colonial Rule*

Robert Trent Vinson, *The Americans Are Coming! Dreams of African American Liberation in Segregationist South Africa*

James R. Brennan, *Taifa: Making Nation and Race in Urban Tanzania*

Benjamin N. Lawrance and Richard L. Roberts, editors, *Trafficking in Slavery's Wake: Law and the Experience of Women and Children*

David M. Gordon, *Invisible Agents: Spirits in a Central African History*

Allen Isaacman and Barbara Isaacman, *Dams, Displacement, and the Delusion of Development: Cahora Bassa and Its Legacies in Mozambique, 1965–2007*

Stephanie Newell, *The Power to Name: A History of Anonymity in Colonial West Africa*

Gibril R. Cole, *The Krio of West Africa: Islam, Culture, Creolization, and Colonialism in the Nineteenth Century*

The Krio of West Africa

*Islam, Culture, Creolization, and
Colonialism in the Nineteenth Century*

⌐

Gibril R. Cole

OHIO UNIVERSITY PRESS ⌐ ATHENS

Ohio University Press, Athens, Ohio 45701
ohioswallow.com
© 2013 by Ohio University Press

Printed in the United States of America
Ohio University Press books are printed on acid-free paper.∞ ™

20 19 18 17 16 15 14 13   5 4 3 2 1

Library of Congress Cataloging-in-Publication Data

Cole, Gibril Raschid, 1955–
 The Krio of West Africa : Islam, culture, creolization, and colonialism in the
nineteenth century / Gibril R. Cole.
   pages cm. — (New African histories)
 ISBN 978-0-8214-2047-8 (pb : alk. paper) — ISBN 978-0-8214-4478-8 (electronic)
 1. Creoles (Sierra Leone)—History. 2. Creoles (Sierra Leone)—Religion. 3. Creoles
(Sierra Leone)—Africa, West—History. 4. Islam—Africa, West. I. Title. II. Series:
New African histories series.
 DT516.45.C73C65 2013
 966.4004969729—dc23
                                                    2013020422

For
Khadija

Contents

List of Illustrations

MAPS

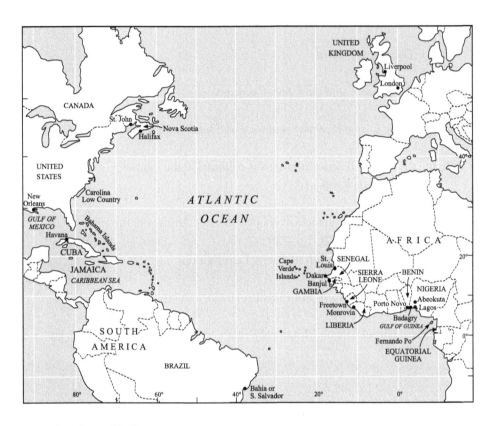

The Atlantic World

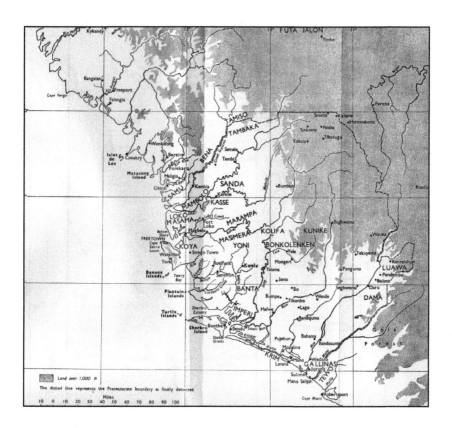

Sierra Leone and the Upper Guinea coast

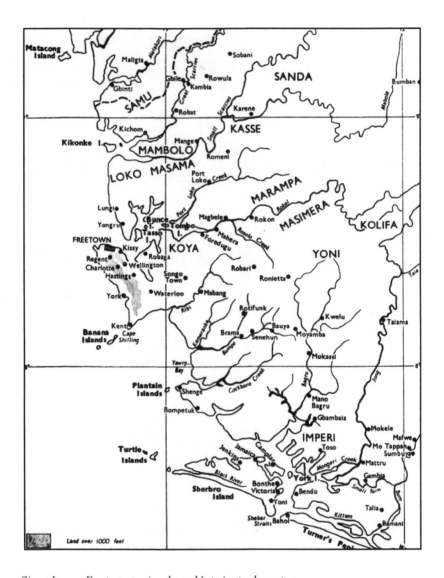

Sierra Leone: Freetown peninsula and Interior trade centers

Acknowledgments

This work is a revised version of a doctoral dissertation submitted to the history department at the University of California, Los Angeles. In many ways, it represents my long-standing interest in the evolution of Krio society, as well as the evolution of the role and place of Muslims in that cultural group. As a young student in Sierra Leone, I was always curious about the inconsistencies between what we were taught in school with regard to the history of the post–slave trade society founded in that country and what the people in Krio society themselves actually thought of their history. Frankly, there was very little discussion of Krio history, or for that matter of African history, in elementary or secondary school. What we learned of Sierra Leone or African history, for the most part, consisted of what happened after the Portuguese explorer Pedro da Cintra supposedly "discovered" Sierra Leone in the fifteenth century. Thus, my earliest consciousness of African history was inculcated, almost literally, at the feet of my maternal grandmother, who narrated her recollections of late nineteenth to mid-twentieth-century Freetown. She and other elderly figures were unabashed in recalling stories of incidents that occurred in the local communities, including embarrassing and sometimes life-threatening events they personally experienced. Some recollections, such as those of the multicultural demographic makeup of nineteenth-century Freetown and the religious fluidity, followed by the creeping encroachment of religious rigidity in both the church and the mosque, as well as cultural praxis, all fueled my budding interest in the development of Krio society and the discipline of history in general. Those formative days ultimately prepared me for the task of conducting research and fieldwork, including archival investigations and oral interviews, in pursuit of a BA (honors) degree at Fourah Bay College and a doctoral degree years later. To my grandmother, and all the "organic intellectuals" of the community who refused to accept the notion of a lack of historical consciousness on their part, I express my deepest appreciation.

I would like to acknowledge the helpful assistance of the personnel at the Sierra Leone Archives in Freetown, Sierra Leone; the Public Record Office in London, UK; and the CMS Archives at the University of Birmingham, UK. Also, the kind hospitality and friendship of Daphne and Reginald Cline-Cole (and Funke!) in Birmingham; Zainab Zubairu; and Ade Daramy in London certainly helped in easing the daily challenges of research work away from home. I would also like to acknowledge the contribution of several other people for their cooperation and support during the course of the preparation of this work, not all of whom I name here but to whom I will always remain personally grateful. Among these people is Haroun Raschid Cole, to whom I extend my thanks for his invaluable help with computer software issues at critical points during the writing process. I spent the summer of 2007 in Nigeria on a research visit, thanks to research grants from the Louisiana State University (LSU) Office of Research and Economic Development and the history department, respectively; while in Nigeria, I also benefited from the support of the department of history and Faculty of Arts at the University of Lagos, particularly Dean Ayodeji Olukoju, who graciously organized a public forum of faculty and students, where I gave a lecture and shared my research interests and during which I was the beneficiary of insightful comments and feedback from students and faculty alike. I remain truly grateful for the experience.

From the preparation of the manuscript proposal through the completion of the work, several friends and colleagues have provided much assistance and informed advice along the way. Foremost among these are Andy Burstein, Reza Pirbhai, Suzanne Marchand, David Lindenfeld, and former history department chair Dr. Gaines Foster (currently dean of the College of Humanities and Social Sciences); all of them read either the original proposal or portions of the manuscript and offered valuable comments and suggestions. I am also grateful to Darlene Albritton and Lois Edmonds of the history department and Interdisciplinary Studies, respectively, for their help in myriad ways during the course of the writing process. I remain very grateful for all their help along the way. Outside of LSU, I also benefited from comments and advice from Mac Dixon-Fyle of DePauw University; and last, but in no imaginable way the least, I owe a particular depth of gratitude to Ismail Rashid of Vassar College for his invaluable critical comments, keen insight on Atlantic World issues, and his thoughtful suggestions for changes to the manuscript. I am indeed also enormously grateful to the anonymous readers of Ohio University Press for their helpful and insightful critical review of the manuscript, and to the editorial director, Gillian Berchowitz, and series editors, Jean Allman and Allen Isaacman, for their patience and kind assistance during the course of this endeavor.

I must cite the Louisiana Board of Regents through the Board of Regents Support Fund LEQSF (2009-10)-RD-ATL-04, which ensured the completion of this project. My successful application for this grant was greatly enhanced by the patience and kind assistance of Ann Whitmer, for which I am very grateful. I should also cite the then LSU College of Arts and Sciences for a semester teaching release and leave of absence to ensure the completion of the book. And finally, to my daughters, Marie and Ajima, I say thank you for all the love and inspirational support, without which this work would have been doubly hard.

Introduction

TWO CENTURIES AFTER ITS ESTABLISHMENT as a haven for Africans freed from enslavement and captivity in the Americas and Europe and on slave ships, the myth of Sierra Leone as a colony of predominantly Christianized and Europeanized Africans has become an ingrained part of the postcolonial historical reconstruction of this West African country.[1] The eminent Sierra Leone historian Akintola Wyse, who argued for the use of the nomenclature *Krio*, instead of *Creole*, in reference to the descendants of the former slaves and captives, and who worked laboriously to establish their credentials as a distinct "ethnic group," has been credited with creating this myth.[2] Despite acknowledging the persistence of African elements in their culture and being critical of British policies toward them, Wyse insisted that the Krio were "in essence Black Englishmen, [who] would eventually be the agents for the propagation of European civilisation 'as beacons of light in darkest Africa.'"[3] It is a view of Krio society that obfuscates its religious, class, and cultural complexities.

There is no doubt that Wyse was among the most eminent and prolific intellectual architects of the Krio myth, but he was not its sole creator. Christopher Fyfe, the British government archivist at the time of independence and author of *A History of Sierra Leone* (1962); and Arthur Porter, the first Sierra Leonean head of the history department at Fourah Bay College, and author of *Creoledom: A Study of the Development of Freetown Society* (1966), also played a crucial role in laying the scholarly foundations of this myth.[4] The myth was systematically fleshed out by various scholars in subsequent decades; however, its most emphatic scholarly articulation was the publication of the volume commemorating the bicentennial of the Sierra Leone Colony in 1987.[5]

1

This work, *The Krio of West Africa*, focuses on the Muslims in the Sierra Leone Colony in the nineteenth century and challenges the underlying paradigms and received wisdom about the development of Krio society in the volume commemorating the bicentenary. It rejects the assumptions that Christianity and Europeanization were prerequisites for inclusion in a society that evolved out of the multifarious groups of Africans resettled in the Sierra Leone Peninsula. It argues that African Muslims played a crucial role in the evolution of Krio society, which included vital contributions to the social, economic, and political landscapes of nineteenth-century Sierra Leone and West Africa. Muslim agency was critical to the development of the evolving Liberated African community during the nineteenth century in several ways. The forceful assertion of their religious worldview and their African cultural praxis in the face of seemingly insurmountable odds, especially in their relations with the established Church of England and colonial state officials, ultimately enhanced the capacity of Krio society in general to maintain their sense of autonomy in the constricted social space of British colonial rule.

The leading scholars of Krio society do paint a complex portrait of the historical experience of the group, highlighting especially its "African" elements, social hierarchies, and economic fault lines, and the racist and deleterious impact of British colonialism on its development. These scholars, however, ultimately derive their intellectual cues from the British "philanthropic" sponsors, imperial proconsuls and missionaries, who narrowly envisioned the Sierra Leone settlement as a Christian- and European-oriented enterprise and loyal subjects of the British Crown. These cues produced the inelegant elitist and gender-biased characterization of nineteenth-century Krio society as a colony of "Black Englishmen" steeped in Victorian English values.[6] They have also been responsible for the production of a historiography that has concentrated largely on the Westernizing impact of the Christian evangelical missions on the manumitted Africans and their descendants, rather than highlighting the multifarious religious, ethnic, and cultural processes that molded their lives and historical experiences. It is a historiography that excludes the contributions of Muslims in the molding of Krio society, and unnecessarily renders parochial the country's historical experience. It is also an interpretation of Sierra Leone history that flies against the observations of nineteenth-century chroniclers, who were much more attuned to the ethnic, cultural, and religious diversity of the Sierra Leone Colony and its environs. Interrogated much more deeply, the historiography stands in stark contrast to the historical and contemporary realities, and indeed the lived experiences of the people of Sierra Leone.

The process of forging Krio identity in nineteenth-century West Africa was a dynamic and deeply contested one that pitted members of Krio society against one another, "outsiders," and British colonialists. Nonetheless, the development of Krio identity and society both allowed for and transcended ethnic, cultural, class, and religious differences. Ultimately, what distinguished Krio society was not its separateness from other Sierra Leonean ethnic groups, but its ability to absorb different elements from a variety of cultural backgrounds, and to continuously re-create itself in response to the changing social and political realities of nineteenth-century British colonialism. The malleability and adaptability of Krio society partly derives from the transatlantic and creolizing experiences of the first batches of repatriated Africans resettled in the Sierra Leone Peninsula in the late eighteenth century. These groups had not only gone through the crucible of enslavement and cultural acculturation in Europe and the Americas, but they had returned "home" to Africa, armed with cultural fragments from the different lands and climes that they had traversed, to reconstitute a new "province of freedom."[7] As shown in the first chapter of this work, subsequent generations of repatriated Africans, though arriving with much more grounded cultural elements, would not only amplify the themes of malleability and adaptability but creatively deepen the processes of creolization/kriolization in Sierra Leone.

It is within this expansive interpretative framework of Krio adapability and creative responses to internal and outside forces that I situate the historical experience of the Muslims within Krio society in Sierra Leone and West Africa. Within the contemporary realities of Sierra Leone, where the Krio as a whole have been politically marginalized, the history of the Muslim Krio has unfortunately become a story of the marginalized within the marginalized. Yet the historical experiences of a group whose endeavors were critical to the shaping of the nineteenth-century West African landscape that became Britain's first colonial enterprise in Africa, in spite of the fact that the group had hitherto been relegated to the margins in the historiography of the region, cannot be overemphasized. The history of Muslim identity within Krio society not only offers new possibilities of expanding the confines of nineteenth-century Sierra Leone history, it also facilitates the rethinking of the various forms of marginalization that characterize the region. Equally crucial, it offers a fascinating lens into dynamic local and global forces shaping religion, culture, and society then as well as now. It suggests a more measured reflection on the recent confrontations and conflict between proponents of Islam and Christianity, especially the demonization of Islam in popular media and scholarly circles.[8] As the history of the Muslim Krio demonstrates, the relations between Christians and Muslims have been complex, spanning centuries and different global locations, and have involved not only conflicts about competing faiths, worldviews, and cultures, but also accommodation and meaningful intercultural exchanges.

RELIGION, ETHNICITY, AND LIBERATED AFRICAN MUSLIMS

Scholars of Krio and West African history are necessarily wrong in utilizing religion as a lens to analyze and delineate the boundaries of Krio society. After all, religion had a profound impact on the development of the Krio from the inception of the settlement of freed Africans in 1787 up until recent times. The Africans repatriated from England, North America, and the Caribbean between 1787 and 1800 came with their plethora of Christian churches and train of missionaries. For these groups, Christianity was not simply an external imposition but part of an identity that had been forged in the crucible of Atlantic enslavement, resistance, and freedom. While they had many disagreements with their abolitionist benefactors, some of them violent, Christianity did provide a common ground for the different groups.[9] The Africans rescued from slave ships on the Atlantic Ocean bound for the New World (Liberated Africans) beginning in 1808 also became the subjects of intensive and rigorous state-sponsored evangelization and socialization designed to Christianize and Europeanize them.[10] In an alien landscape far from home, some of the recaptured Africans no doubt embraced the faith of those who had rescued them from cauldrons of enslavement in the New World, and became active propagators of Christianity within and outside the colony.

There is no doubt that these assimilationist projects profoundly affected the evolution of the religious and social character of the Krio and colonial Sierra Leone. It was the work of the missionaries that propelled Sierra Leone to the apex of modern education in sub-Saharan Africa during the nineteenth century, and earned the Krio elite many accolades in a variety of fields. However, to privilege the achievements of the Christianized and Westernized segments of Krio society to the detriment of those who were Islamized or followed indigenous African religions in chronicling the history of Sierra Leone, as the extant literature has done, is deeply problematic.

From the onset of the Sierra Leone Colony, Christianity never held the field uncontested. The earliest settlers arrived in a landscape that Islam had already a foothold. While it would be on the margins of the Sierra

Leone settlement for the first couple of decades, with the arrival of the Liberated Africans from 1808 onward, Islam moved on to the heart of the Sierra Leone Colony. From this point on, as shown in the work, it would be engaged in intense competition with Christianity and other African religions for the hearts and minds of not only members of the evolving Krio society, but also people across West Africa. Ultimately, Islam would have a much broader impact in the colony and the hinterland. There were simply greater numbers of Muslims in these areas, and Islam won more converts before, during, and after British colonial rule. As David Skinner argues, Islam also "gained influence among non-Muslims because Muslims possessed resources which were highly valued by local peoples."[11]

Long established in the Sierra Leone Peninsula before the advent of Europeans, Islam had the unmistakable advantage of being perceived, in spite of its extra-African origins, as an African religion. Christianity, on the other hand, remained the religion of the European ruling class in the colony, effectively "the religion of the colonial oppressors." Indeed, the perception of the faith as the religion of the Oyinbo was a crucial consideration in the resistance of many a Liberated African to the missionary activities of Christian European and African clergy in the colony. European missionary groups began to arrive in West Africa and elsewhere in the continent in the nineteenth century with the end of the slave trade, while the Islamic presence can be traced back to about the tenth century BCE, when Muslim traders from the Mande empires in the West African savanna region began penetrating the area. The Christian missions were therefore faced with the task of playing catch-up with Islam in terms of the latter's wide distribution and latitude. This challenge was further compounded by the pervasiveness and resiliency of African traditional religions. European missions had to deal with an equally tenacious missionary zeal on the part of Muslim traders, clerics, and scribes, as well as the fealty of believers in the Yoruba orishas and various other gods of the different groups in the colony.

It was precisely due to these challenges in the colonial environment that the colonial and mission officials embarked on a social engineering project geared toward reshaping the lives of Liberated Africans. Undertaken in an atmosphere of European paternalism in colonial Freetown, the instruments of this social engineering included the King's Yard, rural villages and CMS superintendents, parishes, churches, schools, and the courts. New returnees to the colony were relocated into King's Yard, which in many ways represented a way station of sorts for many rescued from slave ships. They were subsequently sent to work in such places as Ascension Island, Fernando Póo, the West Indies, and the Gambia. Those not outsourced to such places were distributed as "apprentices" to the villages, or mobilized as a labor force for the construction of stone churches, public buildings, schools, and provision stores. Liberated Africans were conscious that the project of the state was not simply to ensure that they were skilled or gainfully employed, but also to fundamentally reshape their social and religious identities. Thus many resisted the activities of church and colonial officials and their promotion of cultural and social policies aimed at "Christianizing" and "civilizing" them. Their actions ran the gamut from defiance and protest to migration, outright war, and court battles. The anticolonial resistance actually transcended religious differences.

More than any of the repatriated groups, it was the Liberated Africans, rather than the earlier repatriated groups that had been privileged by leading scholars of Sierra Leone history, who profoundly shaped the transethnic and transcultural character of Krio identity and society. This conglomerate group included Temne, Baga, Bullom, Mende, and Mandinka from the areas surrounding the fledgling Sierra Leone Colony; the group also included Kru, Wolof, Congo, Akan, Igbo, and Yoruba from the farther reaches of West and West-Central Africa. These groups brought a polyglot of languages and religious and cultural practices, including Islam, to Sierra Leone.[12] The different languages ultimately gave way to Krio, which, "through a gradual systematization of its linguistic structures," became the full-fledged native language, with its own syntax and grammar, of the descendants of the repatriated Africans.[13] While the language initially became the hallmark of the distinctiveness of Krio identity and culture, it eventually transcended the boundaries of its original speakers to become the contemporary lingua franca of Sierra Leone.[14] The different African religious systems and cultural practices waned in the face of proselytization from Islam and Christianity, but not without significantly influencing both religions and contributing to the cultural bedrock of the society.

The Yoruba-speaking groups who came from the Bight of Benin, such as the Egba, Ijesa, Ibadan, and Oyo, however, stood apart from other Liberated Africans in terms of their numerical strength and the persistence and depth of their religious and cultural impact on Krio society. Despite the disparate origins of the various Yoruba groups and their different states of origin in the Bight of Benin, they coalesced around shared beliefs and customary, artistic, and cultural practices. In the process, they provided the polyglot Liberated Africans with crucial cultural elements to anchor their shared historical experience and forge a cohesive community. The Yoruba impact on other enslaved and free African groups is not unique to Sierra Leone, and it is in fact emblematic of their enduring historical influence in the many slaveholding and contemporary societies in the Caribbean and Latin America.[15] J. D. Y. Peel notes that Yoruba-speaking groups had "an indigenous religious culture of unusual vitality, adaptiveness, and tenacity."[16] J. Lorand Matory further echoes this view of the vitality of Yoruba traditional religion in his study of the Candomblé in Brazil.[17] As in their native cultural milieu in the Bight of Benin, the Yoruba groups of Sierra Leone demonstrated the ability to make a lucid and fully considered decision as to what religious worldview and cultural outlook they were going to embrace. While the cultural contributions of the Yoruba were crucial in the reconstruction of Muslim and Christian Krio identities and served to bridge the religious divide between the two Abrahamic faiths in colonial Sierra Leone and West Africa, they also posed tremendous challenges for those Krio, especially the elite, concerned about the purity of their monotheistic faiths.

THE 1905 ACT AND THE COLONIAL INVENTION OF THE AKU

At the turn of the twentieth century, the British colonial administrators chose to draw the boundaries of Krio society in its construction of tribal administration to ensure stronger political control over various non-Krio ethnic residents in Freetown. Ordinance no.[19] of 1905, the main legal and political instrument deployed by the state to delineate group identity, insisted on a presumed ethnic and cultural difference between Krio and the tribal "Other." The assimilated and detribalized Krio were conceived of as being exclusively Westernized and culturally assimilated Christians descended from the various resettled African groups. Unlike the "tribal" others administered indirectly through colonially sanctioned tribal heads and customary laws and institutions, the Krio, considered the true residents of the city, were deemed subjects of the Crown. Thus the Krio were ruled directly, through British-derived political institutions, British common law, and their own municipal government. Curiously excluded from the colonially delineated Krio society was a new "tribe" known as Aku, which, under the so-called Tribal Administration System, had its own titular head, the alimami. As far as the purveyors of the 1905 Ordinance were concerned, the construction of Aku as a tribe, as distinct from the rest of the Krio, was solely based on religious differences. The so-called Aku were Muslims, and the Krio, of course, were Christians.

The construction of Aku as a distinct "tribe," separate from Krio, was not simply the consequence of the late nineteenth-century European colonialist drive to pigeonhole Africans into legible racial and tribal categories in order to rule them effectively. In Sierra Leone, the assignment of a tribal identity to this segment of the Krio population is a legacy of the persecution of Muslims. In the early nineteenth century, Liberated Africans were perceived as a serious threat to a Christianized and Europeanized Freetown that evangelical missionary societies and colonial administrators wanted to manufacture. It was a project that was completely at odds with the nature and spirit of the city. Nineteenth-century Freetown was not simply the colonial capital of Sierra Leone, it was evolving as a vibrant West African commercial hub where different religious and cultural traditions intermixed. The determination of evangelical missionaries to foist on all the city's inhabitants a form of Christianity, based on Victorian English values, created social tension and conflict. The dogged determination of some Liberated Africans to adhere to Islam, or African traditional religious practices, repeatedly invited the wrath of missions and colonial officials. Around the mid-nineteenth century, the colonial state, for primarily economic reasons, adopted an ambivalent stance on the missionary project of repressing other religious beliefs and converting all Liberated Africans to Christianity. The improvement of the colony's economic fortunes at the turn of the century witnessed the resurgence of the evangelical forces within the colonial administration; they resumed their efforts to finally put an end to the religious and cultural resistance of Muslims and worshippers of Yoruba orishas, including Sango and Ogun.

The 1905 Act marginalized all non-Christians, who henceforth were "tribalized" and excluded from the mainstream of Freetown colonial politics. In assigning the ethnonym of "Aku Mohammedans" to Muslims within Krio society, the colonial state conveniently obfuscated the reality and historical evolution of the society. From the inception of the rural villages outside the colony to facilitate the relocation and resettlement of those rescued from slave ships in the Atlantic, Liberated Africans of Yoruba origin were known as Oku, a term derived from their common salutation of "Oku'o."[18] With the inauguration of the Tribal Administration System in 1905, British colonial officials merely anglicized the term and appended it to their faith, making it *Aku Mohammedan*; a new epithet that was uncritically appropriated by scholars and interpreted as a derivative of the word *Akuse* (or *Ekuse*), another form of salutation used by Yoruba Liberated Africans. In reality, however, neither the Liberated Africans nor their progeny in Krio society, including such luminaries as Mohammed Sanusie, Hadiru Deen, Sir Samuel Lewis, Bishop Samuel Adjai Crowther, and the Reverend Abayomi Cole, identified themselves as Aku. Without equivocation, they all consistently identified themselves as Oku.

The creation of the Tribal Administration System following the promulgation of the 1905 Act is reflective of the widespread imperial strategies of the British and other European powers to racialize and tribalize Africans. Europeans did not create ethnic and cultural differences in Africa; however, the process of colonial conquest, resistance, and reorganization of the African landscape gave them political and ideological force in many instances that they'd never had.[19] In reflecting on the tragic origins and consequences of the conflicts in Rwanda, Congo, and Darfur, Mahmood Mamdani argues that race and ethnicity in Africa are primarily political identities "imposed through the force of colonial law" and carried out through colonial administrative arrangements.[20] In the case of Darfur, he draws our attention to the fact that "whether colonial rulers invented tribes or acknowledged existing ethnic groups as tribes, the meaning of *tribe* under colonial indirect rule was an administrative unit."[21] So it was in the case of colonial Sierra Leone; the British did not invent the Liberated African people who styled themselves Oku, but they did create an Aku Mohammedan "tribe" that existed in a defined relationship to the other ethnic groups and the colonial state. The construction had clear ideological and political functions; it falsely delineated a monolithic Krio society and signaled their creation as passive "native clones of Western modernity through a discourse on civilization and assimilation."[22]

The intention and power of the colonial state in Africa notwithstanding, the construction of identity was, and remains, a complex phenomenon. The process is sometimes opaque and its outcomes uncertain. While the state insinuates a "coercive force of external identification(s)" on individuals and groups, African individuals and groups can also forge their own modes of identification and identity autonomously or in response to external pressures. In light of this consideration, the Krio of the late nineteenth century identified as members of a common community, even though they were unequivocally aware of their cultural and religious heterogeneity. Whether Muslim, Christian, devotee of Yoruba orishas, or of working-class status or belonging to the educated elite, the members of Krio society embraced their collective identity, in spite of the state's project to categorize its Muslim members as a "tribal" Other. Frederick Cooper and Rogers Brubaker's differentiation between "identification," the process evident among the Krio, and "categorization," the strategy adopted by the state, helps us understand the disjunction between the colonial state's project and Krio self-identification. While acknowledging the fact that "*identification* lacks the reifying connotations of identity," Cooper and Brubaker suggest that state-sanctioned identification will not "necessarily result in the internal sameness, the distinctiveness, the bounded groupness that political entrepreneurs may seek to achieve."[23] Ordinance no. 19 of 1905 clearly failed in generating cultural sameness in Krio society, but it was a society that had a sense of its "group boundedness" that was cognizant of its own religious and class differences.

The process of tribalization and categorization of colonized peoples is merely one facet of the multilayered agenda of the colonial enterprise in Africa, and in the Atlantic World writ large. It aimed not only at fashioning instruments of imperial control; it also desired to re-create and represent the colonized to denizens of the imperial metropolises and to themselves. And in this, the church was complicit. In examining the close relations between European Christian evangelicalism and imperialism in what is described by J. D. Y. Peel as "both creating and representing the colonial and post-colonial worlds of Asia and Africa,"[24] Valentine Mudimbe reminds us that missionary efforts were not limited to the conversion of souls or "the transmission of the Christian faith"; these efforts were motivated by such factors as "cultural propaganda, patriotic motivations and commercial interests." He categorized the church as "the best symbol of the colonial enterprise."[25] The social impact of Christian missions in Africa transcended merely ecclesiastical issues. In South Africa, Jean and John Comaroff point out that from the mid-nineteenth century on, the evangelical activities of protestant missionaries and "their civilizing mission was simultaneously symbolic and practical, theological and temporal." Missions were not only conveyors of religious messages, but also vehicles of a moral economy that celebrated the global spirit of commerce, the commodity, and the imperial marketplace.[26]

While the close relationship between church and state in European colonial projects in Africa is indisputable, care must be taken not to simplify its dynamics or social impact. Peel takes issue with the Mudimbe and Comaroff interpretation of the relationship between church and state, and the social impact of Christian evangelicalism on African societies. He rejects it as "too simple," even as he acknowledges that the "picture of consistency and fit, both within missionary messages and between their project and the secular projects of their age, certainly conveys something of the reality."[27] Peel reminds us that missionaries and colonial officials often disagreed not only on policies, but also in the treatment of the colonized. In nineteenth-century Sierra Leone, the character of the relationship between the church and colonial state is closer to the interpretations of Mudimbe and the Comaroffs than to that of Peel. In a period when the overriding agenda of the state was the resettlement and control of the disparate Liberated African groups, a close cooperation existed between the colonial state and the Church Missionary Society (CMS), both of which shared a common objective of molding them into a generally legible and pliant population.

The CMS and the British colonial administration closely worked together in organizing the Liberated African population in the rural villages outside Freetown. Colonial administrators placed the material resources needed by the resettled Africans in the hands of the European evangelical officials. These officials made deliberate efforts to privilege Africans who adhered to the teachings of the church and toed the official line. In the process, the church and the state consciously or unconsciously engaged in a process of producing social stratification. The resultant social engineering, championed by European officials, was not limited to the allocation of resources such as foodstuffs, clothing, and housing; it involved the far-reaching agenda of "detribalizing" the Africans who converted to Christianity. In reciprocation for the resources dished out by the church and the state, these Africans were expected to jettison all indications of their Africanness, including their "native" attire in favor of garments imported from England. Pupils from the Liberated African communities enrolled in the mission schools were prohibited from speaking patois on pain of severe flogging and other forms of penance.

The enactment of Ordinance no. 19 was clearly consistent with the long-pursued intent of the founders of the original settlement to establish it as a "Christian city." It was also in consonance with the colonial agenda of creating a bifurcated society in which the Christianized educated elite of Freetown would not only serve as an appendage of the colonial state, but also serve the socioeconomic interests of the imperial metropolis. The bifurcating agenda, however, failed to recognize the extent to which the indigenous groups, the "tribes," were also crucial to the making of nineteenth-century Krio society. Indeed, by the late 1830s onward, colonial administrators began to realize that the economic viability of the colony depended on the growth of the colony-interior trade.

An important factor in this colony-interior trade was the Liberated Africans who held steadfastly to their Muslim faith and utilized it as a vital bridge in their relations with the different groups in the Sierra Leone hinterland. The sustainability and vitality of the trade came to heavily depend on the cordial and cooperative relationship between Muslim Liberated African traders of Freetown and their coreligionists from the interior. Commerce did not only bring economic benefits to the Krio, it also provided an avenue for Muslim Krio to redefine their place both within and outside the Krio community, and in relationship to the colonial state in nineteenth-century Sierra Leone. As trade flourished between the colony and the interior, Muslim and Christian Krio traders became increasingly connected to the interior peoples, through intermarriage and other "cross-cultural encounters," over the ensuing decades.

COLONY-INTERIOR TRADE AND THE MAKING
OF KRIO SOCIETY

The Liberated African Muslims did not create the trade networks that the Sierra Leone Colony became increasingly dependent upon in the nineteenth century; they merely tapped into and extended them. Commercial activity between people in the Sierra Leone hinterland and Europeans predated the foundation of the colony in 1787 and the formal takeover of the Freetown settlement by the British Crown in 1808. Officials of the Sierra Leone Company were acutely aware of the vibrant commercial landscape in the hinterland in the eighteenth century and, consequently, sought to tap into that trade very early on. The company was also immediately aware of the almost symbiotic connection between Islam and commerce. By the late eighteenth century, the territories in the interior were already under the control of Muslim rulers, who subsequently came to play a pivotal role in trade between the coast and the interior. Upon their assumption of control of the settlement after 1787, the Sierra Leone Company officials recognized the usefulness of the interior states to the economic development of the coastal settlement.[28]

Mande Muslim trading and clerical families supplanted most of the indigenous ruling houses in the vicinity of the "province of freedom" before 1787. The Mandinka ruling families, as well as the Soso, Sarakoulé, and Jakhanke, were considered important enough that the agents of the Sierra Leone Company established relations with them by the late eighteenth and early nineteenth centuries.[29] Company officials reported a thriving long-distance trade system involving a wide distribution of agricultural and mineral resources. They also mentioned the role played by Islamic institutions in this trade system. David Skinner observes that the Sierra Leone Colony government developed a growing interest in the Northern Rivers precisely because of the crucial role played by the river system in regional and long-distance commerce, as well as "its influence as a centre of Islamic education and missionary activity."[30] The region produced substantial quantities of rice, salt, palm oil, poultry, camwood, groundnuts, benniseed, and other sundry trade items, including tobacco, cotton, coffee, and cloth.

The continued traffic in captive Africans in the region after the promulgation of the Abolition Act of 1807 also engendered an active engagement by the Sierra Leone Colony government with the Muslim states of the interior in the early nineteenth century. On 3 October 1808, the administration of Governor Thomas Ludlam initiated diplomatic contact with one of the interior rulers, Almamy Amara of Moriah, advising the latter that the colonial government would not allow slave trafficking to continue.[31] However, Ludlam and his successors, Thomas Thompson and Charles Maxwell, recognized the need to maintain peace and mutually beneficial relations with the interior states. The colony government remained constantly aware of the pivotal role of these states with regard to the economic viability of the colony. The rulers of the interior states were equally conscious of their indispensability to colony-hinterland relations; they frequently reminded colony officials of their sovereign rights whenever they perceived any appearance of interference in their economic and political activities. The ruler of Moriah, for instance, dispatched a letter to Governor Maxwell, written in English and signed in Arabic, dated 2 March 1814,reminding the latter that he was but a stranger in the region, while "we are the proprietors of the land."[32]

The implicit assertion of sovereign authority and a not-so-subtle determination to defend that sovereignty by the local rulers had the desired effect. The colonial government subsequently regulated its relations with the interior states through formal diplomatic ties. Four treaties were signed between the interior states and the colony between1818 and 1820, formally recognizing the colony's economic and political interests in the hinterland. Two more treaties were entered into in 1826 and 1827, guaranteeing the participation of colony subjects, including the growing merchant class of Liberated Africans and their progeny, in trade with the interior states. While these treaties were aimed at helping the colony government solidify its control over the neighboring territories, they also had the effect of making it easier for Mande merchants and other interior groups to settle and establish trading communities in the colony. Consequently, Freetown and the adjoining rural villages continued to attract a growing number of Mandinka, Fula, Soso, Bambara, and other trading groups from the interior throughout the nineteenth century.[33]

The increasing population of immigrant traders in the colony strengthened trade relations between the colony and the interior. The emergence and growth of identifiable Muslim communities in the colony in turn served to attract itinerant Muslim clerics, scribes, and others, while also facilitating the flow of commerce.[34] The interaction between immigrant Muslims and their coreligionists in the Liberated African communities, consequently, served to enhance the development of Islam in the colony. The developing relations also helped link the colony of Freetown with the interior Islamic regional centers of Timbo, Kankan, and Dinguiraye in the

Senegambia valley, as Allen Howard has noted.[35] These developments were occurring at a time when the social environment of the colony was recovering from the protracted struggle, discussed in chapter 3, between adherents of Islam and the Christian evangelicals and colonial establishment. Thus, between 1831 and 1833, the colony government sought to restrict the movement of Muslim scribes from the interior who were characterized as "aliens," due to the strong belief within the colonial establishment that they (Muslim scribes) were largely responsible for the spread of Islam in the colony. However, such efforts to curtail the further impact of itinerant Muslims were strongly protested by merchants, including Christian and Muslim Liberated Africans, as well as Europeans who were concerned about the potential impact of such restrictions on trade with the interior.

But even prior to the protestations of the various merchant groups, the colony government was already noticing a trend in colony-interior trade relations that it could not afford to ignore; in 1824, the acting governor, Daniel Hamilton, informed the Colonial Office in London of the financial and economic impact of the Fula, Mandinka, and other immigrant groups on the colony's political economy. During a visit to Freetown by some Fula from Timbo, Hamilton noted that the visitors had "expended . . . not less than five thousand pounds worth of gold."[36] The acting governor therefore advised the secretary of state for the colonies that in order for the colony of Sierra Leone to thrive, a European resident should be posted to Timbo "with sufficient number of the coloured inhabitants as a retinue, [so] that in a few years a very expensive and beneficial trade will be established."[37] In correspondence with Lord Bathurst in 1824, Hamilton informed Whitehall that for the first time in his twenty years of residence in Freetown, the increasing trade with the Fula from Timbo offered the best hopes for the colony to become "a place of profit to the mother country."[38]

Hamilton sent thinly veiled threats to interior rulers whose activities he deemed inimical to colonial interests along the trade routes. In June 1824, he sent word via a messenger to Pa Kompa, the ruler of Racon, advising him to cease and desist from creating obstacles to Fula traders trying to reach Freetown. Hamilton reminded Pa Kompa of assurances the latter had once communicated to the colony that he would not "do anything to keep those traders from coming down here."[39] He therefore advised the ruler of Racon to clear the way for the Fula traders to get to Freetown, or "I am afraid we shall not long remain on friendly terms." By 1840, when a new administration under Sir John Jeremie was inaugurated, colonial policy was henceforth concerned less with religious than with economic issues.

Jeremie took office with the immediate and pressing mandate from Whitehall to address the deteriorating financial situation in the colony and to secure the viability of the colonial economy. The Colonial Office in London was concerned about the increasing financial uncertainty of the colonial treasury and was no longer prepared to undertake the responsibility of using British taxpayers' money to sustain the colonial budget. Jeremie directed his attention to colony-interior trade and sought to de-emphasize the colony administration's policy regarding religion, which had weighed heavily against Islam. He was clearly interested in forging "paths of accommodation" with the Muslim community and therefore advised the secretary of state for the colonies, Lord John Russell, to desist from carrying out the policy of the previous administration aimed at expelling all Muslims from Freetown, and provided assistance to the Muslim Krio community at FulaTown, which had seen its mosque destroyed by arson during the administration of Col. Richard Doherty. Jeremie had a cooperative dialogue with Russell, who was committed to the idea of maintaining good relations with the interior states in order to facilitate British commercial interests in the region. The governor was astute enough to recognize the centrality of Muslim Krio traders in colony-interior trade and therefore to the revivification of the colonial economy.

The arrival of traders from the interior increased significantly just before the 1870s as a result of the construction of "a stone Grain Market" at Susan's Bay, which freed the immigrant produce traders in Freetown from the stranglehold of the "landlord-stranger" relationship that hitherto existed. This development served to ensure the centrality of Muslim traders in the period after the mid-nineteenth century. By the 1850s, the main thoroughfare in central Freetown, Kissy Road (later renamed Kissy Street), saw an influx of immigrant traders plying their wares.[40] Many of these traders were already congregating in the neighborhood of Bambratogn (Bambara Town), about a mile south of Susan's Bay, which became the most cosmopolitan locality in the colony. Established in 1821, the Bambratogn neighborhood was mostly inhabited by Bambara, Mandinka, Soso, and other Mande traders, who were later joined by Temne, Krio, Fula, and other groups, ultimately making it an important center of cross-cultural interactions in colonial Freetown. The area continued to attract additional immigrant groups, including Yoruba, Hausa, and others entering the commercial life of the city following the turn of the century.[41] Bambratogn ultimately came to exemplify the importance of indigenous groups to the cultural growth of Krio society. The neighborhood constituted, in effect, "substantive evidence of the interpenetrating influences that largely accounted for the ability of Krio society to imbibe multifaceted African cultural mores that the Krio upper class, socialized in Victorian English values, could not have provided."[42]

The cosmopolitan community of itinerant traders from the interior of Sierra Leone and other parts of the Upper Guinea coast also positively contributed to the process of creolization and the making of Krio society. Largely due to its proximity to Susan's Bay, Bambratogn continued to attract more immigrant traders from the interior, thereby becoming the prime location for non-Krio cultural groups in the late nineteenth and early twentieth centuries. These groups did not demonstrate any evident interest in political affairs, instead restricting their attention to their commercial, religious, and social lives. A variety of goods, including kola nuts, shea butter, gara/fente clothes, gold, and other commercial items, changed hands and were widely distributed from this center.

This locality could be compared to Saint-Louis during French colonial rule in mid-nineteenth-century Senegal.[43] Like the trading communities of Saint-Louis, where African traders handled commercial transactions between the coast and the interior, immigrant traders at Bambratogn moved fluidly between Freetown and the interior, often spending "several months each year" in the centers of production in the interior and subsequently returning to Freetown with items of trade procured in interior trade centers. The more prosperous "big men" among these traders often stayed for extended periods in Freetown, relying on the ability of young men in their employ to travel inland in order to obtain the requisite trade goods.[44] Like Saint-Louis, Freetown was "a place of opportunity" for the immigrant traders. The cosmopolitan nature of the community allowed immigrants to practice their Islamic faith without any encumbrances and, like their counterparts in Saint-Louis, to maintain "a strong consciousness of being members of *Dar al-Islam*,"[45] even if they did not necessarily rule themselves in Sierra Leone.

The Bambratogn community thus facilitated the creolizing, "interpenetrating influences" that allowed Krio society to emerge with the "multifaceted African cultural mores" that solidified its authenticity as an African ethnicity. The shared cultural space inhabited by Christians, Muslims, and others devoted to religious syncretism (or dualism), significantly contributed to the complexity of an emergent Krio society by the late nineteenth century. Christians worshipped in their respective Methodist congregations at Gibraltar Church at Kissy Road and Ebenezer Church at Circular Road; while Soso, Hausa, and other Muslim immigrants adhered to their faith by congregating at their mosques located on Regent and Sackville Streets. But, as was the case with Muslims in Senegal, to employ Robinson's formulation once again, "the paths into the colonial and regular relations with the administration [for the Muslim Krio] were not simple. What was required was a transition from a world where people assumed they were part of the Dar al-Islam to one in which Islamic identity could be maintained underneath, or in spite of, European over-rule."[46] Before the Muslim Krio could come to the realization of a need to forge "paths of accommodation" with the colonial state, a protracted struggle for control of their social and religious lives and resistance to the requirements of social subservience by the colonial state would occupy the Muslims, a subject addressed in chapter 2.

The "path of accommodation" necessitated not only Muslim adjustment to the realities of colonialism, but also the recalibration of British paternalism to meet the needs of its non-Christian subjects. In the engagement with African Muslims, British paternalism lagged behind French paternalism. The French in Senegal developed a "reputation for working with Muslim societies," acquiring what Robinson characterizes as "symbolic capital." Thus the French experience led to a reduction in the need for constant deployment of violence in their interactions with, and control of, Muslim communities under their rule.[47] Only later in the nineteenth century, after a protracted struggle with the Muslims in Sierra Leone, did the British colonial state come to appreciate the need to develop this "symbolic capital." Just as in French-ruled Senegal and Mauretania, the development of this capital was a dynamic process emerging out of not only conflicts but also sites of mutual interests.

KRIO NOMENCLATURE AND LANGUAGE

It is evident from efforts by the colonial state to "tribalize" Krio Muslims, and the highly contentious scholarly debate that raged in the 1970s and 1980s on what to call the descendants of Africans resettled in Sierra Leone, that the group nomenclature is important. *Creole* or *Krio* continues to be deployed, depending on the perspective of the author. I choose, with cogent reasons, the term *Krio*, instead of *Creole*. The extant literature is replete with attempts made in earlier scholarship to ascribe the origins of the nomenclature *Krio* to extra-African provenance. It should be noted that the term *Krio* is not an adaptation of *Creole*, denoting the "offspring of Old World progenitors born and raised in the New World." To the extent that the term Creole literally means "of the place" or "homegrown,"[48] as used in the New World context, particularly in colonial Louisiana, a case can be made that the progeny of the manumitted population resettled in the "province of freedom" could indeed be classified as Creoles. However, the

Louisiana or Caribbean understanding of the name Creole is plausible in the Sierra Leone context only as a referent for the multifarious ethnicities assembled in the Sierra Leone settlement before and after the promulgation of the Abolition Act of 1807; the creolizing environment of that settlement allowed for the ultimate coalescing of these ethnicities and cultural groups into what became Krio society in the late nineteenth century.

Notwithstanding the perception by scholars over the years of a correlation between the nomenclature of *Creole* and *Krio*, the evidence suggests otherwise. While *Creole* has been used historically in reference to persons of mixed European/African descent, the term *Krio* has no such antecedents. Its etymological roots are decidedly African (that is to say, Yoruban). As used in reference to the culture and language of the descendants of the freed Africans in Freetown in the late nineteenth century, it is derived from the original Yoruba *Akiriyo*.[49] The term has been interpreted as denoting the proclivity of Liberated Africans "to walk about and be satisfied." Its usage in the literature has been associated with the practice of Christian and Muslim Krio going from place to place visiting relatives, especially after Sunday church services and Friday juma'a prayers, respectively.[50] However, the term entered the lexicon of colonial Freetown in the context of the post–Atlantic commercial landscape.

The term could be traced to the Yoruba verb kiri (to trade). In the entrepreneurial environment of early Yoruba society, it was customary for potential buyers in the marketplace, or along the village path, to inquire from traders about their wares by posing the question "Kilo'on kiri?" (What are you selling?).[51] The initial inquiry about the trade items from potential buyers would then lead to a process of haggling between seller and buyer, a process that almost invariably resulted in a sale. As Solimar Otero notes, "In the Yoruba oja, the key component is the negotiation of the value of something through verbal barter."[52] In Sierra Leone, the noun *Akiriyo* was used initially to refer to Yoruba-speaking Liberated Africans who opted for commerce in the rural villages, rather than the farm labor prescribed by the CMS mission officials placed in charge of the villages. According to oral tradition in the Muslim Krio communities, the name was originally used as an *oki/oriki* (praise name) for petty traders in the villages who went about plying their wares.[53] The term was used by Yoruba-speaking settlers from the Bight of Benin in reference to other Yoruba-speaking traders in the rural villages; however, other non-Yoruba speakers in the Liberated African communities appropriated the term as a generic referent for all speakers of dialects of Yoruba in the villages, especially as their penchant for commerce became even more pervasive in the colony. Over time, the term Akiriyo evolved to kiriyo, and finally to its present formulation, *Krio*.

The etymological roots of the term *Krio* have been a source of debate among scholars of Sierra Leone history in the recent past. Wyse maintained that the term simply refers to the habitual practice of visiting with relatives by Christian Krio after church services on Sunday. He later acknowledged that this practice was not exclusive to Christians in Krio society, as Muslims also engaged in this practice.[54] The emphasis on visiting with relatives by Christians and Muslims after worship in Krio society, however, neglects the historical significance of commerce not only in Yorubaland, but especially in the economically challenging circumstances of the Liberated African villages in nineteenth-century Sierra Leone. The raison d'être for the peripatetic activities of Yoruba-speaking inhabitants of the rural villages was simply trade as a source of livelihood, especially in a colonial environment, where they were mostly left to fend for themselves by the colonial government for extended periods of time without official supervision following their recue from slave ships in the nineteenth century. The term *Akiriyo* was, as noted, an oki (or oriki); by definition, praise names are not used as pejoratives by people who would later appropriate the term as an identifying nomenclature. The term was not used by non-Yoruba speakers, nor by those speaking the language, to ridicule, but to identify Yoruba-speaking Liberated Africans by their vocation or avocation, not unlike other parts of the world throughout history where people were primarily identified by their respective trades or vocations as individuals or as corporate groups (e.g., tailor, sawyer, mason, shoemaker, goldsmith, etc.). Thus the claim that it was used as a pejorative is simply speculative and untenable.

A NOTE ON METHODOLOGY

It is imperative that some attention be devoted to the sources and methodology employed in the production of this work, especially given the instability and difficulties that have plagued Sierra Leone in the recent past. Research on this work was pursued and completed in an atmosphere of immense challenges, not the least of which was the protracted, decade-long war in Sierra Leone. The war initially made it almost impossible to conduct research in the country, thereby necessitating the postponement of several trips to the country and delaying the completion of the project. Once I was eventually able to make the trip, the deaths of many of the elders in the Muslim Krio communities during the course of the war (though not necessarily as a direct result of it) meant that I could not effectively tap into their repositories of knowledge and wisdom about their communities. The Sierra Leone National Archive at Fourah Bay College, which was already faced with severe logistical challenges, was badly impacted by the war. The collections in the archives are still poorly cataloged, and the organization remains poorly funded and understaffed. The archive did yield significant resources about the lives of Liberated Africans, which are reflected in the book.

The avalanche of European evangelical missionary societies in the postabolition period of the nineteenth century in West Africa generated a trove of resources about their endeavors in Sierra Leone and West Africa. Missionary societies in West Africa did not only threaten the hegemony of Islam in the subregion, they also had a significant effect on the social and cultural landscapes of the societies of the West African littoral. In addition to converting the vast majority of Liberated Africans to Christianity, the missions also successfully proselytized among the indigenous groups, thereby converting a significant proportion of these groups. Unlike Islamic proselytizing in West Africa, European evangelicalism required a systematic collection of information on the local populations. For example, church officials in charge of the Liberated African communities in the rural villages of the Sierra Leone Colony were expected to maintain journals of their day-to-day activities and interactions with their congregations.[55] They were also required to keep the central committees of their respective parent groups in London abreast of developments in Sierra Leone and West Africa in the form of letters and quarterly and annual reports.

The texts generated by church officials do pose significant challenges for the reconstruction of the history of the Muslim Krio of West Africa. As pointed out earlier, church and mosque were frequently in fierce competition for the souls of the inhabitants of the colony and surrounding region. Needless to say, the missionaries did not see or record their impressions of Muslims through unadulterated lenses. The church documents are littered with pejorative characterizations of Muslims as "Mohametans" (or "Mohameddans" or "Marabouts"), epithets that continue to be used by non-Muslims (and some Muslims!) up to the present. Indeed, Muslims across western Africa returned the favor, as it were, by labeling Christians as "Nasara." With sensitivity to the biases of the church documents and a careful reading against the grain in many instances, the writing of this book undoubtedly benefited from the letters, reports, and journals of CMS missionaries, which are presently housed at the University of Birmingham in the United Kingdom.

Contemporary works on the Krio and other African societies in the postcolonial era are obligated to closely interrogate the production of knowledge by evangelical missionaries and other European groups vis-à-vis the peoples they interacted with during the nineteenth century. This is not necessarily to discount the significance and usefulness of the literature left us by missionaries; notwithstanding the peculiar interests of the authors of the journals, reports, and letters, they often prove quite useful in understanding the interactions between church officials and their Muslim counterparts. The journals of Bishop Samuel Adjai Crowther, for example, are particularly important for our understanding of not just the attitude and assumptions of Crowther and other Christian clergymen toward Muslims and orisha (particularly Sango) worshippers; they also provide a very useful representation of the integrity of orisha adherents who, for instance, not only resisted what they considered the intrusiveness of the likes of Crowther on their sacred ile, but were always ready to point out the doctrinal contradictions and perceived "hypocrisy" of church officials with whom they came into contact. The ethnographic information provided by Crowther on cultural institutions such as the Egungun, while not without its limitations, also proves to be quite useful.

Indeed, the sources left us by the European missionaries are important; however, interviews conducted in the local communities in Sierra Leone tell us another story. Such interviews provide the basis for further critiquing of colonial literature used as a primary source. The nuances of Krio culture, especially the essential or characteristic customs and conventions of Krio society, much of which was preserved in the Muslim communities and less so in the Christian sector, could have been ferreted out only through oral interviews. The Krio in Sierra Leone and elsewhere in West Africa have retained the social mores transmitted to them across several generations, which became manifestly clear in the interviews.

Muslims were rather cognizant of condescending, and often inaccurate, epithets such as "Marabout" and "Mohammedan" used with reference to them by church officials. The use of such epithets in defining and characterizing the "Other" was all too common among church and colonial state officials. Thus, in consulting the primary sources located at the Public Record Office in London and those at the Sierra Leone National Archive at Fourah Bay College in Freetown, I was always cognizant of the need both for context and for a close interrogation of the sources, an awareness bolstered by an early experience in conducting oral interviews. Archival sources, sans oral interviews, thus tell us only a partial story. The complementary utility of both sets of sources has ultimately helped immensely in bringing this work to fruition.

The dispatches, official correspondences, private letters, Governor's

Letter Books, Government Blue Books, and so on, as well as the informed voices of the elders in the Muslim communities, have thus been pivotal to the production of this work. While the bulk of archival research was undertaken between 1995 and 1998, I also benefited from earlier consultations, albeit on a limited scale, with archival material as an undergraduate honors history student at Fourah Bay College. The oral interviews conducted at such places as Fula Town and Fourah Bay were undertaken with a view toward providing an insight into the oral traditions and customs of the people of these communities. These interviews ultimately served as a countervailing factor vis-à-vis the journals and reports of church and colonial state officials.

OVERVIEW OF THE BOOK

The Krio of West Africa starts with an examination of creolization and (krio)lization in the making of nineteenth-century Sierra Leone, with the interactions among and between the constituent ethnicities and their resultant congealing into Krio. It examines the diffusion of Yoruba culture and its impact on an emergent Krio society. The second chapter examines the growth of Islam in the Liberated African community and the reactions and policies of mission officials and the colonial state toward Muslims in nineteenth-century Freetown. It also investigates the efforts of the European clergy to suppress not only Islam, but also African forms of religious worship and modes of thought, and the reactions of Muslims and adherents of Yoruba orishas in particular. Even though the CMS and other Christian missions were highly successful in proselytizing among the inhabitants of the colony, they encountered much cultural and religious resistance in Freetown and the rural villages.

In chapter 3, I embark on a discussion of the pivotal role of Muslims and their Islamic values in the development of trade relations between the colony and the societies of the immediate hinterland of the colony. The Islamic faith also had a tremendous impact on the movement of Krio merchants and others in what became a Krio diaspora along the Atlantic coast of West Africa during the nineteenth century. I pay attention to individual personalities, including influential women merchants in Sierra Leone and West Africa, whose trade activities were crucial in the local economies and in those of their diasporan communities. The role of women traders reflected not only the capacity of women, often neglected in the literature, to navigate the constricted social environments of colonial society, but also their ability to facilitate their own social and economic empowerment in spite of the efforts of the European colonial and evangelical officials. In chapter 4, I undertake a social analysis of the diasporan Saro community in the Bight of Benin, the destination of choice for many of the manumitted Africans and their progeny in the nineteenth century. The emigrants from Sierra Leone and their counterparts from Brazil and Cuba, the Aguda, played a crucial role in the growth of the colony of Nigeria.

Following a period of intense persecution by the colonial state and Christian evangelical missions up to the 1830s, Muslims in the colony were able to establish their own identifiable communities and practice their faith. Islam consequently came to play an increasingly central role in the growth and development of these communities. Chapter 5 explores the tensions and conflicts arising from the religious institutions and cultural processes around the reconstituted communal life of Muslim Krio in the nineteenth century. It examines the ways in which traditional culture and the customary practices of Krio society collided with the growing influence of conservative Islam in these communities, especially at Fourah Bay, leading to a socioreligious schism that resulted in a landmark case in the 1890s. Krio society attained a largely hegemonic status in colonial Sierra Leone up until the Hut Tax War era, primarily due to the achievement of the people in the area of education. The European Christian missions, in a bid to effect the conversion of Liberated Africans and others to Christianity, founded schools in the colony and across West Africa.

Thus education and the founding of schools became central to the promotion of European Christendom and to the agenda of *mission civilisatrice* undertaken by both the church and the colonial state, with schools becoming crucial instruments of proselytization and acculturation. Given the competing interests of the Islamic and Christian missionary activists, Islamic education was also emphasized by Muslims. Chapter 6 therefore looks at education and educational reform in the Muslim Krio communities and the ushering in of a period of cooperation and accommodation in relations between the Muslim Krio and the colonial regime.

In the postscript, I draw attention to the resiliency of African cultural praxis in Krio society and the strong sense of cultural nationalism among the people that transcended religious differences. I reflect on the fate of Muslims within the evolving history of the Krio, a group that paradoxically has been progressively marginalized in contemporary Sierra Leone, even as its cultural imprint permeates the entire country.

1 ⇜ Creolization and (Krio)lization in the Making of Nineteenth-Century Sierra Leone

CONTRARY TO THE EARLY SCHOLARLY NARRATIVES, nineteenth-century Freetown and the colony of Sierra Leone harbored a heterogeneous and dynamically changing population. The colony and its emerging capital settlement were not only ethnically pluralistic, but they continuously absorbed different groups that brought along their own cultural influences. Of the more than one hundred linguistic "liberated" African groups that Sigismund Koelle noted in his *Polyglotta Africana* (1854), the various subgroups from Yorubaland would have the most cultural impact on the evolution of Krio society. These Yoruba subgroups may not have constituted the largest cultural group taken across the so-called Middle Passage during the transatlantic slave trade, but undoubtedly their cultural influences in the Atlantic World, particularly in the post–slave trade settlement of Freetown, have been enormous. Primarily due to the outbreak of war in early nineteenth-century Yorubaland, these groups came to constitute the largest proportion of the African population recaptured from slave ships and subsequently resettled in the colony from about the 1820s onward. They provided the heterogeneous community of resettled Africans much of the cultural foundation on which to reconstitute new identities and cultures in the creolizing environment of nineteenth-century Freetown.

How, and in what ways, did the Yoruba speakers successfully exert their cultural influences on the other groups within the colony? What were the cultural and social institutions brought from the old country, and how did their diffusion in the new colony serve to facilitate the process of cultural fusion and/or creolization in Sierra Leone? Given the cultural pluralism of the group, from the inception of the freed slave settlement to its emergence as an identifiable linguistic and cultural group in the late nineteenth century, it is imperative that we discuss the process of creolization and indigenization involving the groups with extra–Sierra Leonean provenance, including the Yoruba-speaking population and people living in the hinterland, and their coalescing into what we know as Krio society. The creolization process underwent a complex mix of resistance, indigenization, and accommodation to the realities of the sociopolitical and cultural dynamics on the ground in the Sierra Leone Colony. Even though they did not create radically new institutions, as was the case for those West Africans distributed across the Atlantic World in earlier centuries, the Liberated African community forged novel identities and structures that generally embraced Yoruba institutions and, to some extent, those of the Temne, Mende, Mandinka, Soso, and other groups in the colony.

The cultural diversity or pluralism that characterized nineteenth-century Freetown was itself the source of its "cultural vitality." As Ulf Hannerz has observed, "Creole cultures like creole languages are those which draw in some way on two or more historical sources, often originally widely different."[1] As dissimilar as the constituent groups may have been in the beginning of the process, they came to "develop and integrate" while cultivating a "political economy of culture." The Temne, Mende, and other groups from the hinterland that were subsequently integrated into Krio society by the late nineteenth century came to develop a consciousness of, and familiarity with, cultural forms that hailed from outside their own cultural context.[2] Such a development is not unprecedented in human interactions, for, as Hannerz observes in the context of "the expansion of the present world system into non-Western, non-northern areas," the developing social structures of early Krio society "provided the matrices within which an international flow of culture … continuously entered into varying combinations and syntheses with local culture."[3] Thus Krio society came to constitute in many ways the characteristics of what could be described as a "complex society," with its attendant "differentiation of experiences and interests," all of which ultimately allowed for a "differentiation of perspectives among members of the society." This was best exemplified by the conscious embracing of Islam by a segment of the emergent Krio, a development that non-Muslims were not unaware of and that did not in any meaningful way threaten the social fabric of the new society.

In spite of this differentiation of religious and cultural perspectives in the making of Krio society, a common group identity ultimately emerged by the late nineteenth to early twentieth century. Krio identity both allowed for and transcended religious differences. While the identifiable Muslim communities of Fourah Bay, Fula Town, and Aberdeen retained their fealty to Islam and the Islamic *Umma* (community), their social and often consanguineous ties to their non-Muslim Krio compatriots remained undiminished. The religious differences between Christians and Muslims in late nineteenth-century Freetown may have been attenuated by what Lamin Sanneh ascribes to "deep theological affinity supported by real social and historical experience, all of which would make religious exclusiveness unappealing."[4] This is not to suggest that there was an absence of personal biases among practitioners of the respective faiths with respect to the other. Far from such an impression, it is here suggested that in spite of instances of religious dogmatism, the common cultural affinities of Muslims and Christians served to mitigate the undermining implications of such dogmatic tendencies. In the main, Muslims in Krio society tended to represent Islam as the better facilitator for the preservation of African cultural authenticity, as opposed to the teachings of the European Christian evangelical missions, which, from the perspective of Muslims, "remained superficial to black culture."[5] Thus, rather than religion being the most important factor in Krio identity, African (mostly, Yoruba) culture was deemed the most important common denominator.

Like Hannerz, Frederick Cooper and Rogers Brubaker have considered the question of identity and of "how people see themselves and their society" vis-à-vis others. As Cooper and Brubaker posit, "Identity, too, is both a category of practice and a category of analysis. As a category of practice, it is used by [people] . . . to make sense of themselves, of their activities, of what they share with, and how they differ from, others." Nineteenth-century Freetown and Krio society was a classic example of this effort at "categorical relationships." In a colonial environment that was largely based on a distinction between natives and non-natives, Krio leaders used the concept of identity to "persuade" their "people to understand themselves, their interests, and their predicaments in a certain way . . . [and] that they are . . . 'identical' with one another and at the same time different from others, and to organize and justify collective action along certain lines."[6]

This was especially so following the extension of British colonial administration into the interior of Sierra Leone in 1896. Indeed, as we are reminded by Harrell-Bond, Howard, and Skinner, the colonial government struggled with the challenge of delineating the legal and cultural differences between "citizens and subjects" in Freetown. Unlike the Krio (descendants of settlers), who were "regarded legally as British subjects, the situation was not so clear as regards the Native residents—that is, both those who had immigrated into the Colony and those born there."[7] I employ the term *identity* in this context to denote the "fundamental and consequential sameness" among members of Krio society that "manifest[ed] itself in solidarity, in shared dispositions or consciousness, or in collective action."[8] This shared consciousness remained central to the development of Krio ethnicity, religious differences notwithstanding.

CREOLE SOCIETY AND ITS DISCONTENTS: RETHINKING REPRESENTATION IN THE LITERATURE

In discussing the emergence of colonial Sierra Leone, the extant narrative has tended to focus primarily on the centrality of the manumitted Africans from Europe and North America, the so-called Black Poor, Nova Scotians, and Maroons, and only secondarily on the Liberated Africans in the foundations of Creole/Krio society. The narrative has also privileged the triumphal impact of the European evangelical missions on the returnee population and the elitist culture that emerged from it. The importance of these returnees and the scriptural influences of the Christian missions in the making of nineteenth-century Krio society are undeniable. However, a critical rethinking of the history of the group needs to be undertaken beyond the oft-repeated narrative of the abolition, and the triumph of the social engineering project engendered by the evangelical and colonial officials that produced a hegemonic social entity based on "the three C's" (Christianity, commerce, and civilization).

The emphasis on the European Christian evangelical movements and their impact on the free Africans and so-called recaptives in the extant literature has had the unmistakable, perhaps not unintended, effect of pushing other religious and cultural identities to the periphery. This emphasis also rendered the history of Krio society as nothing less than a triumph of the hegemony of the Euro-American cultural ideas espoused by the Christian missions, relative to that of marginalized entities. Yet it should be noted that while these other identities may have been relegated to the periphery in the historiography, the censuses undertaken by the colonial state and other sources always seem to refuse to ignore these people. The narrative on the Krio should be much more multicentered, multicultural, and inclusive of those groups that were necessarily excluded from the social engineering project of the Europeans.

The historiography of the Krio, and thus public memory, has been largely shaped by the scholarship of those responsible for the production of knowledge in Sierra Leone during the colonial and immediate post-colonial periods. Such scholarship has rather uncritically attributed the development of Krio culture to the primary influences of the European missions and colonial officials in nineteenth-century Freetown.[9] Even as Akintola Wyse, for instance, was attempting to set the record straight, as it were, by calling for a consideration of the role and place of other groups in the making of Krio society, he was paradoxically giving primacy to the impact of European influences that he believed to have shaped "the unique nature of the society which the Krios evolved."[10] Wyse even made an uncritical reference to the oft-repeated characterization of the Krio as "Black Englishmen"; he consequently privileged the Black Poor, Nova Scotians, and Maroons, whom he identified as having "formed the Western foundations of the society, which were reflected in their Christianity, education, politics, ideals and aspirations, civic pride and high sense of individualism, their mode of dress, their articulateness and their language." Wyse could identify only "a few cultural survivals that recalled from some distant past their African roots."[11] Obviously, such observations were in reference to the above-mentioned groups; however, he was unequivocally crediting Western civilization as the cultural anchor of the new society. Paradoxically, Wyse had been foremost in advocating a reexamination of the makings of Krio society, due to what he perceived as an overemphasis on the extra–Sierra Leonean factor, at the expense of indigenous cultures, in the constituent groups that coalesced to emerge as Krio in the late nineteenth century.

Leo Spitzer has been among those whose scholarship has uncritically attributed primacy to the European factor in the makings of Krio society.[12] And, like the other sources of production of knowledge on the Krio in the early postcolonial period, Spitzer sought to define Krio culture based on the limited outlook of the upper stratum of the emergent society in the late nineteenth century. He appropriated the description of the group as "Black Englishmen" by one of its more socially prominent members, A. J. Shorunkeh-Sawyerr, and thus sought to interpret the term as reflective of the general cultural outlook of the society. Even as he took pains to demonstrate that European influences were, in the main, much more impactful on the upper-class Krio, Spitzer nevertheless concluded that Krio society in general was pervasively European in outlook.[13] However, the fact that upper-class Krio "aspired to and inculcated European social values" did not necessarily render the society uniformly European in cultural outlook. Also, simply because members of the upper stratum of the group may have affected European speech patterns, and attitudes and assumptions, that did not necessarily account for the cultural evolution of the society as a whole. Certainly upper-class Krio sought membership in European social institutions such as the Freemason lodge in colonial Freetown; nonetheless, the vast majority of Krio belonged to the working class and developed a decidedly different cultural outlook from that of the upper-class educated elite. Working-class Krio were less interested in entering the restricted social environment of the Freemason lodge than they were in undergoing the ritual (*Mawo*) ceremony into the equally esoteric Yoruba-derived cultural organizations like the Orjeh, Egunuko, Akpansa, Gelede, and Odeh.

Thus, the critical and erroneous assumption of the Krio as having embraced English values, which has been responsible for the much-repeated characterization of the Krio as "Black Englishmen," is unsustainable and in need of revision. Clearly, the suggestion of cultural alienation on the part of the Krio does not take into consideration the complex historical evolution of the group. If the suggestion of cultural alienation did indeed constitute a historical accuracy, how, then, do we account for the role and place of the Temne, Baga, Bullom/Sherbro, and Soso in the process of resocialization in nineteenth-century Freetown? Tracing the ethnic provenance of a significant proportion of Liberated Africans to any number of these groups, and the cultural contributions of these ethnicities to the making of Krio society, will have the inevitable consequence of undermining the oft-repeated, but erroneous assertion of the Krio as but a caricature of Victorian English culture. A quick perusal of the Trans-Atlantic Slave Trade Database will reveal that while many of the Liberated Africans resettled in Freetown beginning in 1819 began their transatlantic journey from such diverse locations as Badagry, Bonny, Calabar, Cape Grand Mount, Cameroons River, Gabon, Lagos, Little Popo, Whydah, and unspecified ports in the area of the Bight of Benin, many others embarked from "ports unspecified" in Sierra Leone.[14]

While the early returnee groups (i.e., the Nova Scotians and Maroons) and their progeny may have aspired to Western cultural values, they were hardly representative of the society that congealed into what became Krio by the late nineteenth century. Indeed, the Black Poor, Nova Scotians, and Maroons constituted around 10 percent of the population of the colonial settlement that by the late 1820s and early 1830s was being dominated by the Liberated Africans who had not experienced life in New World environments. The Liberated Africans who landed on the Sierra Leone Peninsula from the 1820s and after entered a "stratified and élite-oriented society," dominated by the former groups; however, Liberated Africans, due to their numerical strength and their entrepreneurial skills and disposition, soon experienced an upward social mobility that closed the gap between them and the more established early settlers.

Contrary to Wyse and other scholars who presupposed a Christian prerequisite for Krio identity, this work argues that no such requirement existed. There was a significant number of Muslims in the Liberated African community and in what subsequently became Krio society. There were undeniable tensions between Christian and Muslim Krio, but there was also extensive cooperation, which allowed for the development of a shared identity that transcended religious differences. Their shared Yoruba-derived culture frequently provided a bridge for accommodation, and enabled Muslims and Christians to work for their common good. Trade networks developed between Muslim Krio and their coreligionists in the interior states became vital in providing the trading alternative that was taken up by a large number of Krio, Christians and Muslims alike, which proved crucial to their economic survival during the nineteenth century, a subject that will be addressed later.

Rather than regurgitate the uncritical rendering of the "social acculturation" of the Liberated Africans as evinced in the works of Fyfe and Porter,[15] this work represents a departure from the extant literature as it locates the development of Krio culture in a historical context in which the Liberated Africans consciously sought to develop their 'cultural identities on the basis of continuity in African traditions,' outside of the constrictive social environment of the nineteenth-century colonial establishment. It considers the linguistic and cultural contributions of such groups as the Temne to the development of Krio society. The Temne and other indigenous groups within the geographical boundaries of modern Sierra Leone complemented the Yoruba, Igbo, Fante, Wolof, Hausa, and others, the vast majority of whom were uncompromisingly devoted to their customary ways. The linguistic contributions of the host community to the development of the Krio language thus cannot be overstated.

The Sierra Leone Peninsula has long harbored a heterogeneous and changing population. Long before the arrival of the first batch of repatriated Africans in 1787, it had been home to the Bullom/Sherbro, Baga, and the Temne peoples, one of whose rulers leased the land for the colonial settlement to the Sierra Leone Company. Little is known of the ethnic makeup of the first group of settlers, the so-called Black Poor, whose initial endeavors were largely unsuccessful and whose mortality rate was high. Five years after their arrival in Sierra Leone, only about forty had survived.[16] The so-called "Nova Scotians," the second batch of settlers, were more successful, and some, including John Gordon and John Kizzell, traced their ancestry back to the Sierra Leone hinterland among the Yalunka, Koranko, and Sherbro.[17] The "Maroons" who returned to West Africa from Jamaica via Nova Scotia can trace their provenance to the area of modern Ghana.

The earlier groups of settlers brought diverse religious, cultural, and social experiences to the evolving society on the Sierra Leone Peninsula, but much of the "African" element of their experiences had been denuded by their forced migration and enslavement in the Americas. In their struggle to forge a new, common sociocultural identity, they drew from their experiences, the influences of their benefactors, and their indigenous African neighbors. From 1807, however, the Liberated African settlers would outnumber the earlier returnees; they were less influenced by Europe and America, and would contribute the elements that came to constitute the African bedrock of Krio society. The largest proportion of the Liberated African community comprised Yoruba speakers (or proto-Yoruba), Igbo, Popo, Fante, and other groups from outside the geographical boundaries of present-day Sierra Leone.

Nineteenth-century Freetown thus constituted an admixture of cultures and language groups that resulted in "new configurations of identity."[18] The various groups speaking different languages, and with a variety of ethnic, cultural, and religious backgrounds, in a colonial environment not particularly dissimilar to that of New World societies, experienced close social and cultural encounters in what was an undeniably creolizing environment. In these circumstances, the various Africans sought "opportunities for networking," especially as the colony continued to receive incoming groups of rescued captives along the Atlantic.[19] The Temne, Baga, Bullom, and the exogenous groups in the colony interacted with one another in Freetown and in the rural villages of the colony. The Liberated Africans demonstrated astuteness in realizing, very early on following their arrival in Sierra Leone, that the key to their survival and progress in the colony lay in their developing close relationships with the local groups, particularly the Temne. This was partly made necessary by the limited agricultural potential of the settlement, and by the fact that they had to, consequently, find an alternative means of economic sustenance based on commerce.

The strength and resiliency of Yoruba-derived cultural institutions had a tremendous influence on the endogenous groups, as is evident in modern Sierra Leone society, with such institutions as the Ojeh (Egugu), Untin (Hunters), and Egunuko (Gunugunu) embraced by the Temne, Mandinka, and others. However, the Liberated African community was likewise acculturated by the indigenous peoples with whom they interacted, thereby facilitating a process of constant "change and adaptation" not unlike the concept of creolization.[20] But first, a look at the diffusion of Yoruba culture in nineteenth-century Sierra Leone.

The people from the area of the Bight of Benin who were rescued from slave vessels along the Atlantic and resettled in Sierra Leone did not arrive in the colony as Yoruba. They invariably arrived as Egba, Ijesa, Ife, Ibadan, Oyo, Ijebu, and so on. The dispersal of these various groups across the Atlantic World was well under way before the constituent parts came to be identified as Yoruba. Indeed, it has been suggested that it may have been as late as the nineteenth century that the nomenclature *Yoruba* came into use as a collective referent for these groups.[21] The collective self-identification may have been engendered by the experiences garnered from the Atlantic trade system by peoples taken from the various political units in the Bight of Benin and their recognition of shared cultural and linguistic commonalities. The cross-cultural encounters with non-Yoruba speakers in the Atlantic World may have had the consequence of inspiring a process of identity-formation among the Yoruba-speaking peoples. This was also true of Liberated Africans from the Bight resettled in the colony of Sierra Leone after the Abolition Act of 1807.[22]

It has been suggested that it was in fact among Liberated Africans relocated to Freetown that "a sense of common ethnicity" initially developed among the various Yoruba-speaking peoples, and ultimately spread in the old country as a result of the return of Saro emigrants from the late 1830s.[23] Peel reminds us that the fall of "the old order of Yorubaland" was largely engendered by the "decline of the long-dominant regional power of Oyo and the destruction of many old communities in its wake." As Peel further notes, the "sometimes prolonged" and widespread wars led to the enslavement of "tens of thousands of people, some of whom ended up as Christian converts in Sierra Leone." Given Peel's particular interest in the "mutual engagement of Christianity and the Yoruba people," he did not take cognizance of the presence of Muslims in the displaced Yoruba-speaking groups that were resettled in nineteenth-century Sierra Leone.[24]

J. Lorand Matory also notes the implications of the decline of the Oyo Empire and the rise of the Dahomean kingdom between "the last quarter of the 18th century until the middle of the 19th" for the dispersal of captives from such places as Egba, Oyo, Egbado, and Ijesa.[25] While a good number of these captives embarked on slave vessels from coastal ports at Lagos, Badagry, Porto-Novo, and Ouidah bound for Brazil and Cuba, a significant number were relocated to Freetown by British sailors. While the Oyo, Egba, Egbado, Ijesa, and Ijebu captives who disembarked in Brazilian ports came to be identified as Nago, their counterparts in Sierra Leone were identified as Oku. Unlike Peel, Matory recognizes the presence of Muslims in the dispersed population of enslaved Africans in the Atlantic World. Indeed, it was these Muslims who engaged in a series of "insurrections and conspiracies" in Bahia between 1807 and 1835.[26] Without any evident correspondence and/or cooperation between the coreligionists across the Atlantic, Muslims in Sierra Leone were also engaged in similar insurrections around about the same period. While many of the insurrectionists were expelled from Bahia by Brazilian authorities, those in Sierra Leone were prosecuted in the first treason trial in the colony and sentenced to jail, a watershed event in the history of the colony. The two groups were seemingly destined to share social and geographical space later in the nineteenth century when Afro-Brazilians from Bahia and Saro from Freetown relocated to and embarked on a variety of commercial and sundry activities in Lagos, Badagry, Porto-Novo, and other coastal and inland towns of West Africa, along with Afro-Cubans from Havana.

According to Matory, the presence of Oyo, Egba, Igbado, Ijesa, and other Yoruba-speaking groups in close proximity in Sierra Leone "made them cognizant of their similarities, particularly in the context of their *shared difference* from the populations of the local Sierra Leonean interior."[27] It was in this context that a Pan-Yoruba identity developed in Sierra Leone, to be further developed in subsequent years, particularly through the efforts of educated Yoruba-speakers such as the Anglican minister Samuel Adjai Crowther, who in 1844 delivered a sermon in his native language to a nondenominational congregation, including Muslims, in Freetown. Crowther was quite conscious of the importance of delivering his sermon in Yoruba, precisely because of his strong consciousness of an Oku social fabric that transcended religious differences. The rendering of the Christian gospel in the Yoruba language, which was preceded by the publication of A *Vocabulary of the Yoruba Language* in 1843, only served to reify the common ethnocultural "unity of these peoples and named that unity by a term previously used by outsiders and reserved for the Oyo—that is, Yoruba."[28] The "literacy and literary accomplishments" of "proto-Yoruba" people in both Sierra Leone and Brazil, Matory argues, accounted for the emergence of a Pan-Yoruba identity across the Atlantic World. Interestingly, the Yoruba people in Sierra Leone preferred to be identified as Oku; while they did not necessarily question their Yoruba-ness, they did not share the propensity of the CMS scholars to identify speakers of the Yoruba language in the colony as Aku.[29] An Oku consciousness was in many ways the key to the development of a Krio identity in Sierra Leone by the late nineteenth century. Yoruba cultural practices, whether traditional or "plastic" (in Sandra Barnes's formulation), were critical to the making of Krio society.

The literature on the dispersal of Africans in the Atlantic World is replete with differing perspectives on the survival of African cultures in the New World. It has been argued that the slave trade across the Atlantic not only uprooted millions of Africans of various ethnicities from their natal communities and relocated them to distant places across the Atlantic World, it invariably distributed peoples from a diversity of cultural and linguistic environments. Thus, the narrative on this cultural and linguistic heterogeneity has all but declared it virtually impossible for traditional cultures of relocated African ethnicities to survive the journey across the seas.[30] The World War II era debate between Melville J. Herskovits and E. Franklin Frazier on the capacity of African cultures to have survived the rapacious environments of slave plantation societies in the Americas best captured the conflicting views on the question of cultural diffusion and survival. In spite of the contending points of view on the subject of survivability of African traditional cultures, it could hardly be disputed that the resiliency of African cultures is manifest in the ways in which "language, religion, family structure, and institutions" in the diaspora have been influenced by the cultures of the various African peoples taken across the Middle Passage.[31] Yoruba cultural influences are prominently evident in diaspora communities in the New World from Bahia to Cuba in religion, language, and other forms. But hardly anywhere in the Atlantic World, outside modern Nigeria, are such influences more pervasively evident than in Sierra Leone.

From the nineteenth century, when the first batch of Yoruba-speaking peoples were landed at the Freetown harbor, through the twentieth century, Yoruba cultural influences were widely diffused in the colony and remain an important feature in modern Sierra Leonean culture. The vitality of Yoruba cultural influence is primarily reflected in its ability to remain relevant in Krio culture, in spite of the "civilizing" agenda of the European Christian missions and the rise of Islamic orthodoxy in the Muslim Krio community. While the worship of Yoruba orishas may have been marginalized by the ascendancy of Christianity and Islam, Yoruba religious beliefs and practices remained relevant and continued to inform the existential reality of the Krio during and after the nineteenth century. Such cultural activities as komojade, awujoh, and other traditional ritual ceremonies in Krio society attest to the resiliency and continued influence of Yoruba religious traditions. The secret societies transplanted from Yorubaland also remained a relevant and "integral part of life" in modern Sierra Leone. It is indeed not an exaggeration to describe the country's contemporary popular culture as primarily derived from the Yoruba heritage of Krio society. Indeed, the magnet that attracted people from various ethnicities in the colony to an emergent Krio society was the "prestige" of Yoruba culture. Matory rightly points to what he calls the "Aku masking societies" derived from the Egungun ancestral masquerades of the Oyo and Egba.[32] The Ojeh, Gelede, and Egunuko in effect served to reify Krio cultural hegemony in the colony, and thus engendered much effort on the part of non-Krio immigrants to the colony to imitate the former.

Yoruba religious practices may have retained their organizational forms relatively intact in the New World, particularly in Bahia and Cuba, although not in Sierra Leone. Nonetheless, traditional religious practices on both sides of the Atlantic did not differ much. In Bahia, Candomblé emerged from the religious traditions of enslaved Africans in Brazil, and served as a source of strength and succor for enslaved persons, and continues to do so for their descendants in modern Brazil. Yoruba adherents of Candomblé worship spiritual entities whom they identify and/or "associate with forces of nature," and to whom they offer ritual sacrifices in their religious temples; these entities or orishas, such as Sango and Ogun, were and are as relevant to the Afro-Brazilians in Bahia as they were in the Yoruba Liberated African communities in Sierra Leone during the nineteenth century. Not unlike the practice of Sango worshippers in the rural villages of Hastings and

Waterloo in nineteenth-century Freetown, "Candomble is . . . a spirit possession cult where some devotes, by different initiation processes, are prepared to embody or to impersonate these deities, who during public ceremonies will dance for hours to the sound of the drums."[33] In Sierra Leone, as in Bahia and Cuba, divination remains a very important part of traditional religious praxis. Unlike their counterparts in the New World who belonged to "cults," such as that of the Oricha Ifa in Cuba, diviners in Sierra Leone did not belong to groups established for, and devoted exclusively to, the practice of determining a person's or group's destiny. Sango and Ogun worshippers in Sierra Leone who engaged in divination were usually members of the Egugu, Ordeh, Egunuko, or some other secret society of Yoruba origin. As in Cuba, the diviner in Sierra Leone also had the Yoruba moniker of *Babalawo*, but was generally known as the "Juweni Orisa" or "merecin man."

The reverential treatment of the Juweni in nineteenth-century Freetown was reflective of the strong and 'unshakeable faith in the healing power of the Yoruba gods.' the most revered of these was Sango, the god of thunder and lightning. The European Christian missionaries and the African clergy were quite conscious of the enduring fealty of the members of their congregations to Yoruba religious traditions and the efficacy of the Juweni or merecin man. They therefore sought to disabuse Christian converts of their continued faithful adherence to Yoruba cultural tenets by primarily seeking to undermine the credibility of the Yoruba gods; they generally described every aspect of religious traditions as witchcraft and ascribed religious praxis to what they perceived and characterized as the general depravity of the local population. Members of the clergy often made appeals to the inhabitants of neighborhoods in the colony that were considered to be strongholds of Sango adherents, as did the Reverend Thomas Dove, who denounced the Liberated Africans in the Grassfields community in the late 1830s for having "brought with them from their native country their own filthy idols." Dove lamented that the people of Grassfields were incorrigibly devoted to "idolatry and superstition, and the most abominable practices."[34] The clergyman accurately observed that Yoruba groups taken off slave vessels in the Atlantic had arrived in Sierra Leone with material culture from their natal communities, all of which helped to facilitate the diffusion of Yoruba culture in the colony.[35]

Yoruba cultural praxis had by the mid-nineteenth century become widely diffused in Freetown, thereby giving rise to a religious and cultural practice of dualism, if not syncretism, that threatened the effectiveness of the evangelical agenda of the Christian missions in particular. A Sierra Leonean clergyman, the Reverend E. W. Fashole-Luke, later observed that "Christian people seem to live a dual existence; they hold firmly to the doctrines of the church, but hold equally firmly the traditional beliefs of their Fathers."[36] Reverend Fashole-Luke noted that while the church regarded "traditional beliefs, rites, and customs as pagan and has ruled that they are inconsistent with the doctrines of Christianity . . . the Church has never had enough authority either to banish these African beliefs from the minds of their members or to abolish the African rites and customs."[37]

In attempting to explain the continued relevance of Yoruba religious practices in Freetown, Reverend Fashole-Luke called attention to the failure of Christianity to take cognizance of the relations between the living and the dead in the life of Africans. He noted that

> it is true that the Church believes in the communion of Saints, but it has failed to develop this doctrine in Freetown, primarily because the manifestations of Christianity in the city have been of the Protestant type, which have tended to undervalue the doctrine and to frown upon prayers for the dead. Nevertheless, the Christians in Freetown continue to go to the graves of their departed relatives, on the great Christian festivals, as well as on New Year's Day, when going on journeys outside the country, or when they are about to undertake some new and responsible task; they also visit the graves at moments of crisis, when misfortune strikes the family, or when someone is about to be married.[38]

Such visits to the graves of deceased family members usually involved readings from the Bible or the Qur'an (depending on one's creed), as well as a strict adherence to Yoruba traditional ritual ceremonies. Thus both Islam and Christianity came to be influenced by Yoruba religious practices and customs. This was even more instructive given the fact that both the church and the colonial state sought to create a constricted environment for the adherents of orishas in Freetown and the adjacent rural villages of the colony. The colonial government enacted police ordinances in the mid-1800s to curtail Yoruba traditional religion; however, many in the Liberated African communities in the colony simply ignored the official edicts, mostly aimed at worshippers of Sango, prohibiting the "public worship of thunder" in what was considered a Christian city.[39]

John Peterson characterized the determined resiliency of Sango adherents in the colony as an "example of the general level of independence in the recaptive group." Even as he sought to explain the continued influences of traditional religion as a function of class differences in the Liberated African population, with Sango worshippers belonging primarily to "the lower strata of the class structure," Peterson nonetheless was careful to observe that Yoruba religious traditions were widely influential. In instances in which converts to Christianity continued to participate in traditional ritual ceremonies, he provided at least three possible reasons for this phenomenon; he posited that this was caused by (1) a disenchantment with the dominant influence of Christians in the society; (2) a disapproval of the absolutist control of European missionaries; and (3) a strong belief in the capacity of Sango or Oduduwa to better attend to the existential needs of traditionalists "than did Jehovah."[40] Thus, the Christian missionaries in the colony made a determined effort to eliminate Yoruba religious practices in the rural villages, especially at Hastings and Waterloo, and in the neighborhood of Oke Mauri in Fula Town.

The success, or the lack thereof, of the Christian missionaries to disabuse the Liberated Africans of their allegiance to traditional religion was at once spiritual even as it was based on existential realities. The Reverend Samuel Adjai Crowther, and his CMS counterpart, Rev. James Johnson, were quite aware of the relevance of Yoruba religious traditions to the lives of the people and sought to educate their fellow missionaries on this subject. Both Crowther and Johnson made strenuous efforts to convey to their European counterparts the need to contextualize the pervasiveness of traditional religion in the colony. They were acutely aware of the belief in a Supreme Being among the Yoruba and other African peoples. Yoruba traditional religion is based on a belief in Olorun (or Olodumare), who is said to have created the universe, following which he assigned lesser divinities (or orisha), such as Sango, Ogun, Osun, and the others, to "mediate between him and humanity." Crowther thus sought to put in perspective the role of Sango and other lesser gods in the religious pantheon of the people; he informed his fellow clergymen that the people were not oblivious to the existence of God, and God's unquestionable authority and power, but simply perceived the orishas as intermediaries between humanity and Olorun (God).[41]

On a secular and more practical level, there were those for whom traditional religion had an economic impetus. As Peterson noted, Crowther encountered an Ifa diviner who informed the Anglican minister that it was imperative that he maintained his belief in Ifa, lest he run the risk of undermining the basis of his vocation as a "doctor"; "for him to forsake his god," he informed Crowther, "would be to put himself out of business."[42] Perhaps in an effort to accommodate the concerns of Crowther and his fellow clergymen, another Ifa diviner decided to incorporate Christian liturgy into his practice; he made it a point to impress upon his clientele the importance of calling upon Jesus Christ prior to carrying out any traditional ritual ceremony. The strong and pervasive belief in traditional religion was also necessitated by an increased incidence of diseases, and a consequent increased mortality rate in the colony. The deplorable conditions on board slave ships that facilitated the spread of diseases and caused the deaths of many of the slave trade captives at sea often continued after they had been rescued and resettled in Freetown and the rural villages of the colony. It is said that "about one-third of the Liberated Africans died within a few weeks of arrival in the colony from illnesses contracted on board the slave ships," primarily due to the incapacity of the Liberated African Department to provide adequate medical care to the increasing number of ex-slave captives being landed at the Freetown harbor.[43]

Environmental conditions in the colony also did much to engender the spread of such diseases as smallpox, yellow fever, and influenza, combined with persistent maladies such as dysentery, dropsy, ulcers, and ophthalmia. Faced with these often-fatal afflictions, for which the colonial government seemed unprepared for or incapable in handling, Liberated Africans turned to traditional religion for answers to their existential challenges. With a high incidence of mortality arising from the outbreak of smallpox, the colony government was found wanting in instituting a consistent and conscientious program of vaccination. According to Peterson, "Even when regular supplies of vaccine did arrive during periods of the century, it was oftentimes of such poor quality or so old that it was useless. On occasion, ordered vaccine never did arrive."[44] Consequently, the Liberated Africans found spiritual and medical assurance from propitiatory acts performed for the gods in traditional ritual ceremonies. By the turn of the century, Muslims as well as Christians were consulting with herbalists and traditional healers such as Daddy Adaba and Adekumbile Cole at Fula Town.[45]

Yoruba cultural influences in nineteenth-century Sierra Leone, and their impact in present-day society, was largely reflected in social groups and esoteric societies, membership into which was open to all the inhabitants of the colony and the rural villages, with gender restrictions in some cases. The rural villages were the central loci of the secret societies, as the

Liberated Africans relocated to these places preserved Yoruban cultural items they had brought with them from their native communities. Items of material culture, including carved wooden replicas of animals, faces of human beings, *bata* (drums), and cloth costumes (such as handwoven "Oku lappa" fabrics), were used in the Liberated African communities where the transplanted Yoruba and their progeny soon replicated various types of traditional organizations into which they had been initiated in the old country.

While a good number of the cultural associations were of an esoteric nature, with membership restricted to initiates only, several others existed simply for purposes of entertainment and often commenced in an impromptu manner. Such impromptu performances were primarily identified with the Ajuba, Agbay, and Bata'a koto, which were open to every member of the community. The performances mostly involved drumming, singing, and dancing, with the drummers drawn from the Ojeh (or Egugu) and Odeh societies, which were exclusively male secret societies; however, women were quite prominent in the Ajuba, Agbay, and Bata'a koto performances, almost invariably providing the lead singers as well as most of the chorus. The impromptu nature of the Ajuba, for example, necessitated the use of instruments that were readily available, including wooden boxes, bottles, and the clapping of hands by participants. There was hardly a distinction between performers and audience, as everybody often joined in. The Ajuba dance is evidence of the diffusion of Yoruba culture in the Atlantic World, stretching from West Africa to North America.

According to Babatunde Lawal, a version of the Ajuba, referred to as the "juba" dance, was a common feature in the community of enslaved West Africans in Wilmington, North Carolina; Cuba; and the Caribbean. While Lawal is uncertain about the "exact origin and the meaning of the term 'juba'" in the New World context, he notes that the term "means homage or obeisance, and often refers to the gesture or dance accompanying it" among the Yoruba. In much the same way as the Yoruba did in the Americas, the Muslim Krio version of the dance in the communities of Fula Town and Fourah Bay was characterized by "intensive body movements and intricate footwork."[46] Ajuba and Agbay performances were sometimes organized by women on the occasion of certain *rites du passage*, such as komojade (child-naming ceremonies) and weddings, providing "colour, glamour and gaiety" to these social events. While the Ajuba, Agbay, and Bata'akoto may have been open to all members of the community, many of the other cultural societies, including the Ojeh, Odeh, and Egunuko, involved ritual initiation ceremonies, the details of which were known only to the initiated.

Among the leading secret societies most reflective of the diffusion of Yoruba culture and through which traditional Yoruba customary practices found expression in nineteenth-century Sierra Leone was the Ojeh (or Egugu). The rural villages of the colony, particularly Hastings and Waterloo, and subsequently the Muslim Krio communities of Fourah Bay and Fula Town, represented the cultural center of Egugu activities during the nineteenth century and after. Members were both feared and respected in their communities, largely because of the society's esoteric nature and its capacity to enforce social order within a constricted social and political environment in the villages. According to Crowther, there was a widespread belief among the inhabitants of the villages that the Egugu was aware of everything that transpired in the community, and therefore had the ability to hold everyone accountable.[47] Paradoxically, while the colonial state and the church sought to suppress Yoruba traditional culture in the quest of "civilizing" the natives, both church and state must have appreciated the capacity of the Ojeh society to maintain an atmosphere of social propriety in the villages. As Peterson noted, "As in Yoruba country itself, the *Agugu* in Hastings was the virtual power behind the throne," a sociopolitical reality that clearly irritated the CMS clergy, but one they could hardly do anything about, in spite of their many efforts to discourage the people's allegiance to Yoruba traditional culture.[48] Christian clergymen were not the only ones concerned about the power and influence of the Egugu in the colony; the Imams and other leading Muslim clerics at Fourah Bay, Fula Town, and Aberdeen also came to disapprove of the secret society, particularly with regard to its capacity to compromise the integrity of the Islamic faith among initiates of the various Ojeh groups. The requirement, for instance, for Muslim and Christian initiates to pledge allegiance to Ogun remained a real concern to both the church and the Muslim jamaats, which of course were committed to the belief in an omniscient and omnipotent God. The tendency of Muslim initiates to "swear to Ogun," rather than to Allah, became one of the primary factors accounting for the schism that emerged at Fourah Bay toward the end of the nineteenth century.

Among the earliest Egugu societies founded in Freetown were the Oke Mauri, and the Awodie at Fula Town and Fourah Bay, respectively. While both of these groups may have been in existence by the mid-nineteenth century, albeit as subsidiaries of the Hastings and Waterloo Ojeh, they emerged into the open in Freetown by the 1880s, but only when their leaders felt sufficiently confident that their activities would not be interfered with by the colonial authorities. The Ojeh developed a reputation for their capacity to heal the sick and afflicted, but especially for the malevolent powers of the resident "merecin man" in the respective societies.[49] Wyse undertook a class analysis of the emergence of the Ojeh in Freetown society before the end of colonial rule, suggesting that the memberships of Oke Mauri and others were drawn from "the lower strata in the country — the unemployed, artisans, unskilled workers and the self-employed." He asserted that upper-class Krio maintained a self-conscious distance from the Ojeh, because this stratum of Krio society "could not reconcile its Christian and Western background with membership of such obviously deviant organizations." Perhaps aware that his fixation with the supposed Western influence on Krio culture was obviously evident in his analysis, he quickly sought to qualify his assertion by noting the presence of educated Krio in the membership of the Ojeh, and the significance of Yoruba culture in the emergent Krio society.[50] The founding of Ojeh societies in Freetown was especially significant, because it transcended religious affiliations, and also because it served to further diminish the effectiveness of efforts by colonial church and state officials to create a fissure between Liberated Africans on grounds of differences in religious worldviews. Muslims and Christians, as well as adherents of Sango and Ogun, regardless of their socioeconomic strata, became members of the various Ojeh societies in the rural villages and in Freetown.

Further reflecting the impact of Yoruba culture on the development of Krio society was the role and place of the Odeh society. Like the Ojeh, the former grew out of a tradition imported from Yorubaland by the recaptives resettled in Sierra Leone in the nineteenth century.[51] Peterson contended that the society emerged in the rural villages, such as Hastings, as a result of the villagers' "need to hunt." He maintained that the society "developed into a distinctly Creole secret society which for many served as a more sophisticated replacement for Agugu." Peterson's assertion is also reflective of the fixation on the "Englishness" of Krio on the part of earlier scholars responsible for the production of knowledge in nineteenth-century Krio society. He sought to identify the Odeh society with the colonial establishment by describing it as a "secret organization of Creole civil servants with the governor as the society's patron."[52] But Peterson failed to provide much detailed information about the civil servants, including their religious worldviews. However, the first organized Odeh society in the colony,

Odileh, emerged at Fula Town in the 1880s under the leadership of the renowned diviner, healer, and herbalist Adekumbile (Odileh) Cole, who remained the *Asipa* (leader) and for whom the society was named.[53] The role and place of diviners and herbalists in the Odeh and Ojeh secret societies not only reflected the centrality of Yoruba culture, these secret organizations also provided an outlet for the activities of practitioners of religious tradition, especially as traditional Yoruba religion was not organized as an institution in the same way as were Islam and Christianity. There were no temples, for instance, dedicated to Sango or Ogun in a colony with a plethora of mosques and churches.

Transplanted Yoruba religious practices also found outlets in such other secret societies as Gelede and Egunuko. Feared as well as revered in nineteenth-century Freetown, these societies remain so in present-day Sierra Leone. The origins of Gelede have been traced to eighteenth-century Ketu, from whence it spread to Yoruba-speaking peoples in Ohori, Egbado, and elsewhere in the Bight of Benin, and, as a result of the transatlantic slave trade, to Sierra Leone and the New World.[54] As in Ketu and elsewhere in Nigeria, the Sierra Leone rendering of Gelede assigned a primary role to women, unlike the Ojeh and Odeh societies. The empowerment of women made evident in the primacy of the female gender in Gelede is not accidental; the society emerged in the old country specifically to acknowledge the inherent capacity of women to enhance the productive capacity of the community. Women were presumed to be even more powerful than the orishas and were thus placed on a pedestal and much celebrated.

Gelede in nineteenth-century Freetown paid homage to the central role played by women in the local markets, not unlike women in Yorubaland. Indeed, this central role played by women in trade is directly related to the growth of Krio nomenclature (i.e., the reference to Krio as traders). Liberated African women in the rural villages and in Freetown displayed a predilection for carrying their wares on their heads, plying such wares in their community and beyond, consequently acquiring the oki (or oriki) of Akiriyo (as explicated in the introduction). All of these organizations served to solidify the bonds between all Yoruba descendants in Sierra Leone, regardless of differences in religious outlook, and ultimately facilitated the "reconstruction" of Yoruba culture in the creolizing atmosphere of colonial Freetown during the nineteenth century.

The foregoing examination of the diffusion of Yoruba culture is partly aimed at debunking the emphasis on, if not exaggeration of, Western influences in the makings of Krio society during the nineteenth century. That some of the early Christianized elders of Krio society were enamored of their status as "subjects" of "Mammy Queen" (Queen Victoria of England) can certainly not be denied. By acquiring Western educations and becoming converts to Christianity, many came to believe in the presumed superiority of Victorian English values and, consciously or unconsciously, came to equate Christianity with "civilization," in consonance with the outlook of the European evangelical missions and the colonial establishment. The British colonial establishment and the evangelical missions were determined to inculcate in the resettled peoples the idea of the cultural superiority of Victorian English values and, therefore, sought to disabuse the descendants of Yoruba-speaking Liberated Africans who had joined the ranks of the Christian elite in nineteenth-century Freetown of any allegiance to their Yoruba heritage. The colonial establishment ultimately assigned the designation of "Creoles" to the emergent Christian elite to distinguish them from non-Christians, regardless of shared cultural homogeneity. While all Yoruba-speaking Liberated Africans and their descendants in the colony had hitherto identified themselves as "Oku," and were so recognized by others, the colonial establishment embarked on a determined agenda to create a bifurcated social environment in which Christians were distinguished from the "Other," primarily based on creed. The emergent Christian elite consequently came to uncritically accept and appropriate the meaning and definition of "Creole" as representative of the nascent community.

It is therefore imperative that we consider the meaning of *Creole* in the context of nineteenth-century Sierra Leone. How accurate was the application of the moniker *Creole* to the Liberated Africans and their descendants in late nineteenth-century Freetown? Was the post–slave trade settlement that produced present-day Krio a truly creolizing environment? In what ways was that environment similar to that of Caribbean slave societies? And if not similar, how dissimilar were they? These are some of the questions that I would like to consider next.

(RE)CONSTITUTING NINETEENTH-CENTURY SIERRA
LEONE II: AUTOCHTHONES IN THE LIBERATED AFRICAN
COMMUNITY AND KRIO SOCIETY

As noted earlier, the Liberated African community included a good number of autochthones, including Baga, Bullom, Mende, Sherbro, and Temne. These groups have hardly been acknowledged in much of the earlier examination of the development of Krio society, which elicits the question of historical precision with regard to the evolution of Krio society. Together with the Yoruba Liberated Africans, these groups also played a crucial role in the cultural growth of the emergent society. Both the Temne and the Mende had a profound influence on the adoption of the female circumcision society, known as Bondo, by the Muslim Krio. These indigenous ethnicities in the Liberated African villages of the colony also subsequently absorbed other Mende, Temne, Baga, Sherbro, and so forth, who were not part of the Liberated African community. Indeed, the development of colony-interior trade soon led to an integration of many more of the interior peoples into the nascent Krio society. But even prior to the fluid movement of peoples from the interior to the colony, there is evidence for the presence of these groups in the colony population. Freetown, contrary to public memory, was hardly an exclusively Krio society. Its heterogeneity was quite evident from the earliest days of the founding of the "province of freedom," and certainly as a consequence of the Act of Prohibition.

Even as Britain was formally proscribing the slave trade, British slave traders continued to work in tacit collaboration with their American counterparts in the selling and transporting of captives from the vicinity of the Freetown settlement.[55] Between November 1807 and March 1808, almost two hundred people captured in or near the Temne town of Ragbana were freed and resettled in the Liberated African community in Rokyamp (Freetown). Their numbers in the community were subsequently increased due to a rise in the social and commercial interactions between the resettled freed captives and the inhabitants of the surrounding communities. In time, many of the offspring of the Temne who joined the settlement and intermarried with the Liberated Africans rose to social prominence in emergent Krio society. The Reverend Crowley Nicol, for instance, who was later appointed native colonial chaplain of the Anglican Church, was the son of a Temne father and a Soso mother. He later married the daughter of Bishop Samuel Adjai Crowther.[56] In addition to the likes of Nicol, one of the earliest graduates of CMS Grammar School, Frederick Karli, was a Temne from Port Loko. To further complicate the cultural makeup of Krio society, one of the villages in the Eastern District of the colony, Koya, had a predominantly Temne population, and also a good number of Bullom, Bunduka, and Kosso (Mende),[57] many of whom became integrated into the Liberated African community.

Among the Liberated Africans taken off slave ships in the Atlantic and set free in Freetown between 1814 and 1816 were many of Soso origin; these were subsequently resettled in the rural villages of the colony. The "General Return of Slaves" report for the period covering 5 January 1814 to 4 January 1816 shows a total of 1, 296 persons relocated to the villages. This group of men, women, and children was recorded as having been rescued in such places as the Rio Pongas, Isle de Los, Plantain Islands, Banana Islands, and their surrounding district.[58] The "Annual Report of Natives of Sierra Leone" for the first decade of the nineteenth century indicates a strong presence of people from autochthonous groups, with names such as Coombah, Jeneba, Cancuu, Balay, Yoro, Kai, Yatta, Balla, and Musu, all of which are common to the Mende, Temne, Limba, and Sherbro peoples, among others.[59]

The increasing number of people captured by slave traders and, subsequently, released at Freetown during the second half of the nineteenth century can be attributed to increased activity by slave traders in the area. In 1827, Governor Sir Neil Campbell warned his superiors at the Colonial Office in London of the threat posed by slave traders. He advised Whitehall that the only way to safeguard the fledgling colony was to reinforce and increase the patrols of the antislavery squadrons along the Sierra Leone River and the Atlantic Ocean.[60] He urged Viscount Goderich, secretary of state for the colonies, to impress upon the Portuguese governor of Bissau the potential consequences of continued Portuguese slaving activities in the vicinity of Sierra Leone, especially along the Nunez and Scarcies Rivers. Campbell reported to Goderich that the constant traffic of boats manned by natives of the Rio Grande had caused him to serve notice to rulers of the towns along the river that the colonial state was not going to tolerate further slave trading activities. Campbell was all too aware that the trade in human captives was thriving in the Gallinas and Sherbro areas as well. Thus Comm. Alexander Gordon was assigned the task of intercepting slave vessels in these areas; in 1829, he successfully intercepted the slave vessel *La Laure* along the Sherbro coast and took into custody the crew and about one hundred captives.[61]

Further evidence for the presence and contributory role of indigenous elements in the evolution of Krio society can be traced back to as early as 1797, when Zachary Macaulay left Sierra Leone for Britain, accompanied by "twenty boys and four girls, some of the children from up-country whose education he had been supervising." Most of the young people taken by Macaulay returned to Sierra Leone following the completion of their education at Clapham, with the male graduates subsequently integrated into the colonial bureaucracy. Among those employed by the colonial state was John Macaulay

Wilson, whose father was the leader of Kafu Bulom.[62] Evidence exists for the inclusion of still other indigenous ethnic groups in the demographic composition of the communities that evolved into Krio society. Hogbrook Village (renamed Regent) was originally inhabited by "a shipload of Vai." Captives taken by slave traders in Mende country were among the earliest inhabitants of the PaSanday village (renamed Lumley). It was certainly not unusual for the British navy to record the point of embarkation of captives found on board a slave ship simply as "the coast adjoining the colony." The Trans-Atlantic Slave Trade Database, edited by David Eltis and David Richardson, shows evidence of the practice by the British navy, perhaps not without cause, to simply record the area of embarkation of rescued captives (e.g., Bight of Benin, port unspecified, Sierra Leone, port unspecified, Cameroons River, etc.).[63] In the 1820s, Regent village was marked by its cultural diversity; the inhabitants included Kono, Soso, and Bullom from the colony neighborhood; Bassa, Kroo, and Gola from the Cape Mesurado region; and Igbo, Efik, Kalabari, Yoruba, and Hausa shipped from the Bights. Among the inhabitants of Gloucester could be found many of Temne, Mende, Mandinka, Fanti, Igbo, and Congo origins. Captives from the Congo region predominated Congo Town.

Invaluable sources of evidence for the presence of captives from the interior of Sierra Leone are the "Liberated African Register" and the "Register of Alien Children in the Colony." The colony administration sought to distinguish Africans rescued from slave ships from those who immigrated into the colony from the interior by classifying the latter as "Aliens." The "Liberated African Register" thus contains the names, ages, gender, and other statistical data on slave trade captives released at Freetown, while the "Register of Alien Children" includes the names, ages and gender of young people in the colony as shown in figure 1.1.

Name	Age	Gender	Height
Abasey	29	M	4′11″
Brema	10	M	4′3″
Demba	20	M	5′6″
Massah	26	M	5′3″
Cumba	27	F	n/a
Yenno	18	F	n/a
Yamba	26	M	n/a

Figure 1.1: Liberated Africans originally captured in interior of Sierra Leone

Some of the individuals noted in the colonial records were distributed in the rural villages, but no precise locations were entered in the volumes. Others either were apprenticed to residents of the colony or were recruited into the Second West India Regiment.[64]

By the second half of the nineteenth century, the Liberated African population in the colony villages included young children from the hinterland of the colony, most of whom were distributed to colony households as "wards," and in time became disconnected, for all intents and purposes, from their native cultures and became fully integrated into emergent Krio society. It would not be illogical to suggest that the immense linguistic contribution made to the Krio language by the various indigenous ethnic groups was made possible by the presence of these young people in the colony. Figure 1.2 reflects the ethnic diversity of young Liberated Africans found in the colony in 1865.[65]

Name	Age	Gender	Ethnicity
Binty	9	F	Timmaney
Caramoko	6	M	Mandinka
Condeh	4	F	Kooranko
Damma	8	F	Sherbro
Fatmatta	11	F	Foulah
Fudia	11	F	Mandinka
Isata	7	F	Sooso

Figure 1.2: Ethnic provenance of young Liberated Africans in the colony

AUTOCHTHONES AND LOANWORDS IN KRIO

The significant contact between, and among, the various ethnicities, languages, and cultures within the Liberated African community in the villages, and between the latter and others who were never taken across the Atlantic to the slave plantations of the New World, facilitated the development of a Creole language, and hence the multicultural identity of the emergent Krio in nineteenth-century Sierra Leone.[66] Thus, further evidence for the significance of autochthonous contributions to the evolution of Krio society can be found in loanwords in the Krio language. J. Berry and Eldred Durosimi Jones, leading scholars on the language, are agreed on the crucial role of indigenous cultures in the development of Krio as a lingua franca in the colony during the nineteenth century; both assertively pointed out the role of Temne, Mende, and other local dialects as primary sources of loanwords in Krio, in addition to other extra–Sierra Leonean languages such as Hausa, Igbo, Wolof, and Yoruba.[67]

While no other groups have more loanwords in Krio than the Yoruba and the English, the Temne and Mende, for example, made quite significant contributions to the development of the language and, given the dynamic nature of language development, continue to do so. Loanwords from the latter two cultural groups include plant names, animal and bird names, and words for cooking utensils, as well as more abstract nouns.[68] For instance, the word *woto*, as in *babu woto* (ugly person), is derived from the Temne word *ka-wotho*, denoting the same. Other loanwords with autochthonous provenance are included in figure 1.3:

ETHNICITY	LOAN	MEANING	ETYMOLOGY
Fula	Chuk	Stab/Pierce	Chuk
Limba	Shuku	Basket	Shuku
Mende	Mumu	Mute	Mumu
Themne	Kombra	Suckling Mother	Kom'ra
Themne	Behl	Sweet Talk	Behl
Themne	Kongosa	Gossip	N'konkosa
Vai	Titi	Girl	Titi

Figure 1.3: Krion loanwords from Sierra Leone groups

Figure 4 (below) includes borrowings from Yoruba and other West African groups:

ETHNICITY	LOAN	MEANING	ETYMOLOGY
Hausa	Alafia	Peace/Serenity	Alafia
Hausa	Wahala	Problem/Trouble	Wahala
Igbo	Unu/Una	You	Unu
Yoruba	Aje	Witchcraft	Aje
Yoruba	Akpa	Extravagant/Wasteful	Akpa
Yoruba	Dabaru	Deceitful	Dabaru
Yoruba	Dobale	To prostrate	Dobale
Yoruba	Okoyawo/Yawo	Groom/Bride	Oko Iyawo/Iyawo

Figure 1.4: Krio loanwords from Yoruba, Hausa, and Igbo

Jones draws attention to the fact that little or no phonetic changes occurred in the transfer of loanwords from African languages to Krio. The loanwords from Temne, Mende, Yoruba and other African languages were necessitated by a profound need for fluid communication in the multiethnic Liberated African community. In time, a pidgin or Creole language developed that facilitated fluid means of communication in the post–slave trade colony. The new language, Krio, would subsequently transcend its creolized state and develop into a fluid, full-fledged identifiable language with its own syntax, phonology, lexicon, and grammar. The language, along with a common culture and development of customary practices embraced by members of the community, served to enhance the capacity of the returnee population to coalesce into the new Krio ethnic group by the late nineteenth century.

This new entity was remarkable for its cultural as well as its religious diversity, in spite of suggestions to the contrary.[69] There were Christians and Muslims, as well as those who did not belong to either of the two monotheistic faiths, even though the majority had by the mid-nineteenth century been converted to Christianity; while a significant minority elected to retain a Muslim identity, many others steadfastly retained a preference for traditional religious practices, with the adherents of Sango and Ogun being the most resistant to efforts by Muslim and Christian missionary activists who sought to convert them to one or the other Abrahamic faith. Even more recent scholarship has served to complicate, or perhaps improve, our understanding of the progeny of the many words common in the vocabulary of Muslim communities in West Africa, including those of the Muslim Krio in Sierra Leone. The transnational implications of long-distance trade in the trans-Saharan trails have been investigated by scholars like Stefan Reichmuth (1998), who was cited in Peel's *Religious Encounter and the Making of the Yoruba*, thus revising our understanding of the spread of Islam in West Africa and the origins of words like *Imale*. It was long held in the Muslim Krio communities that words like *alfa* (Muslim cleric), *walaa* (writing board), *saraa* (alms), and *awe* (fasting period of Ramadan) came to be part of the lexicon of the Muslim communities from Arabic via Hausa. However, Peel uses the work of Reichmuth to show that, rather than Hausa, these loanwords were transmitted by Songhai immigrants along the Niger.[70]

CREOLIZATION AND (KRIO)LIZATION
IN COLONIAL FREETOWN

The official appendage of "Creole" placed on the new society-in-the-making in nineteenth-century Freetown may have been informed by the evident similarity between colonial Freetown and New World social environments that engendered the development of Creole societies in the Caribbean and colonial Louisiana; but it was also a convenient political act, as it was an instance of intellectual indifference, at best, on the part of scholars who subsequently examined the evolution of the emergent society and rather uncritically adopted the colonial moniker. The colonial officials who attached this moniker to the post–slave trade society in Sierra Leone acted on the basis of a cursory understanding of the ecological environment that was nineteenth-century Freetown. The understanding of Creole, on which the designation was based, hinged on the thesis that the descendants of the resettled manumitted slaves and Liberated Africans were born in Sierra Leone, outside the native communities of their parents. This notion of Creole was itself born out of New World understanding and definition of the progeny of immigrants from the Old World.[71] Africans taken across the Middle Passage were distinguished from their counterparts born in slave plantations by such tags as "salt-water negroes" and "creoles," with the latter term reserved for those born in the plantations. The term *Creole* was also applied to children born to interracial couples. Based on such definitions, and with the development of a common language, with English as its foundational anchor, colonial officials and ethnographers identified the language and people speaking an evolving pidgin (or patois) that later developed into a full-fledged language as "Creoles." The accuracy and relevance of the designation has been accompanied by a great deal of ambivalence, especially because the word is often confused with *Krio*, which is the preferred ethnonym of the people in modern Sierra Leone. The attendant ambivalence vis-à-vis the use of *Creole* in reference to the language and people is itself a consequence of the colonial environment in which Krio society developed.

The Krio language, the mother tongue of the people of the same name and the lingua franca of modern Sierra Leone, grew out of a need for a common medium of communication in the "province of freedom," not unlike the ways in which Caribbean Creole languages emerged during the days of plantation slavery. As obtained on the Caribbean islands, the Krio language in Sierra Leone was successfully utilized to bridge the communication gulf, as it were, between the multiple language groups in nineteenth-century Freetown. The cultural and language diversity that made necessary the development of a common mode of communication occurred in what was clearly a creolized environment.[72] Nineteenth-century Freetown was not necessarily the destination of peoples who were involuntarily made to leave their natal communities. However, the reality with which they were confronted, and the realities of the colonial environment into which they were thrust, was not dissimilar to the societies in which people who had been forcibly taken across the Atlantic to the Americas were relocated. Freetown, like the Caribbean islands, posed severe ecological challenges to the relocated groups during the late eighteenth century and for much of the ensuing decades of the nineteenth. It was in these conditions, with the attendant existential challenges, that the various groups devised the communicative and other critical mechanisms to address the daily challenges of life in the colony, making the necessary adjustments in every facet of their lives as the situation demanded.

What distinguishes Sierra Leone Krio from its Caribbean counterparts is the unique contribution of the Yoruba language, and to a lesser extent of Temne and other African languages, to its vocabulary during the nineteenth century and after. Even though Krio had its foundational basis in English, and includes words from Portuguese (e.g., *sabi*: to know) and French (e.g., *boku*: plenty), the European influence was ephemeral relative to that of Yoruba and other African languages. With about two hundred languages spoken among the various ex-slaves and "recaptive" groups in the colony by 1850, Yoruba culture and language, and Islam (for some) served as the most important creolizing influences in the colony. With Yoruba Liberated Africans constituting the largest ethnic group in the colony, they retained the ability to maintain their cultural identity and preserve the traditional institutions they had brought from the old country.[73] Some individual Yoruba personalities, particularly clergymen, such as Rev. Samuel Adjai Crowther, and other luminaries like Sir Samuel Lewis, were integrated into the colonial establishment; however, the vast majority were removed from the upper stratum of colonial society, and did not have the financial wherewithal to make their way back to the old country as some of their more financially successful countrymen did in the nineteenth century. They therefore found it necessary to adapt to their new home in Sierra Leone by developing 'new alliances transcending ethnic . . . origins.' Islam was at once an agency of creolization, as it was an agency of resistance to Westernizing, Christian influences. While upper-class Christian Krio were inculcated with a sense of cultural superiority and, therefore, remained aloof and detached from the "natives" (the Other), Muslims in the nascent Krio society took a different path and sought to identify with the African value system(s) of the indigenous ethnicities, especially in the colony villages. Outside the upper class of Krio society, Muslim and Christian Krio were thereby able to absorb, consciously and unconsciously, aspects of indigenous cultures and cultural forms that remained "foreign" to their upper-class kin.

Ultimately, the emergent Krio society came to reflect an amalgam of cultural heritages, including autochthonous elements, such as the local Temne, Baga, Soso, Mandinka, Mende, and exogenous groups like the Wolof, Fula, Igbo, Fante, Popo, Congo, and others, with the Yoruba as the dominant cultural factor. In this instance of historical creolization, these groups were ultimately able to create 'new social and cultural forms that integrated characteristics of their various heritages.'With the Yoruba constituting the largest ethnic and cultural faction within the Liberated African community, the religious, economic, and social institutions of that group remained the dominant integrative forces, and the growing significance of Liberated Africans of Yoruba provenance in the colonial establishment and Christian clergy only served to solidify their cultural hegemony in the colony. Knorr notes that "due to the ongoing mixing of the various immigrant groups, the distinction between the 'indigenous' and 'exogenous' persons and groups became increasingly obsolete and gradually all people were characterized as 'creole' who descended from former slaves on the one hand and between members of different heritages and skin color on the other." The question of skin color, however, was irrelevant to the Sierra Leone situation, in that there was hardly any instance of race mixing in nineteenth-century Freetown.[74] "Race," as it played out in the New World context, was not significant in the creolization process; its impact was more political — resistance against colonial racism — rather than demographic.

The demography of colonial Freetown did not reflect much evidence of race mixing; however, like all societies under European imperial control in West Africa, it was an environment "characterized by dominance and subjugation." Such an environment facilitated an imperative need on the part of the dominated population for social cohesion and ultimately engendered a shared cultural identity, transmitted, inter alia, in a common language. Yoruba traditional institutions, along with those of the other cultural groups, were successfully utilized to create a new Krio society, without destroying the unique contributions of the individual cultures. The new society was significantly influenced by the teachings of the European

Christian missions and, as a result, integrated aspects of Victorian English values; however, those values did not create the oft-repeated society of "Black Englishmen." The emergent Krio society preserved its fundamental African (primarily Yoruba) heritage, and the people remained ever cognizant of the role and place of the colonial and metropolitan culture in their subjugation as well as in the earlier slave trade. By the late nineteenth century, the people were already developing a sense of belonging to an identifiable ethnic group, sometimes self-identified as "Sierra Leoneans," or "Creoles." They had "become indigenized" and no longer primarily identified themselves as anything other than people of Sierra Leone. The creation of the new society was by the turn of the century completed, with the group reflecting a sense of shared identity as members of an identifiable ethnicity, with a common language, culture, and values.

The Krio culture that emerged out of the creolizing environment of nineteenth-century Freetown was unmistakably African, albeit with significant input from European Christendom in so far as the vast majority of the people were concerned. A small minority of Krio, which is the focus of this work, steadfastly elected to adhere to the Islamic faith. An even smaller faction clung to aspects of traditional religion, with many engaging in spiritual practices that can be characterized as religious syncretism, or of dualism. Indeed, not only did many Krio demonstrate a propensity toward religious syncretism, this became a feature of the emergent society. Whether they were members of the Christian faith and/or Muslims, many Krio alternated between their monotheistic creeds and traditional African religious practices not only in the nineteenth century, but long after the turn of the century.[75] Muslim and Christian Krio were monotheistic in so far as their religious beliefs were concerned; nonetheless, they were not reluctant to consult with the merecin man or diviner.

A prominent Krio theologian, Rev. E.W. Fashole-Luke, openly acknowledged that Christianity faced a "tremendous problem," because of what he perceived as the religious duality of Christian Krio. According to Reverend Fashole-Luke, "They hold firmly to the doctrines of the Church, but they hold equally firmly the traditional beliefs of their fathers. The two are kept in watertight compartments and are seldom, if ever, allowed to come together or interact upon each other." He sought to explain this "dual existence" by ascribing it to the unwillingness of the church to accept traditional religious practices; he noted that "the Church had always regarded all African traditional beliefs, rites, and customs as pagan and has ruled that they are inconsistent with the doctrines of Christianity; but the Church has never had enough authority to banish these African beliefs from the minds of her members or to abolish the African rites and customs."[76] The pervasiveness of traditional practices may have facilitated the development of another form of mixing that enabled Krio society to demonstrate an inclusiveness that is not necessarily reflected in public memory. This is the notion of what I refer to as (krio)lization, which was the mechanism used, post-creolization, to incorporate members of other ethnicities in the colony, and from the hinterland, into Krio society.

With the process of creolization, which gave rise to the coalescing of the returnee population into the Krio, completed by the late nineteenth century, another, altogether new, process of integration was taking place in the colony. This involved the assimilation of peoples from various ethnicities into Krio society. The latter was to prove its capacity to absorb people from other ethnicities and cultures, and to demonstrate its cultural flexibility, when Krio sojourners in the interior began to return to the colony with young children from hinterland families who were adopted and raised, for all intents and purposes, as Krio. This was the beginning of the "ward" system, which became the primary means of (krio)lization for a significant proportion of people who underwent a process of acculturation that enabled them to, in effect, become Krio. The act of *becoming Krio* had the effect of not only increasing the population of the group in the late nineteenth and early twentieth centuries, but in virtually eviscerating the ethnic identity of the (krio)lized person. Many Loko, Limba, Themne, Mende, and Sherbro would ultimately replace their "primordial culture" with that of a Krio identity, firmly effected by means of education, socialization, politicization, and the adoption of "Christian" names in place of "native" ones.[77]

The beginnings of (krio)lization may have been born out of sheer altruism on the part of some of the itinerant Krio traders in the interior states, Christians and Muslims alike. These traders often returned to the colony with young boys, and sometimes with young girls, with the understanding that they would grow up in an environment in which they would be able to attend school, thereby having the prospect of a better life relative to what they would have obtained in their native communities. But sheer altruism as a motivation for the adoption of young hinterland children into Krio families in Freetown was only one of the factors accounting for (krio)lization. The missionary factor (i.e., the evangelization of non-Christians), could also be used to explain the utility of an assimilationist mechanism through which the population of Krio society was increased. Young children and adolescents adopted into Christian Krio households were brought in with the caveat that they were to be baptized, and they were required to attend church services and Sunday school.

The European evangelical missions had recognized very early on that the establishment of schools constituted the most effective means of distributing the Christian gospel, and by the mid-nineteenth century had founded several grammar schools in the colony. The CMS and Wesleyans were the first of the missions to recognize the efficacy of educational institutions to advance the Christian faith, with the former taking the lead in founding seminaries and schools. By 1814, the CMS had bought land at Leicester village for the construction of a Christian institution in which to train the children of Liberated Africans who would be sent out into the interior and elsewhere to serve as teachers and missionaries; however, the planned school at Leicester was abandoned and a small group of prospective students were relocated to Regent village in 1820.[78]

The need for replacement of European missionary personnel who were experiencing an increased incidence of mortality in the challenging tropical environment made the development of African personnel even more urgent. It was therefore decided that the Christian institution be expanded and relocated to a larger estate in the colony; a more suitable plot of land was purchased from Governor Charles Turner at Fourah Bay for £335 on which a new institution, renamed Fourah Bay Institution, was founded on 4 April 1827.[79] Following the establishment of a seminary at Fourah Bay, the CMS founded a grammar school in 1845, followed by a female institution (later named the Annie Walsh Memorial School) in 1849. While these schools were obviously founded for the children of Liberated Africans, in time they came to serve the broader (krio)lizing process under way in the mid-nineteenth century. The elementary and secondary schools run by the Christian missions served the purpose of improving not only the English-speaking skills of the young wards from the interior, but, more importantly, their capacity to read and understand the gospel.

Many of the young children and adolescents enrolled in the schools were of Mende ethnicity; however, the Mende presence in the colony in the late nineteenth century was also a consequence of the need for labor. The administrations of Governors James Hay and C. A. King-Harman were committed to a program of road construction connecting the coast and the Northern Rivers, and both acknowledged the need for large-scale recruitment of labor forces in areas outside the colony. The colony administration also recognized the importance of having strong labor leaders upon whom the colony government could depend to facilitate not only a successful recruitment, but also a disciplined labor force that would ensure the successful and timely completion of the road construction project. One such labor leader emerged in the person of Alimamy Lamina, who was eventually given the title of headman of his Mende people in the colony in the 1880s. Lamina proved to be an effective recruiter of Mende workers during the Hay administration and, subsequently, under Governor King-Harman.[80] He proved quite useful to the colony government in the mobilization of troops for the Benin Expedition, the 1895 Boundary Commission, the Karene Expedition, and other operations during the 1898 uprising.

As Lamina's role in the recruitment and organization of a competent labor force grew, he was gradually integrated into the colonial establishment and subsequently came to experience an upward social and professional mobility in the colonial bureaucracy. He soon began to emulate and assumed the ways of his Krio associates and ultimately became acculturated and, as it were, underwent the process of becoming Krio. He eventually dropped his former name of Lamina, and assumed the new name of George Cummings. But he was certainly not the first to undergo the process of (krio)lization in late nineteenth-century Freetown. Mende workers in the colony had been trying to get the colony government to recognize a single leader of all Mende in the colony for quite some time, and in 1873 elected John Blair Campbell. The group petitioned the administration to officially recognize Campbell's election, but the administration proved to be partial to Cummings, who received the official nod as Mende leader in 1896.[81] Perhaps taking a page from Cummings and Campbell, many other Mende adopted names like Palmer, McCarthy, Caulker, and Johnson, and inculcated Krio values and manners, thereby completing the (krio)lization process.

The Kroo were another group whose members also gravitated toward the Krio, with many eventually shedding their Kroo heritage and becoming (krio)lized. The Kroo had been a known quantity in the Sierra Leone Colony for an extended period, going back to 1793. They were first recruited to serve on board ships and as stevedores by the Sierra Leone Company, and later expanded their role to other industries, including the timber and other trades. They were also largely transient, and went back and forth between their native communities around Cape Mesurado to the south of the Sierra Leone River; however, by 1819, the Kroo community was increasing significantly, and their contribution to the colonial economy as consumers was slowly gaining notice in the colonial establishment.[82]

They were officially recognized and included in the "tribal" administrative structure put in place during the Hay administration, with a headman of their own; Kroo leaders, like their Mende counterparts, soon became integrated into the Freetown establishment and gradually became (krio) lized. Kroo leaders like Prince Albert, King William, Thomas Peters, Jack Savage, and many of their successors subsequently became fully assimilated into Krio society.[83]

The (krio)lizing process ultimately had the further effect of complicating the history of Krio society, even as it also served to enrich its culture and language. It is indeed almost impossible in modern Krio society to distinguish the descendants of Liberated Africans and the earlier settler groups from those of assimilated Krio. Many of the latter would certainly perceive it an act of unmitigated gall if one were to even suggest the possibility of their ancestry originating in the interior of Sierra Leone. It is no secret that most Krio would rather be identified with the Yoruba, Igbo, Fante, and other extra–Sierra Leonean provenance than with such endogenous heritages as Mende or Temne. That has, however, not been without its implications with regard to questions of ethnic essentialism.

One of the subtle, but very significant, effects of the act of becoming Krio was the undeniable question of what some came to perceive as Krio "purity." Sierra Leone society, or perhaps Freetown, to be more precise, has long had to confront issues related to the subject of who was a "real" or "blue-blooded" Krio. The Krio language itself is reflective of this cultural conundrum. It is not uncommon to hear reference to *kangbeh* Krio (or one who is descended from a [krio]lized person); in effect, one whose Krio ethnicity is suspect. Nonetheless, the overall impact of the (krio)lization process is one of a positive nature, with the Krio language and culture, for instance, enriched through loanwords and other cultural attributes introduced by assimilated immigrants.

Perhaps in much the same way that Sigismund Koelle (1854) may have perceived it, the society that emerged in late nineteenth-century Freetown was of a polyglot nature that continued to absorb incoming groups in the ensuing period. What ultimately came to be Krio society was reflective of its ability to be inclusive, and its plasticity. Krio society developed as an identifiable ethnocultural entity precisely because of its demonstrated ability to develop a sense of "sameness" among the heterogeneous collection of peoples who were able to develop a mode of communication in a creolizing environment via a pidgin/Creole language that itself evolved to become a full-fledged language with its own morphology, syntax, and rules of grammar. The group of formerly exogenous units ultimately became indigenized, with a shared set of practices and identity that is an amalgam of various Yoruba practices and others contributed by speakers of various other languages from the Atlantic, and the interior of Sierra Leone. That cultural diversity was itself the source of its "cultural vitality," as I have argued. The speakers of dialects of Yoruba, as well as the speakers of such divergent languages as Temne, Mende, Mandinka, Soso, Wolof, and so on, all eventually came to embrace aspects of other exogenous cultural praxis. In the process, Krio society came to constitute the characteristics, as I have noted, of a "complex society," with differentiated social classes and religious worldviews. The conscious embracing of Islam by a segment of the emergent Krio, while it appeared to threaten the status quo of the colonial environment, did not in any meaningful way subvert the social fabric of Krio society.

2 ᗖ Islam, Christianity, and the State in Colonial Freetown

Ile la ba Ifa, ile la ba Imale, osagangan ni ti Igbagbo

(We met Ifa at home, we met Islam at home, but only later in the day did we encounter Christianity.)

—Yoruba aphorism

AS IN THE OLD COUNTRY IN YORUBALAND, Islam had successfully penetrated the Sierra Leone Peninsula long before the British founded a settlement for Africans freed from enslavement in Europe, and later for those recaptured from slave ships in the Atlantic Ocean. Notwithstanding the assumption by the founders that the first settlers on board the *Nautilus* who landed at the Sierra Leone Peninsula in May 1787 would be building a Christian city, a new "province of freedom," envisaged to be an extension of European Christendom, the British were well aware that they would have to deal with the long-established Islamic faith and other indigenous religions in the region. As in the French-controlled city of Saint-Louis in Senegal, British colonial officials in Sierra Leone "did not will the presence of Islam, much less control its growth" in the colony.[1] As the Muslim presence became more noticeable and challenging relative to the spread of Christianity, colonial officials and Christian missionaries were determined to rein in adherents of any faith other than Christianity. From the earliest stages of the founding of the settlement, colonial officials relentlessly pursued a policy of assimilation in their relations with the inhabitants of the settlement. While the earlier arrivals (i.e., the so-called Black Poor and Nova Scotians) were baptized Christians, many of the Liberated Africans who arrived in Freetown following the Abolition Act of 1807 had not been converted to Christianity prior to their landing in Sierra Leone. The settling of the Black Poor and Nova Scotians in Sierra Leone in the late eighteenth century, and, later on, the Maroons, constituted what amounted to two failed private ventures undertaken by shareholders in London, for whom the colonial settlement was less religious than economic, but who nonetheless utilized religion as an instrument of political and social control. The formal takeover of the colony by the British Crown in 1808 did not usher in a fundamental change in policy. Consequently, the colonial state and the established Church of England entered into a religiopolitical pact that effectively transferred authority to the church for overseeing the day-to-day activities of the inhabitants of the rural villages of the colony. The church, through the Church Missionary Society (CMS) of London, became directly responsible for the schooling, clothing, and feeding of the returning ex-slaves and former captives. With the political authority and tacit cooperation of the colony administration assured, the CMS embarked on accomplishing an agenda of assimilation among the inhabitants of Freetown and the rural villages of the colony.

British officials did not start out seeking accommodation with Muslims or worshippers of orishas, both of which groups the British evangelicals perceived as "pagans." The reluctance of colonial officials to seek accommodation with Muslims was due to the nature of the "three C's" project and also because of the strength of the missionary lobby, although they were quite aware of the importance of regional commerce to the sustainability of the colonial economy. Thus, the colony administration ultimately sought commercial and political accommodation for reasons of self-interests, even as the church was being given a politically hegemonic role in the colony. The use of the church as an arm of colonial control in Sierra Leone was substantively different from the approach taken by the French in Senegal. In his analysis of Franco-Islamic relations in Senegal and Mauretania in the late nineteenth and early twentieth century, David Robinson utilizes several themes, including "knowledge and power," "capital," "hegemony and civil society," in an attempt to demonstrate how the French were able to pursue and succeeded in creating "Paths of Accommodation" with the Muslims in the region. While the British ecclesiastical and secular officials were interested in establishing unchallenged control over all of the inhabitants of the Sierra Leone Colony from the beginning without seeking to undertake a substantive study of the role and place of Islam in the region, the French demonstrated an "interest in knowing." As Robinson notes, the French pursuit of knowledge about the Muslims, and others in the region, was based on the realities on the ground. This "practical" approach "was focused on finding enduring alliances, maintaining order, and securing support for the colonial economy."[2] In doing so, the French administration was able to accumulate social prestige and power, "symbolic capital," which clearly arose out of the French "reputation for working with Muslim societies." The French were not the only beneficiaries of this "symbolic capital," as Muslim commercial and religious leaders who accommodated the French also gained "prestige and power" through their capacity to show "the compatibility of their faith with European rule." Thus Robinson posits that the "symbolic capital" garnered by the French served to make unnecessary the "constant application of force." The French approach in Senegal, had it obtained in the period immediately after the formal British takeover of the Sierra Leone Colony, would have averted the political chaos that attended relations between the colonial state and Muslims in the Liberated African community in the early nineteenth century. A "path of accommodation" was eventually pursued in Sierra Leone, "in which colonial authorities were forced to face the pluralism of power and develop new ways to exercise hegemony," but not before a period of confrontation between the colonial state and Anglican mission and non-Christians, primarily Muslims.[3]

The Anglican mission was made up of men who were influenced by an assumption of cultural and religious superiority vis-à-vis the inhabitants of the colony and were guided by their Christian obligation to continue the liberation of Africans not only from the shackles of slavery and slave trading dungeons and vessels, but also from "paganism" or "fetishism." CMS officials who took charge of the Liberated African villages were not constricted by the philosophical and political concerns of later British colonial officials who were required to consult Frederick J. D. Lugard's *Dual Mandate in British Tropical Africa* on the guidelines for the administration of the settlements.[4] Operating in a colonial environment with few established administrative guidelines, CMS officials were free to conduct affairs in a manner that they believed was in accordance with their Christian faith and obligations as ministers of the church. To the English missionaries in Freetown and the rural villages, the inhabitants of the colony were in dire need of religious and social transformation. They concluded that the most effective way to accomplish this was through a policy of assimilation, that is to say, developing a social environment in which the repatriated African settlers would identify with "the mother country," primarily through baptismal ceremonies and direct administrative control of the villages by church officials. The CMS did not directly or openly advocate assimilation, since doing so would have suggested a resultant basic equality between the missionaries and the village inhabitants. Having been socialized within a hierarchical

British society, the missionaries sought to reinforce the development of a socially stratified society in Freetown and the rural villages. Those who opted for Christianity and took an active role in the affairs of the established church came to constitute the upper stratum of the colony's African population, in essence the elite, while those who were nominal Christians occupied the middle tier. Non-Christians were relegated to the lower stratum of society. Officials of the CMS and other European missionaries sought to create a Victorian middle class out of the African elite, who would become an appendage of the colonial state and exemplify all that was supposed to be good in British rule.

Even though the CMS and the colonial authorities were highly successful in proselytizing among the inhabitants of the colony, they encountered much cultural and religious resistance in Freetown and the rural villages. The group that bore the brunt of the material deprivations and physical assaults of the colonial state due to their resistance was the Yoruba-speaking (or Oku) community. Many of these people had been converted to Islam prior to their captivity, and many more were further influenced as a result of the proselytizing activities of Muslim scribes, teachers, and traders from the Sierra Leone interior who frequented the colony. They were therefore less predisposed to respond positively to the entreaties of the European missionaries, particularly the CMS, after the latter were given direct charge of the rural villages.

I argue that the colonial authorities and the European missionaries developed the colonial constructed Oku[5] as an ethno-religious entity separate from other Liberated Africans, and subsequently the Krio, in order to create and maintain a dichotomy between Muslims and Christians within Freetown society. The colonial state and mission officials in essence utilized religion as the basis of determining who would properly be part of the society the British had envisaged Freetown to be. While Christians would be clearly identified with the colonial power structure, Muslims in the Liberated African community, and ultimately Krio society, would constitute the "Other." However, the reality was that the entity that emerged in the late nineteenth century as Krio society was the logical result of a settlement that had evolved culturally, linguistically, and with the same traditional ethos. This common historical environment was what allowed the Krio to coalesce into an organic society, albeit with differentiated social, religious, and professional categories.

Why, then, did the British adopt policies and utilize measures that were patently designed to construct a binary within Liberated African society of nineteenth-century Freetown? We may locate part of the answer in the agenda of the established Church of England to convert the "heathen" Africans. In a colony where religion was utilized as an instrument of political control, the church and the colonial state deemed it imperative to have religious homogeneity in order to advance British colonial interest in Sierra Leone. Hence Christians were allowed to become part of the colonial fabric, while those who embraced Islam or continued their fealty to Yoruba orishas were excluded from the mainstream of colonial society and consequently categorized as "tribal" and "uncivilized." Contrary to the colonial construction that Christianity was the single most important determining factor for the emergent Krio identity in the nineteenth century, a significant minority in the Sierra Leone Colony remained Muslim. In spite of the admonition of the church, and to the great frustration of the European missionaries, religious affiliation in colonial Freetown during the nineteenth century was fluid and dynamic.

ISLAMIC ORIGINS AND EARLY INFLUENCES

The Fulani jihads of the eighteenth century were the first organized events to have a widespread impact among a high proportion of the populations of the highlands of the Upper Guinea coast, and they ultimately led to the formation of Muslim states across the interior expanses of West Africa. However, even though Sierra Leone itself did not experience much of the political changes engendered by the Islamic reformist movements of the eighteenth century, it did not entirely escape the conquest of Futa Jallon.[6] As a result of the jihads of the period, the coastal areas that were adjacent to what became the colony of Freetown saw an influx of Soso, Fula, and Mandinka peoples, a good number of whom were Muslims.[7] These new immigrants subsequently had a strong influence on the coastal Temne, Baga, and Bullom among whom they settled. The nineteenth century saw a continuation of the trend, with an even more significant movement of Mande traders and scribes to Freetown. In 1794, the directors of the Sierra Leone Company perceived an imperative need to penetrate the hinterland of the Freetown settlement for purposes of trade. Consequently, the company dispatched to Futa Jallon two of its employees, James Watt and Matthew Winterbottom, by way of the Rio Nunez and overland to Timbo, as emissaries to the Fula theocratic state. The company was primarily interested in obtaining information on the expanding Muslim states along the Northern Rivers, including the Melakori, Bereira, Rio Pongas, and the Rio Nunez. The emissaries may also have been charged with ferreting out information regarding the activities of the French in the Temne country south of the

Scarcies River.[8] Watt, a former planter in Dominica, and Winterbottom, the younger brother of the company physician, Dr. Thomas Winterbottom, received a warm welcome from the leader of the theocratic state, Ali Bilma, who intimated to his guests his desire to have direct trade relations with the colony. The officials were accompanied on their return to Freetown by deputies of Ali Bilma to facilitate the latter's desired trade relations with the Sierra Leone Company.

The success of the Timbo visit served as inspiration for a second visit to the interior by company officials in 1795, this time by Watt and John Gray, the company's accountant ,who traveled by boat along the Kamaranka and Bumpe Rivers to access the small Muslim state of the Mandinka.[9] The activities of Watt, Winterbottom, and Gray were precursors to the nineteenth-century explorations of Mungo Park, Hugh Clapperton, Richard and John Lander, Réné Caillé, and other Europeans dispatched for similar purposes across Africa just before the onset of European imperial conquests across the continent. It could also be seen as an early indication of British intention to extend political control to the interior of Sierra Leone, as ultimately occurred in the late nineteenth century. Around 1801, Dala Modu, a scion of a leading Muslim Mandinka trading family, immigrated to Freetown, accompanied by fifty of his fellow Mandinka, with the tacit acquiescence of the Sierra Leone Company administration, whose directors perceived these developments as evidence of the success of their expansionist agenda in the interior.[10] Even though Islam did not yet constitute an influential presence in the colony, the commercial transactions in gold and other trade items serviced by Muslims laid the foundations for future conversions in Freetown.

However, it must be pointed out that even though the eighteenth-century jihad of Futa Jallon was one of the first organized movements that would ultimately lead to a wider distribution of Islam in West Africa, this was not the first penetration of the religion in Sierra Leone. As early as 1605, Father Balthasar Barreira, a Portuguese Jesuit priest, became the first Christian missionary to commence large-scale evangelization in the area. He was partly successful in converting several of the political leaders in the area to Christianity and, encouraged by his initial success, proceeded upriver to extend the ministry among the Soso along the Scarcies.[11] The confidence of the Jesuit priest was subsequently shattered when he encountered the influential presence of Islam among the Soso of Bena, whose king had initially invited Barreira to his kingdom. Barreira later reported that his discussions with the Soso king following his arrival were disrupted by the melodious voice of a Muslim *Yeliba* (griot) who was singing the praises of the king and his royal ancestors (*SLI*, 53). According to Father Barreira, the griot "did nothing but revile and decry our faith and, on the contrary, exalt the sect of Mahomet in order to persuade the King and the others who heard him to persevere in it, and not make themselves Christians." Barreira noted that the praise-singer did not "follow the laws of Moses, but the al-coran of Mahomet," as did many of the Mandinka and Soso in the interior of Sierra Leone, especially along the Northern Rivers. Thus throughout the late eighteenth and early nineteenth centuries, the European missionaries and British government officials were reporting on the activities of Muslim scribes and itinerant traders in the vicinity of the colony. In 1788, Lt. John Matthews of the British Royal Navy published the report of his *Voyage to the River Sierra Leone*, in which he described the widespread activities of Muslim proselytizers in the area of Freetown toward the close of the eighteenth century (*SLI*, 85). He further noted the presence of Arabs and Fulani among the leading Muslim preachers. Matthews was firmly convinced that it was due to the Arab presence in the area that "the defeat of the Spaniards before Gibraltar was known at the Rio Pongas within forty days after the action" (*SLI*, 86).[12]

By 1793, Zachary Macaulay was also reporting on the impact of Muslims in the interior of Sierra Leone. He told the story of a Madhi in the Northern Rivers who was of "Moorish extraction" (*SLI*, 86). By 1803, the journals of James Watt and Matthew Winterbottom, the two Sierra Leone Company officials who had been dispatched to Futa Jallon in 1794, were published in a work titled *An Account of the Native Africans in the Neighborhood of Sierra Leone*; the book contained a firsthand account of the extent to which Islam had "emancipated [the Fula and Mandinka] from the gross superstition of their ignorant neighbours." Both Watt and Winterbottom believed that "the customs of these people bear a striking resemblance to those of the Jews, as described in the Pentateuch," noting, furthermore, that "after Mohamed, Moses is held by them in the highest estimation." In 1822, Gordon Laing of the Second West India Regiment visited Falaba to the north of the colony and published a book three years later detailing the jihad of the Muslims (*SLI*, 86).[13] Clearly, by the twilight of the eighteenth century, the Sierra Leone colonial settlement was not unaware of the growth and spread of Islam in the region. However, unlike the French in Senegal, colonial authorities in Sierra Leone did not utilize the information and knowledge of the presence of Islam and its implications for relations between the colony and Muslims to create "paths of accommodation." Knowledge of the

Islamic reformist movements of nineteenth-century West Africa was hardly utilized by colonial authorities to prepare for an eventual influx of Muslims from the interior.

The immigration to the colony of Muslims from the interior in the early nineteenth century ushered in a period of cross-cultural encounter that tested the ability of the church and the colonial state to coexist with Muslims and, for that matter, adherents of traditional religion. Among the first groups of Muslims to establish an identifiable religious community in the colony was the Fula from Timbo, who, by 1819 had established a settlement of their own in what became known as Fula Town. The new community of Muslims soon attracted a significant number of Muslims from the Liberated African society to the neighborhood. By 1821, Bambara and Soso immigrants from the interior also began settling in an area adjacent to Fula Town, which came to be identified as Bambratogn (Bambara Town) (*SLI*, 86).[14] The Abolition Act of 1807 and the consequent resettlement in Freetown of those rescued from slave trading vessels led to an increase in the population of Muslims in the Sierra Leone Colony, including those who had been converted to Islam before captivity as well as others who adopted the faith following their arrival in the Sierra Leone Peninsula.[15] Among the Liberated Africans most impacted by Islam were those from the various subgroups of the Yoruba such as Ijesa, Ijebu, Oyo, Ibadan, Ifa, and others from the southwestern region of what became Nigeria, who had been Islamized directly or indirectly as a result of the jihad led by the Fulani scholar Othman Dan Fodio in 1804. Once they were resettled in Freetown, the Liberated Africans soon gravitated toward their coreligionists from the interior of Sierra Leone. Gradually, the Muslim immigrants from the interior began to have an increasing impact on the Liberated Africans, a development that was clearly not welcomed by the colony government and the European Christian missionaries in Freetown. The mosque became the center of religious worship and "the focus for a common and distinct identity."[16] This development soon irritated the colonial state, and the political and evangelical establishment tried to arrest the development of Islam within the colony.

RELIGIOUS PLURALISM AND UNIFORMITY IN THE 1830S

The growing influence of Muslim clerics among Liberated Africans in the colony seems to have hastened the colony government's resolve to carry out the plan of the founders of the original settlement (i.e., the creation of a Christian society from whence Africans who had been successfully assimilated into English culture would be dispatched to other parts of the

The Jamiul Salaam Mosque at Foulah Town.

Figure 2.1: Jamiul Salaam Mosque at Foulah Town

African continent to spread the Christian faith and Western civilization).[17] It thus became imperative for the colonial state and Christian missionaries not only to instill European Christian values and ideals in the inhabitants of the settlement, but also to subvert the growth of Islam and African modes of thought. The Christian missions were acutely aware of the difference between traditional religion and Islam; however, they sought to conflate the two religious systems in a bid to simultaneously undermine any competing claims to the hearts of the Liberated Africans in the new "province of freedom." It was thus deemed essential to curtail interaction between the converts to Christianity and Muslims and adherents of Yoruba orishas. In 1839, the established church in the colony announced that it "regarded all African traditional beliefs, rites and practices as pagan" and therefore, "inconsistent with the doctrines and practices of Christianity."[18]

The aims and objectives of the CMS and other evangelical missions after 1807 were reflective of a European mind-set at the end of the eighteenth century that assumed "the manners, customs and morality of Europe were ... self-evidently superior," and as such Christian clergymen of the various mission groups in the colony operated in the belief that their evangelizing activities were ultimately aimed at rescuing the inhabitants from centuries, if not millennia, of "wallowing in darkness." As Fyfe noted, "Euro-centrism reinforced the exclusive claims of the Christian religion."[19] The Sierra Leone Colony was an almost perfect theater for the perpetuation of the supposedly superior "civilizing" values and morality of the Europeans, as it was founded as a haven of freedom for manumitted slaves and captives rescued from slave ships. The notion of moral superiority could hardly have been asserted as long as the slave trade continued unabated; however, with the promulgation of the Abolition Act in 1807, British mission groups, to use Fyfe's formulation once again, assumed a posture of "self-righteous zeal of liberators who demanded gratitude from the liberated."[20] Thus the CMS missionaries brooked no nonsense from the inhabitants of the colony villages who were placed in their charge. While earlier colony inhabitants, like the Nova Scotians and Maroons, had generally embraced Christianity, the Liberated Africans posed a challenge to the proselytizing efforts of the European missionaries. The Wesleyan missionaries from Britain who had taken over control of the Methodist Church in the colony were not effective, at least initially, in spreading the Christian gospel. Indeed, Methodism itself was not without its problems in an English colony, where the Church of England was supreme.[21]

To the officials of the established church in Freetown, Methodism, like Islam and African traditional religious beliefs, was a form of dissension and nonconformism. Nonconformist tendencies in the colony were therefore to subsequently come under intense attack following the replacement of the Society for the Spreading of the Gospel to Africa and the East by the Church Missionary Society in 1799.[22] The unwillingness of the latter to tolerate or cede a leading role to another Christian denomination was reflective of the tension between a fluid, evolving society and the desire of the established church and the colonial state to engineer social conformity. Both the Anglican Church and the colony government perceived and dealt with Islam and Yoruba orisha worshippers as essentially the same creed, perhaps for reasons of political and social control. In its zeal to crush any form of dissension or nonconformism, CMS officials were also not reluctant to undermine the interests of a perceivably dissenting Methodist mission. With the latter marginalized, the CMS was left in complete control of the villages and with an enhanced capacity to effect its social engineering agenda.

Among the founders of the CMS itself were some of the leading members of the Sierra Leone Company, and, in accordance with the ideals of the company, the mission group required the Liberated Africans to fully adhere to the doctrines of the established Church of England. As the evangelical arm of the church, the mission was assured of official support and soon became an extension of the colonial administration. By 1810, the CMS had been delegated the responsibility for assimilating the Liberated Africans arriving in the colony. The primary means of assimilation was twofold: (1) conversion to Christianity; and (2) Western education. Thus as early as 1810 Governor Columbine formally appointed the Reverend Gustav Nylander, a German missionary, to the post of colony schoolmaster in addition to his position as colony chaplain, with his salary paid from the colony treasury.[23] The appointment of Reverend Nylander was at once instructive even as it was paradoxical; the agenda of inculcating Victorian English values in the colony inhabitants initially had to be carried out by German graduates of a Lutheran seminary in Berlin, who were required to spend time in England studying English. Nylander was relieved of his duties as chaplain and replaced by the Reverend Leopold Butscher (another German missionary) in 1814, the same year that marked the beginning of a far more significant cooperation between the colony government and the CMS under Lieutenant Governor Charles MacCarthy. The first Englishman in the CMS, John Horton, arrived in the colony in 1816.

MacCarthy gained promotion to governor in 1816, and his period of stewardship was to have a profound impact on the lives of the Africans under his control. As governor, he commenced a form of paternalism that was to have far-reaching effects on the colony inhabitants, and would shape relations between Muslims, Christians, and the colonial state until the mid-nineteenth century. Under MacCarthy, the colonial state sought to impose greater control and organization over the lives of the Liberated Africans, including the control of their spaces and behavior, work and time. In short, the governor was determined to ensure a greater regimentation of the lives of the people. MacCarthy's background and personality largely accounted for his policies and actions during his governorship. He was consumed with his own sense of royal pedigree, to the extent of emphasizing to the colonial office in London that he was descended from "ancient Irish Kings." In 1820, he proceeded to England in order to receive a knighthood, thereby becoming the first governor of Sierra Leone to receive the accolade from the British monarchy.[24]

Following his promotion to governor, MacCarthy proceeded to divide the colony into English-styled parishes. Each parish was placed under the supervision of a superintendent (later designated manager), who was selected from CMS clergy and paid directly by the colony government. The CMS was given political and religious authority in the rural villages, thereby becoming the local representative of the colony administration, and fully cognizant of MacCarthy's instructions to have the Liberated Africans baptized as soon as they showed signs of adopting European ways. The governor was determined to create a regimented society, and Waterloo, Hastings, and the other rural villages became the incubators in which the Liberated African populations experienced a form of "MacCarthyism" that would have a profound effect on the colony. As part of their duties, the clergymen were to ensure that the Liberated Africans engaged in agricultural production for subsistence and export purposes, and were further expected to mobilize the labor forces necessary for the construction of roads and public structures, such as chapels.[25] The construction of chapels, for instance, was deemed essential by parish superintendents in view of the fact that conversion to Christianity was considered to be the key element in the transformation of the Africans from savagery to civilized human beings. As Lamin Sanneh has observed, "MacCarthy's understanding of 'English manners and ideas' extended to matters of ecclesiastical jurisdiction. Accordingly, presented with a chance to place state resources at the service of church and society, MacCarthy set up to draw on Christianity for the cause of civilization."[26]

Colony village managers were given instructions specifying the hours of labor to be expended by field laborers. According to an article of instructions given to the managers, the hours of labor were "indispensable, as in order to make the field labours productive a certain number of successive hours must be devoted to them without any interruption."[27] Inherent in the parish plan was the conversion of Liberated Africans to Christianity, an act signifying the transformation of the ex-slave to a "civilized" person in the eyes of colonial authorities. Thus, Christianity came to be synonymous with European civilization. Consequently, the colony government and the church considered the construction of chapels in the rural villages to be of utmost importance. By 1816, the first concrete church was constructed in the village of Regent. Henceforth, the inhabitants of the village were required to assemble in church upon hearing the church bell in order to listen to the reading of the gospel by the village patriarch, Rev. William Johnson. There was to be no dissent, and attendance was required, "for as superintendents, armed with magisterial powers, he [Johnson] could compel them to come in."[28] Conversion to Christianity and social conformism were thus effected.

The village managers' capacity to distribute lands and other material resources through the government assistance program also enhanced their ability to exercise political authority, always backed by the office of the governor. Indeed, the CMS clergymen were always confident of the support of Governor MacCarthy. In a dispatch to the Colonial Office in London in 1816, MacCarthy sought to justify his plan "to devote a greater part of my time in attempting to give them [the Liberated Africans] ideas of European civilization." The governor was "convinced that in order to civilize the captured Negroes, and to induce the settlers not wanted for the purpose of trade to apply to agriculture, it would be desirable to divide the peninsula in parishes, settling a clergyman in each."[29] MacCarthy assured the CMS clergymen appointed as village managers that their dual role of magistrate and superintendent gave them "real and total" power to "keep the uncivilized in due order and reward the industry of the well behaved."[30] The well behaved were mostly those who did not resist conversion and conformed to European modes of thought and directives uncritically. It was not enough to merely attend church; it was essential to be seen as making "progress" in personal appearances. Therefore, African attire was frowned upon and deemed worthless and undesirable, compared to European clothing, which was valorized as aesthetically sophisticated and refined. Fyfe observed that Governor MacCarthy spared no expense to make the villages reflect his vision: "Bells, clocks, and weathercocks were ordered from England for church towers, forges for village blacksmiths, scales and weights for village markets. Hats were ordered for the men, bonnets for the women, shoes for all; gowns and petticoats, trousers and braces."[31]

But the colony government effort was not limited to aesthetics in art and other forms of appearance. The clothing ordered from England was required to be donned for church attendance, especially on Sunday. However, the village managers expended much energy in disabusing the village residents of the habit of performing any type of manual work or outward physical activity on Sunday. The morning services were usually marked by passionate sermons about the evils of working on the Sabbath. The European clergymen were also firm believers in the biblical adage of "Spare the rod and spoil the child," and therefore missionaries in their capacity as teachers frequently resorted to physical chastisement of the students under their stewardship. The incidence and severity of flogging reached such an alarming rate that the colonial secretary, Walter Lewis, wrote to the secretary of the CMS, complaining of this practice and the effect it was having on the attitude of the Liberated Africans toward the church and state, after one young pupil was flogged to death in the 1820s.[32] The severity in attitude and intolerance of the missionaries soon discouraged many people from attending church service and weekly Bible meetings, an obligation that many were not excited about in the first place. When it became evident that many of the village residents were not enthusiastic about the Christian religion in spite of the efforts of village superintendents, the clergy developed a policy that it hoped would effectively address the problem. By 1819, the Reverend Henry During sought to deal with the general ambivalence toward church attendance in his Gloucester parish by restricting church membership to a select few, consisting of village residents whom he perceived as having a positive attitude toward the church, a policy that was soon universally applied.

The decision to restrict church membership to a select few may have been reached not only to avoid alienating those who were disinclined to conversion to Christianity but, perhaps more importantly, to engender a process of social stratification within the villages, thereby creating a social elite from church membership. The members of the church came to constitute an elite group primarily due to the reward system that had been put in place earlier by Governor MacCarthy, which provided Christian converts access to the much-desired social programs, enabling them, for instance, to live in choice domiciles that were reflective of their socioeconomic preeminence.[33] Becoming part of the constructed social elite amounted to a quid pro quo for membership in the church. Furthermore, church members were also used to enforce the political authority of the clergy by being required to report any perceived social deviations to the CMS missionaries, as well as secretly collect and report information on the activities of nonmembers of the church back to the clergy.[34] Secret meetings were conducted between church members and CMS superintendents wherein authoritarian measures were taken to curb the spread of Islam and the continued reverence for Yoruba orishas.

CMS clergymen continued to perceive a strong link between Muslims and orisha worshippers, in spite of a lack of evidence to support such linkages. Such developments caused much friction in villages such as Hastings and Waterloo, where Islam and the worship of the Yoruba orishas were in competition with Christianity for membership, thereby creating an atmosphere of uneasy tensions between the religious groups in the colony. As in Bahia, Brazil, Cuba, and elsewhere in the New World, worship of the orishas remained strong among adherents of traditional religion. Enslaved Africans, "separated by time, distance, and cruel fate from Africa," continued to remember and preserve their "ancient ancestral culture."[35] Orisha adherents in the colony villages in Sierra Leone engaged in their ritual practices and, not unlike their partisans in the New World, sang traditional songs in "perfect Yoruba." Church officials were acutely aware of the fact that a shared Yoruba culture provided a bridge for accommodation between practitioners of traditional religion and adherents of Islam, and with converts to Christianity. The CMS clergymen therefore sought a constrictive environment with the aim of limiting the influence of other creeds.

The heavy-handedness of the CMS missionaries in the villages with regard to church attendance and compliance with the political dictates of the clergy did not prove to be quite effective in the short run, a fact that was not lost on the church. Reverend Samuel Adjai Crowther advised in a church correspondence that such oppressive policies were counterproductive, as they failed to engender any genuine commitment to Christianity on the part of church members. Many often attended church services, he noted, "merely to please their missionary who was also their [village] manager."[36] In 1837, Crowther observed that the adults in the villages were clearly not interested in Sunday school attendance. He complained that the villagers often engaged in taunting the village schoolmaster after exiting the chapel by scampering through the windows. Crowther also noted that the Liberated Africans in the villages steadfastly held on to their native customs and traditions, including drumming and dancing, and lamented that even the Christian converts, contrary to the teachings of the church, did not see any inherent contradiction in reading the Bible and dancing to the sounds of the drums.[37] Crowther recalled an instance when one Christian Liberated African man reacted with utter disdain to a missionary (Reverend Weeks) who had admonished him and his companions for dancing to the bata. He expressed astonishment at what he perceived as a display of ingratitude on the part of the villager. According to Reverend Crowther, "Instead of being thankful for this kind admonition, he looked on Mr. Weeks as an intruder on their peace; he immediately applied to the manager for permission to play; and that being granted, returned with his company with singing, clapping of hands, dancing and performing somersets [sic] in spite of their admonisher."[38]

The behavior of secular Europeans in the colony did not help in ensuring the success of the missionaries, especially on the issue of rowdiness, including the imbibing of alcoholic beverages. The Reverend W. A. B. Johnson had occasion to express concern about the behavior and activities of certain European officials on the Sabbath when he noted that some

> Europeans have now commenced a new method of showing their ungodliness. They frequently break the Sabbath by going

on horseback round the villages on Sundays. They generally go through Gloucester, Bathurst, to Leopold, where they arrive at such time when divine service is nearly over which they profess to attend, after which they proceed to the waterfalls, get almost intoxicated and then return over Regent town about 3o'clock and many compliments when we are about to go into church.[39]

The efforts at Christian evangelicalism notwithstanding, African cultural practices proved difficult to extinguish in the rural villages, as the Liberated Africans stoutly resisted attempts by the authorities to repress their traditional customs and way of life. The colony government inadvertently contributed to the strengthening of African customs and values when in 1822 it adopted a policy of settling the Liberated Africans according to ethnic origins. Governor Sir Neil Campbell deemed this new policy a more viable option in order to hasten the process of "civilizing" the Liberated Africans.[40] The policy was fully co-opted by Campbell's successor, Alexander Findlay, by 1830. It was to be a regrettable act of political blunder! With the newly arriving batch of rescued captives being placed in the rural villages according to their ethnicity and left largely unsupervised, the immigrants were able to reproduce their way of living, and in the process strengthened their cultural tenets. Waterloo and Hastings, in particular, were dominated by people speaking dialects of Yoruba, many of whom were Muslims or orisha worshippers. Out of nearly 2,000 Liberated Africans settled in the rural villages between 1814 and 1816, 1,162 were without direct official supervision, leading independent lives and free from the constrictive measures of the CMS.[41] The new arrivals received their supplies on a weekly basis during the initial period following their relocation to the villages, but for the most part remained without official supervision.

Between 1816 and 1817, a total of 2,545 recaptives were released in the colony, and virtually all of them (2,122) resettled in the rural villages were left with no official supervision, save for the weekly distribution of rations by mission officials. In 1818, 603 recaptives were resettled in the colony, and 529 of these were left without official supervision.[42] One European official suggested that the lack of interest in the church demonstrated by the new arrivals was "merely the natural effect of the want of a clergyman for several years."[43] In these circumstances, even as Christian proselytizing was making meaningful headway among the inhabitants of the colony, it was still facing significant challenges from traditional religion and the growth of Islam. According to Archdeacon John Graf, places like Waterloo and

Hastings were teeming with followers of traditional religion, with Graf consequently describing Waterloo as "the seat of heathenism." Graf was thus concerned about the "pernicious effect this must have upon the rising generation and what barrier it offers to the increasing prosperity of our school [and religion]."[44]

The frustrations of Graf and his fellow clergymen were compounded by the fact that even among Christian converts, there were many who continued to participate in traditional religious ceremonies. Indeed, Reverend Graf noted that he was "extremely grieved" upon learning that a female member of the congregation, "one of the oldest on the list, had disgraced her profession by having recourse to superstition." The woman in question had an ailing child whose deteriorating health, in spite of scriptural prayers, did not show any discernible improvement. She consequently decided to consult a traditional healer, who advised her to acquire "a sheep, some fowls, rice, [and] rum," which were reported to have been used as part of a ritual ceremony at the communicant's home. The sheep, rice, and fowls were actually used to prepare the food for those attending the ceremony; however, Graf expressed great sorrow over the fact that even though the mother of the sick child had been a member of the congregation for many years and "reads her bible fluently," she could not completely forsake her native customs and traditions.[45]

The tendency of Liberated Africans to hold on to their traditional cultures within their "Atlantic Creole form of Christianity" was not limited to the Yoruba-speaking groups in the rural villages of Sierra Leone. Linda Heywood and John Thornton note that Christians in the Kongo Kingdom attended Mass on a regular basis by the end of the sixteenth century. Kongolese in the capital of Sao Salvador and those in the villages by this time had come to "recognize and accept the principal rituals and symbols of Christianity."[46] As Heywood and Thornton tell it, the people of Kongo "identified the cross, religious paintings, priestly garb and paraphernalia, and other blessed objects . . . as part of their own religious lives." However, not unlike the Liberated Africans in Sierra Leone, Kongolese "retained many of their older beliefs within their Atlantic Creole form of Christianity." Christianized Kongolese "also continued to revere local deities," and "many local customs connected to older religious beliefs" remained a part of the local landscape.[47] The same could be said of other Christianized communities in other parts of Africa, with Christian clergy experiencing great anxiety in their efforts to eradicate the stubborn persistence of traditional religious cultures.

While the Christian missionaries frowned severely upon the continued practice of indigenous religions, especially the adherence to Sango, the god of thunder and lightning in the Yoruba pantheon of orishas, there was no concerted effort directed against them by the church and colonial state, as was the case with regard to Islam. The colonial state and the Christian missions perceived Islam as a very real threat to the social stability of the colony and were alarmed at the presence of Muslim scholars in the rural villages of the colony. Christian missionaries and their counterparts in the colony government were all too ready to remind anyone that "the colony of Sierra Leone was established expressly for the purpose of abolishing the slave trade and the spreading of Christianity and civilization."[48] The colonial state and the missionaries became particularly concerned with the favorable reception of the proselytizing efforts of Fula, Mandinka, and Soso Muslim scholars roving the villages. The converts to Islam consciously received, adapted, and assimilated Islam into their African culture. As explained by Lamin Sanneh, the themes of interaction and of adaptation ran through the entire spectrum of Islamic penetration and its submergence in the Liberated African consciousness.[49] Within the villages, elements of Islamic and traditional religious values often existed side by side without destroying the distinctiveness of each other. Unlike Christianity, the teachings of Islam did not appear to collide directly with the cultural attributes of the Liberated Africans, and, therefore, the latter were inclined to be more receptive to Islamic proselytizing than they were to the Eurocentric teachings of the Christian missionaries.

Despite its concern about the growing influence of Muslim teachers, the colony government had no clear strategy of how to react to them. Many of the Muslim teachers were also traders from the interior, deemed by the state to be crucial to the increasing trade relations between the colony and the trading states of the interior. The Fula and other Muslim teachers, normally found in the rural villages of the colony, were increasingly playing a more prominent role in the developing of colony-interior trade. Mandinka and Fula clerics in Freetown also facilitated the trade, serving as "brokers" for the "big men" in the interior who supplied the gold, ivory, hides, shea butter, and other products for the Freetown market.[50] Consequently, the colony government was reluctant to alienate the Muslim traders from the interior. But the Christian missionaries, especially those of the CMS, had acquired significant power and influence in the colony and were not about to let the increasing commercial and social influences of the Muslim scholars go unchallenged. By 1827, the CMS had become part of the colony government, no longer just a mere colonial agency, and in the rural villages, it was the government. The colony administration was merely the financier of the church apparatus that ruled the village communities.[51] The mission clergy was also confident of its ability to flex its own political muscles. The events of the succeeding years were to have a dramatic impact on social relations in the rural villages and in the colony as a whole.

Between 1822 and 1830, the rural villages of Hastings and Waterloo saw a significant increase of Yoruba, and by 1831 the group outnumbered all others. The dramatic increase in the Yoruba population was primarily due to the outbreak of a series of trade conflicts in the old country that came to be known as the Owu Wars (1822–23); however, others found their way to Sierra Leone as a result of other political developments, including the fall of Oyo in the 1830s and the efforts at state consolidation by residents of Ilorin and Nupe. These developments led to the large-scale capture and sale of Yoruba-speaking peoples into the transatlantic system.[52] The social instability that followed the disintegration of Oyo engendered the movement of significant numbers of Yoruba from densely populated sections of Old Oyo, many of whom became ensnared in the Owu Wars.

The Owu Wars have been characterized as constituting the signal events that engendered the state of instability across Yorubaland. The origins of the conflicts, according to Ade Ajayi, lay in the quest for dominance of trade, especially in the area of Apomu.[53] Saburi Biobaku saw these wars as but episodes of the wider Islamic jihad and the transatlantic slave trade.[54] Oyo's disintegration at a time when the jihad and the slave trade were serving to undermine traditional society only contributed to the creating of conditions that facilitated the forced removal of many people from Yoruba cities. The disruptive effects of the Fulani jihad ultimately gave the slave traders the necessary cover to capture and sell many people into the Atlantic system.

As war created opportunities for slave traders, thousands were captured and subsequently sold into the transatlantic trade system and placed on board slave vessels bound for the New World. A significant number of those placed on board slave vessels for the trip across the proverbial Middle Passage were later recaptured by the British Anti-Slave Trade Squadron and relocated to Sierra Leone. The people thus relocated may not have arrived in Freetown as a "cohesive self-conscious" cultural monolith that came to be identified subsequently as Yoruba. They arrived, as already indicated, as Oyo, Egba, Ijebu, Ijesa, Ife, Ota, Sabe, and others. A good number of the relocated lot also included Igbo and Hausa.[55] Many of these had been converted to Islam before their captivity, as Islam had begun making incursions into Yoruba cities like Ikoyi, Oyo, Ogbomoso, Iseyin, Iwo, and Kuwo even before the fall of the kingdom of Oyo.[56] With Muslims in Oyo constituting a significant proportion of the population, they were soon able to obtain much respectability, especially as a result of their long-distance trading acumen and skills as warriors.

The Fulani jihad and the resultant spread and preeminence of Islam in Ilorin led to the conversion of many Yoruba. Many of these elected to retain their Islamic faith following their arrival in Sierra Leone, in spite of the evangelizing endeavors of the European missionaries. The evangelical missions faced enormous challenges from the increasing influences being exerted by the Muslim Fula and Mandinka clerics in the colony villages, prompting Governor Benjamin Pine to call the attention of the Colonial Office in Whitehall to what was perceived as a growing menace in the rural villages.[57] Even before Pine's report to Whitehall, his predecessors, including Charles Turner, were by the mid-1820s sounding the alarm about the perceived threat posed by Islam to the development of Christianity in the colony. Turner's 1824 memo to Whitehall drew attention to the undermining effects of Islam on the work of the evangelical missions and reminded the Colonial Office of the raison d'être of the colony settlement (i.e., "the introduction of the blessings of Christianity and Civilization to Africa").[58] The correspondence between Pine and Earl Bathurst served as reassurance to the mission groups, who thenceforth became prepared to work in concert with the colony government toward the elimination of the Muslim presence in the villages and in the colony as a whole.

The reluctance of Muslims in the Liberated African community to renounce their faith and convert to Christianity was profoundly frustrating to the colonial establishment, as was made clearly evident by Lt. Col. Dixon Denham of the Liberated African Department when he observed that

> great numbers of "the Acoos" have had their freedom here during the last four years. They are mostly brought in [as] adults and advanced in years and generally remain in their savage state, associate among themselves and can never be persuaded to receive instructions. They are a fierce debauchered race and the most complete kaffers I ever saw, speaking no language but their own barbarous one.[59]

Denham's assumptions and attitude toward Liberated Africans of Yoruba origin largely reflected the general attitude of colonial officials vis-à-vis the older group of manumitted Africans and the newer recaptured African population; the latter were expected to be grateful to the colony government and as such should demonstrate their gratitude with an uncritical embrace of European sacred and secular dogmas. The failure of many Liberated Africans to renounce Islam and/or allegiance to orishas was therefore unacceptable to Denham and other colonial officials, who frequently interpreted such failure as not only reflective of ingratitude, but also as an incapacity on the part of the Yoruba speakers and other Africans to transcend their "savage state." Denham's observation also betrayed the inefficacy of the colony government's policy, born out of Whitehall's budgetary concerns, to allow the Liberated Africans to fend for themselves, without official supervision. In these circumstances, the Muslim clerics in the colony successfully exploited the supervisory vacuum at Hastings and Waterloo, in particular, to spread the influence of Islam. The resultant growing influence of Islam in the Liberated African villages raised the ire of the CMS missionaries and colonial officials, leading to further alienation of the Muslim community.

PERSECUTION OF MUSLIMS AND THE COBOLO WAR

The perceived threat posed by Muslims to the continued growth of Christianity in the colony led to the instituting of policy directives by the colony government in 1826 to arrest the development of Islam among the Liberated Africans. The directives thus instituted were specifically aimed at a group of Muslims who had openly questioned the heavy-handed methods of village managers in mobilizing labor for farmwork and in public works projects, and who, furthermore, openly registered their desire to retain their religious and cultural traditions. Aware of their incapacity to successfully exercise their religious freedom, the group of mostly Yoruba ex-captives therefore left the jurisdiction of the colony government and relocated to Cobolo on the Ribbie River, a few miles northeast of Waterloo.[60] The extent to which the exodus of the Muslims was symbolic and reflective of their knowledge of the Hijra of the Muslim prophet Muhammad is unclear; however, the colonial and church officials perceived it as a direct rejection of their authority in the villages and in Freetown. Consequently, the rector and superintendent of Waterloo, Rev. Godfrey Wilhem, warned his superiors in Freetown that the Muslims of Waterloo were about to lay siege to the village. Every male Muslim in the village, regardless of his affiliation with the renegade group, immediately became a potential suspect or accomplice, as a result of Wilhem's clarion call. In the ensuing volatile environment caused by his own alarmism, Wilhem ordered the arrest of every Muslim Oku (Yoruba). After a search of the homes of Yoruba Muslim residents of the village, thirteen men found in possession of machetes were arrested in 1826 and transferred to Hastings.[61]

Wilhem's action may have been a direct result of his own sense of personal failure to persuade the Muslims to renounce their faith in favor of Christianity, and also because of the open resentment displayed by Muslims and Sango worshippers toward the Christian missionaries and the colonial state. Much of their anger was born out of colonial policy that was intended to enforce what was deemed by authorities in Freetown as moral discipline geared toward character development in the manumitted slaves. The villagers were ordered, for instance, to be out of bed before 5:00 a.m., when they were expected to be in the village chapel for morning service. Immediately following the conclusion of the morning prayers, the village inhabitants were required to be "at the works by 6 o'clock in the morning when the artificers and labourers in Freetown commence(d) labour."[62] Wilhem was eventually replaced as rector and village supervisor, an action that was not unconnected to his record as evangelist and administrator.

The replacement of Reverend Wilhem ushered in a new period of persecution of Muslims in the villages and across the colony under Gov. Alexander Findlay. Findlay, who had served as lieutenant governor prior to his elevation to the top spot, had demonstrated little tolerance for the aspirations and sensibilities of the settlers in general. He was as likely to dismiss the candidacy of settlers for official colony administration positions as he was to accuse dissenters of sedition, as was the case with Maroon sub-managers who protested their dismissal.[63] Findlay soon replaced the village superintendents with managers who were expected to carry out his edicts as swiftly as they were issued. The new governor was not about to allow Muslims and Sango worshippers in the colony to serve as obstacles to the evangelical missions, and he openly displayed a contemptuous attitude toward the colony inhabitants, of whose intellectual capacity he thought very little. Findlay simply demanded obedience and expected the Liberated Africans as well as the earlier settlers, the Nova Scotians and Maroons, to follow orders or face the dire consequences of dissension and/or critical obedience.

Among Findlay's first edicts upon his assumption of office was a directive to the village managers to restrict the free movement of people. He appointed J. Auguin to fill the void made by Wilhem's removal at Waterloo, with the proviso that he provide "every possible encouragement to agriculture and industrious persons and use every endeavour to make the Liberated Africans under your control appreciate the blessings which attend a careful use of their time."[64] Findlay also required the new manager "to attend divine service every Sunday morning having previously mustered the constables and all other persons receiving government pay who must also attend at least once on the Sabbath." In the case of the Liberated Africans, Auguin was instructed to "repress [their] vicious practices," which included "their habit of withdrawing themselves from the service of their masters and mistresses and . . . absconding from the places where they were first located and wander[ing] about from village to village."[65]

Findlay's single-minded desire to spread Western civilization in Africa may have propelled him to the undertaking of decisions and actions aimed at persuading the inhabitants of the Sierra Leone Colony to toe the official line; however his decisions betrayed his unfamiliarity with the local environments in the rural villages. He thus ended up making decisions, the implications of which were not carefully considered, such as the engendering of a religious conflict that may have otherwise been avoided. Findlay could be compared to the French general Louis Faidherbe and his handling of Muslims in Senegal. At this stage colonial authorities in Sierra Leone were not prepared to pursue a policy of accommodation relative to Muslims. While Findlay employed a heavy-handed policy relative to Muslims in Sierra Leone, Faidherbe sought to accommodate Muslims, including allowing the latter to not only construct a mosque, but also issuing a decree in 1857 allowing Muslims to have their own Muslim Tribunal, much to the chagrin of the Roman Catholic community.[66] As David Robinson observes, one cannot overestimate the significance of Faidherbe's actions, and the practical consequences of an image of "French toleration" among the Muslims of Saint-Louis. But Findlay was no Faidherbe. The former was more like the intransigent Governor Genouille, whose penchant for dispatching military units against African communities in Senegal ultimately led to his recall back to France.[67] Not fully satisfied with his order to restrict the movement of Muslims in the Liberated African villages, Findlay issued orders in August 1830 banning traditional religious ritual ceremonies. Two years later, on 24 October 1832, he issued an order-in council that had a fourfold objective:

> 1st. That any person who shall, in future, harbor or entertain any runaway Liberated African in his or their houses, or shall refuse, or willfully Neglect to carry him before the manger of the district, shall be fined, for every offense, in sum not exceeding five shillings.

2nd. That no Liberated African shall be allowed to remove from the village where he is first located to settle in any part of the colony, without permission from the assistant superintendent, in writing, approved of by the Governor; persons found offending against this order are to be treated and dealt with as rogues and vagabonds.

3rd. That the special and stipendiary constables are to be directed to apprehend all strangers they may find within the districts who cannot give a satisfactory account of themselves, and to carry him or them before the manager, who is hereby directed to send such person or persons, in the custody of constables, to the districts to which he or they belong.

4th. And that the foregoing regulations be printed and proclaimed aloud in every town, hamlet and village throughout the colony.[68]

The order-in-council was clearly related to the mini exodus of Muslims from Waterloo to Cobolo. On 19 November 1832, the Muslim Liberated Africans who had been arrested as "suspicious characters" and were still being held in custody were deposed at Hastings. The senior official at the Liberated African Department, Thomas Cole, expressed confidence that those involved in the alleged disturbance plot "will be apprehended shortly." He urged, however, that "those already in custody must be brought [to trial] to answer to the charges [against them], as it would not be legal to keep them longer in confinement without an investigation."[69] Nonetheless, Cole's apparent respect for the principle of habeas corpus was belied by the fact that even though the Muslims in custody had denied any knowledge of the alleged plot to attack the colony, they were kept in jail and subsequently sentenced to imprisonment. Either the colony administration was inefficient in enforcing the laws of the land, or its personnel were willfully negligent of the civil rights of non-Christians.

The colonial government used the twin issues of slavery and the slave trade to justify its repression of Muslims and Sango worshippers in the villages. Cole pointed out that the deposition of the witnesses in the case involving Muslim plotters to lay siege to the colony had only confirmed official suspicions that the Muslims who had left Waterloo had been induced to do so by their coreligionists who were involved in the slave trade. According to Cole,

The object of the peoples who have persuaded them to return to their own country was to make slaves of them as soon as they could get beyond the reach of the jurisdiction of this colony. Three of the discontented Ackoos [*sic*], Ogubah, Odohoo & Joko, came to the office this morning voluntarily and gave themselves up. They state that they are of the Mohammedan faith in their own country, and never having received any instructions since they were brought to the colony on the performance of their religious duties; they declare that none of them have been made proselytes through the intervention of the Mandingoes and Foulahs. They also disavow having entertained any idea of returning to their country, nor have they ever been persuaded to do so.[70]

Nevertheless, Cole vowed to advise the governor to prohibit the presence of Mandinka and Fula scribes in the villages, whom he believed were exercising enormous influence over the Liberated Africans, in spite of evidence to the contrary.

The Muslims at Hastings and Waterloo meanwhile continued to quietly resist official efforts to restrict their religious freedom. Flight from the villages, particularly Waterloo, came to constitute a major form of resistance to religious persecution, especially in the face of increased government intervention in October 1832. The colony government used various means to curb such movement, including attempts to get neighboring polities in the hinterland to join in the subjugation of Muslim Liberated Africans. On 21 October 1832, the assistant superintendent of the Liberated African Department was instructed to send a letter to the ruler of Plantain Islands, Thomas Caulker, requesting his cooperation in apprehending and repatriating to Freetown "a number of Liberated Africans of the Mahomedan persuasion."[71] In order to convince his superiors in London of the propriety of his actions, Governor Findlay reported that the Muslims were poised to attack the colony and advised Whitehall that he was about to "adopt the most rigid measures with a view to bringing these offenders to punishment."[72] Muslims were summarily rounded up and transferred to Freetown, and all those professing to adhere to Islamic tenets were henceforth forbidden to wear Muslim attire. Such measures were, however, mostly ignored, and the Muslims continued to practice their faith, including the donning of kaftan and agbada, actions that incensed the government, especially the governor, who equated dissension with sedition. Negative opinions of the governor published in local outlets were often interpreted as libel in his letters and dispatches to Whitehall in London. As Fyfe noted, "Findlay interpreted the law in his own way." In 1832, when the governor's son was openly mocked for "(losing) his horse-whip in a drunken brawl, Findlay persuaded his Council that libeling his son implied a seditious libel on government, constituted them a Court of Royal Commission, fined [Hamilton] McCormack [the offending party] £100 and sent him to prison for three months."[73]

Thus it was only a matter of time before the governor would seek to employ even firmer measures to deal with the seeming intransigence of the Muslim Liberated Africans. On 13 November 1832, he dispatched a militia group to apprehend the renegade Muslims at Cobolo. Findlay announced that he had received a report earlier that "a large party of Ackoos have unlawfully assembled on the Maharra Road for the purpose of attacking Waterloo and some other settlements on the eastern part of the colony and further that gangs of their country people from other villages are expected to join them."[74]

Unsure of the ability of the militia to subdue the Muslims, Findlay mobilized the police forces of Waterloo and Hastings to serve as support troops at Cobolo. The governor ensured that the assembled troops were provided with requisite armaments, and were also given detailed instructions regarding their objective. John Dougherty, manager of Hastings, was given the task of leading the militia forces, assisted by John Hazely, his counterpart at Waterloo. The troops marched toward Cobolo, arriving at dusk on 13 November, and Dougherty ordered his troops to retire for the evening and be ready for an early dawn attack the next day. On 14 November, he led a group of 120 of his men toward Maharra Road, where the Muslims were said to have assembled; he then dispatched a smaller group of sixty-nine troops under the command of his assistant, Hazely, to enter Cobolo and presumably surprise the Muslims.[75] However, the Muslims were hardly surprised, and the troops led by Hazely were consequently met with stiff resistance, leading the colony militia troops to retreat in disarray, much to the chagrin of Dougherty. Two of the troops suffered severe injuries from the brief skirmish, in spite of the fact that the colony militia troops were better armed.[76] The colony government therefore found it necessary to send in additional, and better equipped, forces from Freetown, including the navy.

Findlay was disappointed with the performance of the troops at Cobolo, but he was determined to subdue the Muslims at any cost, including the use of British naval ships. He believed his Royal African Colonial Corps, backed by the navy, were perfectly capable of bringing the Muslims to submission, so he ordered the commander of the naval forces, Colonel Islington, to proceed up the Ribbie River against the Muslims. Islington was instructed to make it adamantly clear to the militiamen from Hastings and Waterloo that the government would take every necessary measure to ensure discipline among the militia forces, and to warn them that deserters risked summary execution.[77] Findlay also mobilized a British frigate, HMS *Charybdis*, which happened to be docked at the Freetown harbor, for action. The commander of the frigate, Lieutenant Crawford, who was about to set sail for the Gambia, was prevailed upon to move up the Ribbie instead, stopping first at York to take a group of village recruits under one Captain Pratt aboard in order to supplement the mobilized forces assembled at Cobolo. The naval forces were expected to attack the Muslim Liberated Africans from the rear or cut off their retreat across the river. Findlay also ordered the managers of the rural villages to arrest all Muslims suspected of possessing arms. Many were consequently arrested, primarily because they were in possession of such farming implements as machetes and axes.

Peterson characterized the resistance of the Muslim Liberated Africans at Cobolo as "ferocious," which he attributed to their possession of "grisgris and fetishes."[78] Fyfe was equally certain about the role of idolatry in the Cobolo debacle.[79] The available primary sources do not provide much clarity as to what really transpired once the regrouped forces entered Cobolo.[80] Dougherty reported that his forces encountered no resistance from the Muslims the second time around, which the governor interpreted to mean that the Muslims may have been subdued by the local Loko.[81] However, Governor Findlay was satisfied with the action of the colony forces at Cobolo, which he believed would serve "as a salutary example to others" and "prevent a similar occurrence in the future." Furthermore, in his report to the secretary of state for the colonies, Findlay confidently maintained that had it not been checked in time, the rebellion would have greatly endangered the safety and government of the colony.[82]

The governor subsequently informed Whitehall that the captured Muslims would be punished for their participation in the rebellion. Another group of Muslims suspected of supporting their coreligionists at Cobolo was incarcerated for three months with hard labor.[83] Findlay maintained that there was substantial evidence of a planned insurrection by the Muslims scheduled to coincide with the Christmas celebrations in the colony, with the objective of "killing all the white men" in the colony.[84] Findlay was thus determined to curb all Islamic influences in the colony once and for all. He informed the Colonial Office in London of his intention to indict the leaders of the Muslim rebellion for high treason.

The indictment of the Muslims for treason was a watershed in the political and legal history of the Sierra Leone Colony. The colony court strongly asserted its independence and the principle of separation of powers in an environment where the government was virtually a military dictatorship. The governor was "extremely confident" of the eventual conviction of the Muslim leaders, and state prosecutors were hardly prepared for the critical definition of the parameters of the colony's jurisdiction by the counsel for the defense. Findlay asserted that the evidence garnered by the colony justice department would ultimately prove that the Muslims had an elaborate and "concerted rebellious plan" to lay siege to the colony and exterminate all Europeans. However, there was hardly any evidence to this effect offered in court.

On 1 January 1833, the acting chief justice of the Supreme Court of Sierra Leone, Michael Melville, began proceedings in one of the major cases on religious freedom in the constitutional history of the colony. On trial for five counts of treason were four men who described themselves as laborers and who also had the peculiar distinction of sharing what were clearly European names, a fact that was, however, not necessarily uncommon in the Liberated African community. The colony government's case against the accused persons, William Cole, William Cole, George Cole, and George Cole, was grounded on the simple assertion that all four had acted in a disloyal manner against the authority of the British monarch. The clerk of the Supreme Court informed the court that the accused persons were subjects of the British Crown, who, "not regarding the duty of their allegiance, nor having the fear of God in their hearts, but being moved and seduced by the instigation of the devil, as false traitors against our said Lord, the King [of Great Britain] wholly withdrew their allegiance, fidelity and obedience which every faithful subject of our said Lord the King should and of right ought to bear towards our said Lord the King William IV."[85]

Among the charges faced by the accused was that "on divers days, with force and arms at Cobolo . . . in the colony . . . together with divers other false traitors . . . armed and arrayed in a warlike manner, that is to say with guns, muskets, cutlasses, bows and arrows and other weapons, being then and there unlawfully maliciously and traitorously assembled and gathered together against . . . the King with His colony of Sierra Leone, and government of the said colony as by law established in contempt of our said Lord the King and his laws."[86]

Further charges included "subversion and altering of the legislation, rule and government now duly and happily established in the said Colony of Sierra Leone." The Cobolo War thus represented a determined action on the part of the colonial state to assert its authority in the face of what the governor perceived as a resistance movement with religious overtones.

The accused, of working-class status, could not afford private legal representation and so Justice Melville appointed William Henry Savage, a colony lawyer born in England to "an African father and an English mother," to serve as their defense counsel. Savage had considerable experience as counsel in the Court of Mixed Commission, and an equally considerable familiarity with prejudice in the colonial establishment. In an 1828 correspondence with R. W. Hay, Britain's undersecretary of state for the colonies, Savage noted that he had been in Sierra Leone for eighteen years, having arrived in 1810.[87] He lamented in his correspondence with Hay that even though he was "a notary public and the senior practitioner of all the courts of this colony," he could not rely on legal practice for meaningful financial gains, due to a paucity of available work.

His letter to Hay also betrayed his frustration with the racial climate of the colony; the fact that he was part European did not help him avoid the virulent institutional racism in the legal profession. In spite of his experience and skills as a practicing lawyer with the Mixed Commission Courts, he did not succeed in ascending the professional ladder of the colonial judiciary, a fact that accounts for his alternate vocation in trade in the Northern Rivers and in Freetown. Even after he was appointed as Acting King's Advocate, he continued to encounter professional challenges, despite his public assurances that "at all times my exertions shall be made to promote the interests of Her Majesty's government and the well-being and welfare of the colony."[88] Frustrated by the incessant racism of European officials, Savage eventually resigned from government service in 1821 and went into private practice and commerce. Being one of two practicing barristers in the colony versed in the English common law system, the other being a European, Savage usually was the preference of Liberated Africans for legal counseling. In the ensuing years following his decision to leave the colonial judiciary, he grew quite prosperous and amassed a considerable amount of real estate in the colony. Notwithstanding this fact, he still remained conscious of the social inequities that pervaded colonial society.

Savage immediately poked holes in the charges against the accused Muslims, calling the court's attention to what he perceived as a fundamental flaw in the charges, namely the ability of the colony government to bring to trial persons accused of participating in any action that had not occurred within the colony's jurisdiction. The defense counsel reminded the court that Cobolo was located outside the geographical boundaries of the colony, and thus the colony's political and judicial authority did not extend to the territory, and as such the Muslims had been improperly indicted.[89] By removing themselves from the colony and relocating to Cobolo, Savage contended, the Muslims could not be accurately deemed subjects of the British monarch, and furthermore, the accused men could not be justifiably convicted for lack of fealty to the British monarch since they were not born in Britain. Savage's argument clearly succeeded in creating enough reasonable doubt in the mind of the judge, who himself expressed doubts as to the political legitimacy of the colony government's claim to jurisdiction in a territory that was outside its geographical boundaries. Justice Melville agreed with defense counsel and acquitted the accused Muslims.

Governor Findlay, however, did not accept Justice Melville's verdict and ordered the retrial of the Muslims, this time on charges of murder for the deaths of militia members who had perished in the war. The prosecution's lead witness, when pressed to prove that the men on trial and others already serving jail sentences were indeed part of the alleged plot to attack the colony, conceded he could not. The prosecution's lead witness, however, maintained that "all of them pray[ed] in the Mohamedan [sic] mode." The case was once again dismissed by the court, only to have Findlay direct his justice department to seek a third trial, this time for piracy, because the renegade Muslims had allegedly participated in a war near the Ribbie River. Ultimately, colony government lawyers convinced Findlay that the charge of piracy against the Muslims could not be sustained because the act of piracy could occur only on the high seas, and the Ribbie was a fairly small river.[90]

PERSECUTION OF MUSLIMS
IN THE POST-COBOLO PERIOD

Governor Findlay's inability to convict the surviving leaders of the Muslims of the Cobolo War did not dampen his determination to suppress the growth of Islam within the colony, particularly in the Liberated African community. Even before the conclusion of the treason trial, the governor was already busily engaged in formulating policy geared toward the creation of a constrictive environment in the colony and the rural villages that would eliminate any form of social activism by Muslims and others reluctant to uncritically accept the dictates of the colony government. Perceiving the war as a consequence of the impact of the missionary activities of Mandinka and Fula scribes, he ordered that Muslim clerics be kept out of all rural villages, and that all Liberated Africans be required to comply with the European dress code.[91] His contemptuous attitude was hardly restricted to the Muslim Liberated Africans, as even Christians, including colony administration officials, became unwitting victims of his whims and caprices. He once openly frowned on the liberal inclinations of the commissioner of the Court of Mixed Commission, Henry Macaulay, who was in the habit of playing cricket "with a parcel of dirty black boys."[92]

Findlay's resentfulness toward backsliders was particularly demonstrated in the case of those colony residents who had the temerity to openly reject the assimilation policy of the colony government and its cultural appendages. Thus it was not surprising to observers when on 1 March 1833 he issued an official proclamation further restricting the movement of Muslims in the colony. Findlay was doggedly determined to remove all obstacles to the spread of Christianity in the colony, and he identified one such obstacle in the growth of Islam. The colony administration concluded that the Liberated African community was coming under the increasing influences of "wicked and evil-disposed persons professing the Mahomedan religion."[93] Findlay and his executive council were convinced that the ex-slaves and their progeny were being swayed by the Muslim Mandinka and Fula from the interior, who had succeeded in "insiduously" encouraging "many of our subjects . . . to leave their lawful places of abode, and to rebel against the constituted authorities of the colony." Thus the proclamation issued by the governor formally declared that "no strangers professing the Mahomedan faith shall, in future, be permitted to settle in any of the towns, villages or places within this colony, over which we have jurisdiction."[94]

By "strangers," the proclamation clearly referred to, and targeted, the Mandinka, Fula, and Soso teachers and traders who hailed from the Islamic centers of Timbo, Kankan, Dinguiraye, and other parts of the interior to the north of the colony. Findlay did not demonstrate any particular appreciation for the economic relations between these centers and the colony as had some of his predecessors, and he consequently failed to take into cognizance the potential and/or real impact of his policy directives concerning Islam on trade relations with interior states. The vehemence with which the colony government pursued its anti-Islamic campaign under Findlay was reflective of an intense frustration on the part of the colonial state regarding the pace of the proselytizing efforts of the European missionaries, especially among the Liberated Africans in such colony villages as Hastings and Waterloo in the 1830s. Thus the colony authorities resorted to a classic colonial political tactic.

As Howard Temperley observes with reference to Christian missionaries in European imperial territories in Africa, "when preaching failed, they used the arm of the state as their instrument."[95] The colonial administration did not feel constrained by its obligation to consider the implications of its policy for the Muslim inhabitants. To Findlay and like-minded officials in Freetown, the Liberated Africans who elected to embrace Islam, rather than Christianity, deserved nothing better, having committed what colony officials perceived as an act of ingratitude toward the British monarch. The proclamation of 1833 was very clear on this point; it reminded the Liberated Africans of the antislavery efforts of the British government for and on behalf of the ex-slaves by noting that "large sums of money have been expended by the British government, and many valuable lives sacrificed, in rescuing those Liberated Africans from perpetual slavery who are now enjoying in the colony all the benefits and blessings of freedom."[96] If many of the Liberated Africans were disinclined to demonstrate any enthusiasm for the religion and Victorian English values of their benefactors, they were going to be required to do so. The proclamation therefore "ordered and declared that all managers and justices of the peace within the colony aforesaid, shall, in future, strictly prohibit all Liberated Africans under their superintendence or observation, from assuming any other dress than that usually adopted by Europeans."[97]

The proclamation further noted that

> whereas it has come to our knowledge that many of the disbanded soldiers settled in the villages in the colony, who are receiving pensions from His Majesty's government, have retrograded into their original native superstitious customs by following the faith and assuming the garb of the Mahomedans; and as the prevalence of such conduct on the part of individuals whose duty it should be to afford examples of Christianity and civilization to their less enlightened brethren, is shewn from experience to be of dangerous and pernicious tendency; it is hereby ordered that no pensioner shall in future under any pretence be allowed to assume the Mahomedan dress, under the penalty of forfeiture of his entire pension.[98]

In order to ensure conformity, Findlay required the managers of the colony villages to report "every instance of non-observance of this requisition."[99]

The colony government's measures aimed at suppressing Muslims and the growth of Islam generally failed. Indeed, such measures had the effect of strengthening the resolve of the Liberated Africans who had always maintained that they had been Muslims prior to their relocation to Freetown. Rather than renouncing their Islamic faith, groups of Muslims demonstrated their piety by making the long trek from Waterloo and the neighboring rural villages, some twenty miles from Freetown, to the colony in order to attend Friday juma'a prayers at Yadie in Fourah Bay.[100] The frequency of these treks and the evident challenges of making the twenty-mile journey between Waterloo and Freetown led many to remain in the area of their place of worship for extended periods of time. As a result, the leaders of the Muslim congregation made entreaties to the former defense counsel of the Muslims tried for treason, William Savage, who owned large tracts of real estate in Fourah Bay. Savage, as noted earlier, had supplemented his legal career with an avocation in colony-interior commerce. Thus by the 1820s, he was already a fairly successful import-export merchant.

Given the prevailing racial climate in the colony, it is not surprising that Savage identified with the Liberated Africans and became the legal champion of those whom he perceived to be real victims of political and religious persecution. The Muslims within the Liberated African community were not the only recipients of his legal assistance. He also represented the Nova Scotian Wesleyan congregation in 1836, when the group was involved in a fight for control of the Wesleyan Church in Freetown.[101] Even though he consequently earned the enmity and animosity of the European political and religious establishment, Savage nonetheless managed to thrive in his commercial enterprises and amassed reasonably great wealth. Thus when in 1833 the Muslims needed a place to stay, Savage was able and all too ready to offer them a portion of his real-estate holdings at Fourah Bay. The grant of land to the Muslim community has been credited to the efforts of such Liberated African leaders as Mohammed Yadalieu, Sumanu Othman Ajibode, and Badamasie Savage.[102]

By 1836, a significant number of the Muslims at Waterloo and Hastings were relocating to Fourah Bay, even though many others maintained domiciles of choice in the rural villages and continued to make the long trek to Freetown for Friday juma'a prayers. The Muslims in the new community encountered a group of Temne living by the bay under their headman, Pa Foray, for whom they believed the area was named.[103] The outnumbered

Temne were probably subsequently absorbed into the Yoruba Muslim community, because by the end of the nineteenth century the area was an exclusively Oku community. Meanwhile, as the community population increased, some began to move west to live among their Fula coreligionists at Fula Town, which had been established in 1819. In time, the Liberated Africans outnumbered the Fula, but retained the name of the community in honor of their former religious mentors.[104] They constructed houses made of mud and timber, with thatched bamboo roofing. They also built a small Islamic center (*zawia*) to satisfy their religious needs.

CHURCH AND STATE SUPPRESSION OF ISLAM

With the establishment of distinctive Muslim communities at Fourah Bay and Fula Town in the colony proper, dominated by Liberated Africans of Yoruba heritage, Islam continued to flourish in the colony, much to the chagrin of European church and state officials. The missionaries sent out by the CMS found their evangelical activities increasingly challenging and less exciting as a result of the continued growth of a high-profiled Muslim community within the colony. The church and the colonial state thus had to contend with a profound dilemma: how should the agenda of constructing a Christian community based on European values be pursued and attained, given the growing body of Muslims within the colony population? What type of policy (or policies) should the colonial state adopt toward these Muslims?

By the mid-1830s, European missionaries and the African clergy and lay preachers in the colony had become deeply involved in the struggle against Islam. Some members of the clergy made individual efforts to persuade the followers of Islam to renounce their faith and embrace what they fervently believed was the one and only true faith, Christianity. The Reverend James Frederick Schon of the CMS diocese at Kissy reported an encounter with an elderly Muslim man he had been trying to convince to renounce his faith and convert to Christianity, so that the man's soul may be "care[d] for."[105] Unfortunately, as Reverend Schon noted, the man was as fervently devoted to his Muslim faith as was Schon to Christianity. He assured the CMS clergyman that his soul was already cared for by God, "since I do nothing bad, I drink no brandy, no gin, no wine, I do not make *greegree* [amulets]." Reverend Schon recalled that the Muslim smilingly assured him that by God's grace he should go to heaven, especially as he clearly abstained from "Christian liquor."[106] Schon, however, remained unimpressed and still considered the old man a sinner so long as he would not convert to

Christianity. Missionaries like Schon who were not making much headway in persuading the Muslims to renounce their faith became increasingly frustrated, and consequently sought to get the colony government much more actively involved in the suppression of Islam in the Liberated African community. On 13 January 1839, the European agents of the CMS sent a petition to Governor Richard Doherty denouncing the growth of Islam and advocating active governmental action in suppressing the religion. Signed by eight of the leading CMS agents in the colony, the petition was described as a "Memorial of the Agents of the CMS respecting the Spread of Mahomedanism [sic] among the Liberated Africans."[107] The document, inter alia, stated:

> That the agents of the CMS in this colony have marked with no ordinary concern the rapid increase of the Mahomedans and the bold practice of their imposing ceremonies.
>
> That Mahomedan teachers are going about proselytizing in the villages in consequence of which many Liberated Africans have been induced to join their number, and some have even sent their children from the villages to town to have them trained up in the system of heathenism, superstition and Mahomedan delusion.
>
> That the Liberated Africans apprenticed to such persons are, of course, deprived of all Christian instructions and are frequently made to work on the Lord's day, for which the Mahomedans in the town of Fourah Bay, especially, manifest not the slightest regard.
>
> Your petitioners, therefore, beg leave to express to your excellency and your honourable board, their firm conviction that the free and open exercise of Mahomedanism is fraught with danger to the colony in a moral and civil point of view; and humbly request that you will be pleased to consider the propriety of checking so injurious a system, and to adopt such measures as will secure to the Liberated Africans bound to Mahomedanism the privileges of the Lord's day and other means available to their instruction in the Christian religion.[108]

The European missionaries were not the only Christians who were determined to curb the spread of Islam in the colony. In less than a week after the European missionaries delivered their petition to the governor, African lay preachers, responding to Governor Doherty's request for their opinion, followed up with a petition of their own. The lay preachers' petition warned against the continued growth of Islam and "the pernicious effects" of the religion on the colony population. Furthermore, the African lay preachers expressed their concerns about the construction of mosques, which they believed were "intended for entrapping the ignorant into the grossest superstition imaginable." The lay preachers further asserted that Islam and Islamic law regarding polygamy were "contrary and inconsistent to [*sic*] the law of God and the common usage and custom of this colony."[109] The African lay preachers also claimed that "the Muslims believed in witchcraft, incantations and charms, and they are hereby subjected to gross impositions by making a trade in selling charms and using lass-mamy."[110]

The lay preachers also voiced their disapproval of the practice of sacrificial slaughtering of "bulls, sheep and fowls" at Muslim saraa ritual ceremonies, on the grounds that such practice was "contrary to the precepts laid down in the New Testament, and against the common law and usages first established in this colony on its formation." And like their European counterparts, they also expressed concern regarding the Sabbath, noting that "they [the Muslims] dedicate the fifth day of the week [Friday] as their day of public worship, whereas the seventh day is set apart by all protestants as their Sabbath which is universally allowed as the established doctrine and rules of every sincere Christian and are considered as a part and parcel of the ancient laws of Great Britain and of this colony since time immemorial."[111]

Thus the laymen demanded that the Muslims "be made to observe the Christian Sabbath, with the greatest veneration and respect."[112] They implored the governor to use the powers of his office to quell the growth of Islam in the colony once and for all, and concluded their letter to Doherty by lamenting that "the benighted sons of Africa, who have been lately rescued from the misery of second slavery are now plunged into human darkness by the grossest of all evils, the Mahomedan persuasion."[113]

The petition carried the signatures of some of the more prominent African lay preachers in the colony, including Joseph Jewitt, A. Elliott, Thomas Frank, John Leigh, William Williams, J. W. Richards, Serpio Wright, James Jackson, and Thomas Freeman, among others.

Governor Doherty was consequently assured of the support of the Christian missionaries and their clerical counterparts in the Liberated African community to pursue a policy of strict containment of Islam and Muslims in the colony. If religious dissension were one way a group of Liberated Africans was going to express its independence from colonial state domination, the governor was equally determined to assert his political authority. Doherty remained unconvinced, as had several of his predecessors, that the Muslims in the Liberated African community had been converted to Islam before their arrival in Freetown, and suspected that the itinerant immigrant traders and preachers from the interior were responsible for what he believed was a clear effort by Muslims to subvert the authority of the colonial state. Thus on 18 March 1839, he notified the secretary of state for the colonies that there was evidence of Islamic subversion of the colony government. He informed Whitehall "of a somewhat new and curious problem for bringing to the test our principles of religious tolerance."[114] He warned Lord John Russell that

> a large body of Liberated Africas [sic] have settled themselves as a distinct community at Freetown on land given to them for that purpose by a William Savage. They have erected mosques, and are living as Mahomedans, zealously and successfully propagating their faith, taking concubines in addition to their wives, training up the children apprenticed to them by the government in the same belief and practices, addicted to a sort of witchcraft and to pilfering and presenting a serious obstacle to the progress of Christianity and civilization.[115]

The governor meanwhile considered the legal and moral propriety of expelling the Muslims from the colony, ultimately deciding on the issue of ownership of the land occupied by the Muslim community at Fourah Bay, which he promptly pronounced as crown land.

THE LAND QUESTION

Doherty thus proposed to his superiors in the Colonial Office in London to remedy what he perceived as the Islamic menace to the colony by dispossessing the Muslims of their mosque and homes, on the legal ground that these structures were located on crown lands. The governor's proposal was ultimately geared toward the elimination of the Islamic challenge through the displacement of the group from the colony. Doherty's action was clearly illegal, especially because the colony government had never disputed William Savage's ownership of the land. Doherty's actions could only be interpreted as having been the result of religious bigotry. The governor himself was not unaware of the legal implications of his proposed remedy to the Islamic challenge; he was certain that the Muslims would likely contest in the colony courts any attempt to forcibly remove them from their homes, or the razing of their places of worship. He therefore advised the secretary of state for the colonies that the state should exercise caution in its attempt to expel the Muslims from land they had legally occupied for many years. Indeed, Doherty was quick to point out to Whitehall that his proposal to demolish the Fourah Bay community merely because the inhabitants had embraced Islam "seems to me nothing less than persecution."[116]

Nonetheless, the governor was not about to let constitutional precision serve as an obstacle to political expediency; so in order to avoid a clear transgression of the letter of the law, Doherty elected instead to compromise the spirit of the law. He thus proposed to Whitehall that the Muslims be expelled not on the grounds that they had embraced Islam and rejected Christianity, which he conceded would be tantamount to religious persecution, but on the more convenient and legally pliable grounds that they were bad tenants.[117] He then went on to direct the colony surveyor, Frederick Pyne, to furnish the governor's office with the names of persons occupying homes constructed on the purported crown land. The list provided by the surveyor's office was intended to help facilitate the serving of notices of eviction to the inhabitants at Fourah Bay. In the interim, Doherty informed the Colonial Office that he had already put the inhabitants of the other identifiable Muslim community at Fula Town on notice by having their mosque burned down by some colony police officers who had "recently waited upon me and signified their willingness to meet my wishes."[118] He later blamed the arson on the overzealousness of the police.

The "pro-Christian bias" of the governor and the colonial establishment in general was demonstrably clear to the Muslims in the colony, and they appeared ready to relocate to some place outside the colony rather than renounce their faith. However, they were equally determined to demonstrate their disapproval of the governor's action in a public way, albeit within the confines of the law. So on 21 June 1839, the inhabitants of Fourah Bay sent an open letter to the governor expressing their disapproval of the government's policy and disappointment at the actions taken against them. Describing themselves as dutiful and loyal Liberated African subjects of the British monarch, they acknowledged receipt of the official notice of eviction from their homes and expressed sorrow regarding what they characterized as "this melancholy mandate," which required that they vacate their homes within a period of five months, but stressed that they cease and desist from worshipping in their mosque almost immediately. They maintained that the governor's actions were due to prejudice and rejected his having characterized them as "a set of idle lazy people." On the contrary, they informed the governor, they were hardworking people with vocations as sawyers, carpenters, blacksmiths, tailors, hawkers, traders, laborers, and farmers. The letter reminded Doherty that his predecessors had never questioned the legitimacy of their occupation of the land and the existence of their community in the colony and, more importantly, had "never disputed Mr. Savage's right to the said property during his lifetime."[119]

The Fourah Bay Muslims also maintained that Governor Campbell, who preceded Doherty, had even encouraged them to "build a place of public worship previous to his leaving for England." Campbell had even promised to provide the inhabitants of Fourah Bay an official license recognizing their right to public worship.[120] Campbell's action in this instance was not unlike that of Louis Faidherbe in Saint-Louis, when the French governor ordered that the Muslim community of that city in Senegal be allowed to construct their own place of worship. The Muslims also offered a direct repudiation of Doherty's assertion that they had become Muslims only after their arrival in the colony, as a result of the evangelizing activities of the Muslim scribes from the interior states. They steadfastly maintained that notwithstanding such claims, they were already Muslims prior to their resettlement in the colony. They therefore asked Doherty to refrain from compelling them to "renounce that faith which is so deeply rooted and sunk in our minds." They were very much aware of the possibility of their mosque at Fourah Bay being subjected to the same eventuality as occurred at Fula Town, and as such implored the governor not to burn down their mosque and to allow them to exercise their right to religious worship. The letter was signed by three of the leading members of the community, namely Mammadu Savage, Henry Macaulay, and James MacCarthy.

In London, Lord John Russell, the secretary of state for war and the colonies, sent a memo to the solicitor general on 19 March 1840, asking for legal advice on the propriety of the proposal to remove the Muslims from the colony and the best way to effect their eviction, especially "as to the mode in which the governor should be instructed to effect that object.[121] In April 1840, Russell sent a dispatch to Doherty in Freetown acknowledging receipt of his letter of December 1839, and concurring with the governor's views on Islam and the potentially "injurious" consequences of the religion's spread in the colony. Russell also agreed with Doherty "that the persons who openly profess Mahometanism [sic] should be removed to the verge of the colony." He informed the governor that he "will have no difficulty in breaking up their settlement at Foulah Town; and with regard to the other settlement at Fourah Bay, you will take such measures for dispossessing the individuals located there, as upon a view of the facts of the case, the official legal adviser of your government shall consider to be most in accordance to the law."[122]

The decision of the Colonial Office to authorize the expulsion of the Muslims was, however, overtaken by the realities of the colonial economy during this period. The increasing red ink of the colony budget had to be dealt with immediately, and one of the ways of achieving this objective was by increasing trade with the interior states, which were mostly controlled by Muslims. Consequently, the Colonial Office in London recalled Doherty from Freetown and sent a new "man on the spot" in the person of Sir John Jeremie; the new governor (an Irishman), who had the distinction of being the first civilian to be appointed to that position by Whitehall, arrived in Freetown in October 1840 and almost immediately sought ways of accommodating Muslims in the colony as well as those in the interior. The appointment of Jeremie may have reflected a growing debate within the British colonial officialdom, with some being more flexible in their attitudes toward Islam, and thus the colony government would later begin to find ways of reaching religious accommodation. Upon his arrival in the colony, Jeremie hinted at several schemes aimed at addressing the prevailing challenges of the colonial economy, including agricultural projects such as cotton production, and the establishment of a savings bank.[123] Jeremie advised the Colonial Office against the expulsion of the Muslims from Fourah Bay and quietly acquiesced on the rebuilding of the mosque at Fula Town, which left the Christian missionaries perfectly perplexed, in much the same way that Catholic priests in Saint-Louis had reacted to the "religious toleration" of Faidherbe. Like the latter in Senegal, Jeremie's initial activities were informed less by racial and religious considerations than by the economic interests of European merchants who had mostly been concerned about the overly religious antagonisms of the previous administration. Jeremie took a quite dispassionate view of the Muslim presence in the colony, much to the disappointment and chagrin of the Christian clergy.

The discomfort of the clergy vis-à-vis the new administration was compounded by the decision of the Colonial Office to send yet another Irishman, Dr. Robert Madden, to Freetown to inquire into the prevailing state of affairs within the colony. Following an official inquiry, Madden reported that the allegations against the Muslims were unfounded and suggested that much of the antipathy against the followers of Islam may have been motivated by racial and religious bigotry.[124] The Madden Report proved particularly irksome to the retired Doherty, who consequently unleashed a vitriolic attack on the commissioner's findings.[125]

Governor Jeremie's death in April 1841, less than one year after his arrival in the colony, was an unwelcomed development for the Freetown Muslims; his short tenure served as a brief period of respite for Muslims in the colony, and a new period of uncertainty and sometimes outright antagonism was ushered in with the inauguration of Norman Macdonald as governor in 1845. Macdonald had served in several capacities in the colony administration for an extended period and did not share Jeremie's progressive outlook on race relations and religious issues. As governor, he did not limit his rancor to the Muslims of the Liberated African community; he showed outright contempt for Christian Africans as well. The colony inhabitants consequently displayed a general disregard and, indeed, nothing but contempt for the governor. Macdonald declared that Africans were unfit to hold high office in the colony and sought to interfere in the politics of the neighboring interior states. His direct intervention in the politics of the Bullom shore in 1846 so enraged the local Soso that they had his estate at Clarkson burned down, an act that the governor blamed on Muslim Liberated Africans. He lamented the fact that there had "always existed some legal or technical objections to taking measures for removing them and not only is the nuisance thus permitted to remain, but is of course daily increased."[126] He pronounced Muslim Liberated Africans "disloyal subjects and undeserving of the slightest confidence" and therefore initiated a series of ordinances aimed at creating a constricting social environment for the Muslims, on the ground that "they would be the first to aid in any outbreak in the colony." He urged the Colonial Office to assist his administration in ridding the colony of what he described as "a bed of serpents," reminding Whitehall that his predecessors, such as Governors Fergusson and Doherty, as well as himself viewed the Muslims and others in the Liberated African community who were reluctant to accommodate the European establishment as "blisters on the face of our society."[127] The persecution of Muslims, briefly relieved by Jeremie, was thus set to continue.

REVEREND SAMUEL ADJAI CROWTHER AND ISLAM IN THE COLONY

Muslims in the Liberated African community by the mid-nineteenth century constituted a minority in a colonial society in which the power of the colonial state was associated with the Christian faith. Lamin Sanneh draws attention to the perspective of Ibn Khaldun, who maintained that Christianity, unlike Islam, "does not embrace religion as a state idea, and without the state religious truth lacks the necessary political instrument to establish and maintain it." Ibn Khaldun, Sanneh notes, also believed that "religious mission requires political protection."[128] Ibn Khaldun, who was writing in the fourteenth century, may have utilized his observations of contemporary Christian evangelism to conclude that "Christianity is not a true 'missionary religion'"; however, his thesis is unsustainable with regard to the concerted effort of the colonial state and the Christian missions, particularly the CMS, in establishing and maintaining Christianity in colonial Sierra Leone. It would not be inaccurate to note that without the tacit cooperation, and indeed the pivotal political authority of the colony administration, especially in the face of an aggressive proselytizing agenda of Muslim clerics in the hinterland of the colony, as well as within the colony, the European and African Christian clergy would have achieved far less success than they actually did. Not only did the CMS become an intrinsic part of the colonial administration, effectively "integrated into the colonial power structure," with European missionaries assuming stewardship of the rural villages, the colonial state, very importantly, even utilized the military as an instrument of religious assertiveness during the Cobolo crisis.

The ability of the Christian missions and the state to facilitate the establishment and maintenance of Christianity also benefited immensely from the role and place of African "receivers" of the faith, who in turn assumed the role of "transmitters" (both as clergy and as laymen) and actively facilitated the spread of the religion not only in the colony, but to other parts of the West African coastal littoral and points beyond. Liberated Africans who encountered Christianity upon their arrival in Freetown subsequently became very instrumental in the spread of the religion, and in emphasizing the orthodoxy of the established church. As missionaries, they were in close contact with their European counterparts in the church as well as in the colonial bureaucracy and the merchant community. While they may not all have accepted European perceptions of Africans uncritically, some did embrace and share the colonial mission of Christianizing and "civilizing" the Africans.[129]

One Liberated African who was quite accommodating to European civilization, and a champion of the Christian missionary effort in the colony during the nineteenth century, was the Reverend Samuel Adjai Crowther.[130] The leading African evangelist in the CMS mission for most of the first half of the nineteenth century, Reverend Crowther remained grateful to the British, especially the established church for their role in the abolition of the slave trade, and for his own manumission, after being taken captive during the destruction of his native Yoruba town of Osogun in 1821. He was relocated to Sierra Leone, along with others taken off slave ships, in 1822, and resettled in the village of Bathurst, where his assimilation into European Christendom commenced with his baptism and change of name (from Adjai to Samuel Crowther) in 1825.[131] Ade Ajayi describes the new convert as an "industrious, intelligent, humble young man, the type beloved by missionaries." His humility and industriousness soon enabled him to enter and make steady progress in the mission-run elementary and grammar school system, and in the process inculcated and adopted Western cultural values. He was subsequently recommended for further studies at the Fourah Bay Institution, where he studied and became the first graduate of what later became Fourah Bay College. In 1843, after studying theology in Islington, England, Crowther was ordained a minister in the CMS and soon returned home to begin his missionary duties alongside his European counterparts.[132] He was subsequently dispatched to lead the CMS mission in Abeokuta, where he was reunited with his surviving family, including his mother, in 1845.

However, before his departure for his new duties in Nigeria, Crowther was determined to persuade those Liberated Africans who had elected to adhere to the Islamic faith, or to retain their allegiance to Yoruba orishas, particularly Sango, to finally convert to Christianity. The decision of the colony government in Freetown to be less involved in religious matters and to pursue a "path of accommodation" by allowing Muslims to worship freely served to engender an aggressive evangelical agenda among the Christian missionaries. The latter were soon engrossed in their quest to bring light to those among whom "there was nothing but darkness," that is, Muslims and Sango worshippers, all of whom they considered to be heathens. In spite of Crowther's attack on their faith, Muslim Liberated Africans were quite proud of Reverend Crowther, whom they considered one of their own countrymen. When news reached the leaders of the Fourah Bay Muslim congregation of the young CMS minister's imminent departure for Abeokuta, the Imam of the Muslim community sent a delegation to Bathurst village, where Crowther resided, on 17 December 1843, "to ask after my health, and to learn for certainty whether I was going to the Yoruba country."[133] Crowther was moved by the gesture, and observed that the Muslims spoke fluent Yoruba and Hausa.

On 18 December 1843, Crowther made a reciprocal visit to Fourah Bay, during which he seized on the opportunity to impress upon his hosts the blessings of Christianity and to convince the Muslims of "the importance of surrendering to the religion of the Whitemen's Bible, because it leads the sure way to happiness."[134] He later reported that he had, on an earlier occasion, given a copy of the Arabic version of the Holy Bible to the Imam of the community, and had informed the Imam that he had been instructed by the London Committee of the CMS to translate the Bible into Yoruba so "that the people may be able to read this book for themselves in their [native] tongue." Reverend Crowther maintained that he had refrained from objecting to the presence of Muslims in the colony, but had "endeavoured to show them the great blessings Christianity bestows on mankind whenever it is embraced." While the Fourah Bay Muslims were not persuaded by his admonition, Crowther noted that "to my surprise, they gloried at having their countryman to be the first clergyman of the Church of England among the Liberated Africans in the colony of Sierra Leone," even if the Muslims were adamant about retaining their Islamic faith. On 8 January 1844, he formally informed the Imam of Fourah Bay of his impending inaugural service in the Yoruba language at the Mission Church in Freetown, and invited the Muslims to attend. According to Reverend Crowther, "At my asking this, one of them said I was trying to entrap them and begged that I would not urge them, their religion and ours being the same. They said that they acknowledged Jesus to be a great Prophet sent by God, but concerning his sonship, they could not reconcile it."[135]

Crowther reported that he consequently sought to engage his Muslim compatriots by noting that "on that very account it was requisite that they should attend the Yoruba service, because they would have the advantage of hearing the doctrine expounded in their own language which they well understood, and that, thus, the difficulty under which they were laboring would be removed."

His hosts promised to have a presence at the inaugural service and, on the appointed day, Crowther noted in his journal that at least three of the Muslims did attend as they had promised to. In his journal entry, he observed that "the novelty of the thing [service in the Yoruba language] brought a large number of people together, Yoruba, Igbo, Calabar, etc. to witness the reading and preaching [of] the gospel of Christ in a native language in an English church." Perhaps in an attempt to disabuse the Muslims of their reluctance to accept the divine nature of Christ, Crowther sought to address the issue directly, noting that "the text from which I preached was taken from the lesson I had read to them, the 35th verse of the first chapter of St. Luke, 'ohung ti awoh mi inoh reh li aomokhe *li ommoh Olorung.'* (That holy thing which shall be born of thee shall be called the son of God.)[136]

In subsequent Church sermons, Crowther seized the opportunity to address several aspects of life in the colony that were of vital concern to him, especially the worship of Sango, the Yoruba *Orisa* (god) of thunder and lightning. He lambasted traditional religion, reserving his most incendiary comments for the worshippers of the Yoruba deity, and made the point of lecturing them in their local places of worship. On 23 February 1844, on a visit to one such location, he proceeded to question the wisdom of their belief in Sango, prompting an unfriendly reaction from disdainful worshippers who in turn pointed out to the CMS minister what they perceived as the superficiality and hypocrisy of Christians "who were the greatest adulterers that could be met in the whole colony."[137] Crowther was mortified by this outburst of emotion from the beleaguered Sango worshippers, and was astonished when they ridiculed the habit of Christians to claim during church services that they could literally see God. He allowed that he had "to hold my tongue," because "the charges were true." The biting sermons of Reverend Crowther were also aimed at Muslims, whom he maintained were "in the habit of alluring away lawful wives of their neighbours." According to Crowther, "The tenth commandment seems to have struck them hard on their right eye."

In spite of Crowther's indefatigable efforts, Muslims remained devoted to their religion. Unlike the Muslims of Fourah Bay, he noted that the inhabitants of Fula Town never attended his church services. He was also disappointed by the reluctance of all Muslims in the colony to refrain from engaging in manual activities on Sunday, the Christian Sabbath. Nonetheless, Crowther remained determined to continue his evangelical work among Muslims, even though he must have realized that Muslims and Christians in the colony had become entrenched in their respective faiths. The Yoruba cultural commonalities shared by the Oku in the emergent Krio society transcended religious differences, and the developing cohesiveness of the new society showed signs of an inherent capacity to accommodate religious plurality. By 1853, the colonial state did not appear to be in a position to continue the pursuance of a policy of aggressive anti-Islamism. The colony's increasing trade relations with the mostly Muslim interior states, which we will address in the next chapter, was by this time contingent on continued cordial relations with Muslims in the colony. Economic and political expediency, rather than the religious preferences of the colony inhabitants, seemed to be the guiding force in determining colonial policy by the mid-nineteenth century.

Whether for reasons of commercial or political expediency, there was by the 1850s a growing evidence of accommodating tendencies on the part of colonial authorities and some of the Christian clergy, like Reverend Crowther, and some of the leaders in the Muslim communities. Crowther, albeit without much enthusiasm, would agree to make room on board ship for some of the Muslims who expressed a desire to return to the Bight of Benin along with their Christian counterparts by mid-century. A perceived common Yoruba heritage of Muslims and Christians in the colony was by this time engendering efforts at accommodation within an "imagined community" of Krio. On the official front, colony administration authorities were fast coming to the realization that Muslims at Fourah Bay, Fula Town, and Aberdeen were potentially instrumental to the development of what could be a flourishing trade relationship between the interior states and the coastal colony. Muslim familiarity with the Arabic language also came to convince the colonial state that Liberated African Muslims could be utilized as interpreters and translators, thereby facilitating the development of avenues of accommodation and cooperation between the colony and interior Muslim states. What remained was the tapping of such resources in the colony Muslim population, individuals who, as Robinson discovered in Senegal, "had clear credentials of piety, learning and prestige in the faith," and who could work in cooperation with the colonial authorities "without compromising" their religious and personal integrity.[138] Such individuals would be found in the likes of Mohammed Sanusie, Hadiru Deen, and Amadu Wakka in subsequent years as commercial relations grew in intensity between the colony and the interior.

The change in colony administration policy vis-à-vis Islam in the 1850s and after was reflective of the increasingly pivotal role of Muslims in the colonial economy. By mid-century, colony government policy demonstrated a deliberate "interest in knowing" about the Islamic faith and Muslims in the colony and the interior. Black and white traders alike soon echoed the need for a more flexible colony government policy toward Muslims, noting that the moribund colonial economy would be much revived by a less dogmatic approach to Islam and an equally less prejudiced attitude toward Muslims. But the change in colony government policy and attitude was also a result of the demonstrated strength and resiliency of the Muslim community. As noted earlier, the failure of the joint assault of the colony government and the church on Muslims in the colony and rural villages only served to strengthen the resolve of Muslims to consolidate their faith and institutions in the colony. Always consistent in their assertion that they had embraced the Islamic faith prior to their being relocated to the Sierra Leone Colony,

Liberated African Muslims traversed the forested landscape between the rural villages and Freetown, where they succeeded in building a mosque, thereby serving notice that theirs was a religion that was not about to be eliminated in spite of the efforts of the colony government and the established Church of England. The colony government may have finally come to appreciate the especially important economic implications of this reality and, consequently, sought to engage colony Muslims in accessing the pivotal trade systems of the interior Muslim states.

3 ∾ Trade, Religion, and the Colonial State

THE ACCOMMODATION ACHIEVED BETWEEN MUSLIMS, Christians, and the colonial state by the mid-nineteenth century enabled Muslim Liberated Africans to participate more vigorously and creatively in the commercial life of the Sierra Leone Colony. The colonial administration recruited educated Muslims to develop a bridge with their religious community and to aid in the interactions between the colony and the peoples of the Sierra Leone hinterland. Muslim traders became crucial in expanding the Sierra Leone economy through their trade networks with the hinterland initiated in the eighteenth century, participation in local urban markets, and in Krio diaspora communities along the West African coast in the late nineteenth and early twentieth centuries. The role and place of Muslims in interregional commerce, in fact, long predated the establishment of British colonial influence in West Africa, which had a tradition of Muslim and non-Muslim traders traversing the economic landscape covering the Upper Guinea coast.

The pivotal intersection of trade and Islam in Sierra Leone and West Africa was clearly appreciated by the supervisors of the Freetown settlement long before it was transformed into a formal British Crown colony in 1808. The origins of long-distance commerce involving Muslim merchants can be traced back to the medieval period (certainly between the tenth and thirteenth centuries), when Dyula/Wangara merchants began establishing trading diasporas linking the empires of Ghana, Mali, and Songhai with societies outside the jurisdiction and regions of the respective political units. The "commercial diasporas" thus established were anchored by Islam, with Shari'a serving as the recognized judicial system. To the Muslim traders, the Islamic legal system ensured an atmosphere of general trustworthiness in the merchant community. Thus, those who wished to participate in the developing trade system considered it imperative to convert to Islam and become a part of the regional commercial network.[1]

The Islamic faith also had a tremendous impact on the movement of Krio merchants and others in what became a Krio diaspora along the Atlantic coast of West Africa during the nineteenth century. The wide distribution of Krio traders in the region has been documented in the literature; however, women traders have not always received an equitable treatment in the historiography, perhaps due to a paucity of written sources. The lack of available written sources on women traders may have been due to the reluctance of influential male personalities to acknowledge the pivotal role of women traders in local and regional commerce. In Sierra Leone and other parts of West Africa, women were instrumental in local markets; their activities transcended merely commercial activities, as they usually utilized their organizational skills to cater to the social and cultural needs of their communities. Women traders in the Liberated African communities laid the groundwork for the entrepreneurial success of the group and their subsequent ascendancy over the earlier returnees, primarily through the plying of vegetables and other farm produce in the villages outside the colony. This role was subsequently expanded and had become quite pivotal by the mid-nineteenth century, with Muslim women playing an important role in local trade in spite of the constricted social parameters of the colonial space.

By 1854, trade between Freetown and the interior was picking up steam, and the once threatening red ink of the treasury seemed to be largely a thing of the past. The administration of Sir Arthur Kennedy was by this time reporting to Whitehall that, rather than impending financial disaster, the colonial economy was flourishing.[2] Colony traders who elected to remain in Freetown rather than journey to the interior sought to take advantage of the growing trade with the interior by establishing relations with incoming merchants who brought their goods by canoe from the Northern Rivers to Government Wharf and the Grain Market at Susan's Bay. Traders from the nearby Muslim Krio communities of Fula Town and Fourah Bay located their stalls at Kissy Road (later renamed Kissy Street), just south of Susan's Bay, to take advantage of the increasingly flourishing trade. Many hawked such imported items as hide, kola nuts, benniseed, and shea butter.

The increasingly pivotal role of Muslims in colony-interior trade relations would have profound consequences for colonial policy regarding religion. Cognizant of the significance of Muslim rulers and traders in the interior and their coreligionists in Freetown for the economic viability of the colony, the administration adopted what amounted to an ambivalent attitude and policy toward Islam. While assuring the Christian missions of continued government support, open antagonism toward Muslims in the colony was discouraged, and some Muslims were soon co-opted into the colonial administrative machinery. Meanwhile, acting Governor Robert Dougan sought to reassure Soso cattle traders from the interior of government protection for their trade caravans en route to the colony. In May 1855, Dougan sent a letter to the ruler of Medina, Alikali Modu, imploring him not to reduce trade with the colony, with assurances that the cattle merchants would enjoy safe passage and "unmolested" transactions in Freetown. Dougan implored Modu to "dispel the erroneous impression" that Muslim Soso traders were not welcome in the colony.[3] It was thus clearly evident in official circles in Freetown that Muslim merchants in the colony, as well as those from the interior, were becoming virtually indispensable to the sustainability of the colonial economy. Hence the evident volte-face in colony policy regarding religion, and a cessation of the persecutory stance regarding Muslims. Rather than an emphasis on religious and political persecution of Muslims, the colony government seemed willing to pursue a policy of accommodation vis-à-vis Muslims. For one thing, given the growing importance of trade with the interior states, there was a dire need for Muslims with expertise in Islam and Arabic. As obtained in Senegal, "a translation service for Arabic correspondence" became essential to colony-interior trade in Sierra Leone. In much the same way as Faidherbe did in French-controlled Saint-Louis, the British would come to utilize the Office of Government Interpreter as a sort of "diplomatic operation." Faidherbe enlisted "persons who had clear credentials of piety, learning, and prestige in the faith."[4] Faidherbe's example was eventually to be adopted by British colonial officials in Sierra Leone.

MUSLIM INTERLOCUTORS IN THE COLONIAL SERVICE

The Sierra Leone Colony government only had to identify capable personalities in the Muslim communities within Krio society who, as in the case of Muslims in Saint-Louis, could work for the colony government "without compromising their Islamic practice or their standing among most Muslims" in Sierra Leone. The colony government signaled its willingness and capacity to work in cooperation with educated Muslims, thereby forging a "path of accommodation" with Muslims, with the appointment of Mohammed Sanusie, a Muslim Krio who was educated in Freetown and Futa Jallon, in December 1872 to the post of government Arabic writer in the Native Affairs Department, with an annual salary of £78 (seventy-eight pounds sterling) paid out of the Colonial Revenue Fund (CRF).[5] Shortly after Sanusie's appointment, the government announced the appointment of Hadiru Deen and Momodu Wakka as government clerk and assistant government interpreter, respectively. Sanusie's role proved very crucial to relations between the colony administration and the Muslim traders from the hinterland states. As the official Arabic writer, he also served as assistant to the government interpreter, in which position he became the official liaison between Freetown and the Muslim interior states. Sanusie, Deen, and Wakka represented an emergent generation of educated Muslims, fluent in Arabic and English and the indigenous languages. The one-time CMS missionary and Pan-African pioneer Edward Wilmot Blyden observed that they "can not only read and write, and with ease and propriety converse, in the language of Arabia, but can also translate readily from Arabic into Aku and English, and from English into Arabic and Aku."[6] Sanusie's fluency in Fulbe made his services indispensable to colony-interior trade relations especially at a time of increased commercial transactions with merchants from Timbo, Kankan, and the Senegambia valley. Fula caravans bringing gold, hides, ivory, and a host of other trade items going back to the early nineteenth century were now playing a significant role, along with the Mandinka in the colonial economy. Sanusie impressed the English explorer William Winwood Reade (1838–1875), whom he had encountered while the latter was in Sierra Leone as one of several British personnel deployed in West Africa to investigate the source of the Niger River, and other river networks in Africa, in the nineteenth century. Sanusie shared his love of poetry and literature in general with Reade, and exposed the Englishman to his vast library of Islamic literature.[7] Quite impressed with the scholarly interests of Sanusie, Reade consequently urged Governor Kennedy to recruit Muslim personnel for the colonial civil service.

The Muslim personalities recruited into the colonial civil service became vital to colony-hinterland trade over the years, to the extent that a separate office designated as the Aborigines Branch was created in 1878 to oversee interior trade relations. Sanusie, for instance, was well placed to assuage the anxieties of the Muslim traders from the interior who had shown an inclination to work in concert with their coreligionists in Freetown.[8] The change in government policy toward Islam and the increasing, and undisturbed, presence of Muslims in the colony generated an increase in trade caravans arriving in Freetown. On 2 April 1879, the government interpreter reported "the arrival in Freetown during the March quarter . . . of 1,176 caravans."[9] The colonial government was by now fully cognizant of the need for a less confrontational policy and attitude toward Muslims in the colony, especially given the cooperative role played by Muslim rulers in securing the trade routes connecting the colony and the interior. The cooperation between the colony government and Muslim rulers along the trade routes was not lost on the caravan merchants; an emissary of the ruler of Dinguiraye, who accompanied a caravan sent from that chiefdom in 1879, informed the government interpreter that Muslim rulers of the interior were aware of, and grateful for, the efforts of the colony government to cooperate with Muslim rulers in securing the trade routes connecting the interior to the coast. As a reciprocal gesture, the interior rulers promised to ensure smooth relations between the colony and the hinterland states.

The 1880s ushered in a period of increased incidence in caravan arrivals in Freetown. Sanusie reported that some of the trade items sent to Freetown included "some very heavy and large ivory" and gold.[10] The gold reaching Freetown between 1878 and 1879 originated from Segu and Buré, which had been the centers of gold production going back to the medieval period. Hides and other wares sent by the Sangarahs were exchanged for flints, guns, and gunpowder; the Sangarahs were at this time feeling threatened by the Sofa warriors of Samori Touré, hence their need for weaponry. In addition to the gold and ivory taken to Freetown by the traders from Segu and Buré, those from Dinguiraye and Futa also transported such sundry articles as country gowns, shea butter, calabashes, and fine country cotton cloth.[11]

By 1886, even more caravans were reaching Freetown from the interior; the government interpreter, T. G. Lawson, reported the arrival of new caravans in the colony via Port Loko. The traders started their journey from Sangarah, while others originated from Kankan, Sanankoré, Buré, and Segu.[12] The colony government in Freetown was usually called upon to intervene whenever the caravans encountered obstacles along the trade routes. When, for instance, a group of interior traders was required to pay what they perceived as exorbitant and illegitimate fares by canoe operators on a river in Port Loko, the group reported the incident to the colony administration in Freetown and asked for assistance from the government in preventing a recurrence of such irregularities.[13] Caravans were "the basic institution" for moving goods overland, and their movement across great distances was often a difficult and challenging undertaking. Thus, given their increasing importance in trade between the colony and the hinterland, the colonial government took serious measures to ensure that trade missions from the interior states experienced as little difficulty as possible.[14]

Muslim Krio merchants who made the journey to the interior via the Northern Rivers facilitated increased commercial exchanges between the colony and the interior. By the end of 1886, many colony-based traders were actively transporting much of the trade goods from the north to Freetown. Consequently, such items as India rubber, palm kernels, palm oil, benniseed, cattle, beeswax, gold, rice, and hides became readily available in the colony.[15] The Muslim civil servants Sanusie, Deen, and Wakka in the Native Affairs Department have been acknowledged as crucial to the increasing cooperation between the interior traders and colony government and Krio traders; in his role as Arabic writer, Wakka also served as emissary to hinterland rulers, and was often able to observe interstate relations between interior rulers. In this capacity, and from information garnered from colony-based traders in the interior, he remained quite knowledgeable of political and economic developments in the interior, which he constantly relayed to the authorities in Freetown, thereby allowing the colony government to take advantage of such developments; rulers in precarious positions vis-à-vis their neighbors were invariably rendered assistance by the colony government with an eye toward obtaining favorable economic benefits in return.[16]

During a period of increased rivalry between European imperial powers for land appropriation in West Africa, the relations between the Muslim Krio and their coreligionists from the interior also served to keep the colony government apprised of the activities of the French in the territories to the north of Sierra Leone. Muslim traders from the interior who were opposed to the French presence in areas adjacent to their territories were quite willing to share information about French activities with the British in Freetown. The ability of Sanusie and Wakka to communicate with the interior traders enabled the colony government to maintain surveillance on the activities of interior rulers as well as the French.

The ruler of Futa Jallon thus made it known that he was inclined to join forces with the anti-French Mandinka jihadist leader Samori Touré, in order to keep open the Tamisoe Road through Sammayah down to Freetown along the Atlantic coast.[17] The Futa Jallon ruler was obviously less motivated by reasons of religious and political concerns than by trade considerations. The singularly most important factor behind his overture to Samori was his desire to keep open the road to Freetown. Access to the Tamisoe Road, which was known as the best route for the traders, had been restricted since 1885, due to the activities of Samori's Sofa warriors. Some caravans had been plundered and life had been made generally miserable for traders; thus, the Futa ruler found it politically and economically expedient to enter into an accord with the Mandinka leader, who was at this time also interested in establishing cordial relations with the British in Freetown.[18] Samori's interest in establishing a diplomatic dialogue with the British was made all the more urgent by the French occupation of Buré in 1885, thereby cutting off the jihadist leader from the gold of that region, which was of central importance to the economy of his Mandinka Empire.[19] Realizing the ultimate implications of French expansion for his empire, Samori determined to strengthen his military forces in order to meet the French threat. He thus resolved to develop close relations with the British in Sierra Leone, if only for the politically expedient purpose of eliminating the French from Mandinka country. After his occupation of Falaba the year before the French takeover of Buré, Samori sent word to the colony government in Freetown suggesting that the British take control of his Mandinka country. As Gueye and Boahen have noted, this offer was merely an expedient proposition, calculated to give the French pause in their land appropriation.[20] He did not succeed in obtaining British protection vis-à-vis the French, but succeeded nonetheless in signing an Anglo-Mandinka treaty in May 1890, which allowed him to procure modern weapons from Freetown. His activities thus had great repercussions on the trade routes between the interior states and coastal Freetown.

IMPACT OF TRADE ON ISLAM IN THE COLONY

As a consequence of increased trade relations between the Muslim states of the interior and the colony, there was a concurrent rise in Islamic influences in Freetown as a result of Muslim missionary activity. In addition to the influx of traders from the immediate hinterland of the colony, including the Limba, Temne, and Loko, "streams" of Muslim merchants flowed into the colony from Buré, Futa, Bambara, Timbuctu, Jenne, Segu, and Kankan.[21] Blyden noted that the "Houbous, those renegade Foulahs, who for thirty years have been a terror to caravans passing through the districts which they infested, have been scattered by the military energy of Samudu [Samori]." Consequently, there was a fluid movement of traders and trade goods between the interior and the coast, and with them an increasing spread of Islamic influences in the colony. The "same vocal sounds which may be heard in the streets of Cairo and Alexandria, of Morocco and of Tunis" became commonplace in the colony by the late nineteenth century. The *Azan* (call to prayer) subsequently became a part of the social landscape of Freetown, as Muslims were reminded of their obligation to pray five times a day by the muezzins. While the Muslim merchants did not forget their religious obligations, their crucial role in the colonial economy was becoming increasingly evident. By 1882, the colonial economy was growing quite significantly, as evidenced by some statistical data on import/export exchanges between the colony and Atlantic destinations made available to Blyden, as agent to the interior, by the governor-in-chief, which he subsequently reproduced in his *Christianity, Islam and the Negro Race*:[22]

Exports to Britain £189,120.11.6
Imports from Britain £272,195.6.2
Exports to America...£23,354.8.6
Imports from America... £34,436.16.8
Export to France £77,861.2.11
Imports from France £15,790.3.1
Exports to Germany £23,152.17.0
Imports from Germany £20,639.19.6
Exports to Belgium £217.4.0
Imports from Belgium... £0.0.0
Total value of exports from Sierra Leone..........................£420,015.2.8
Total value of imports £398,814.19.9

The growing colonial economy may have assisted the growth of the Islamic faith in the colony, especially as colonial officials sought to encourage the continued movement of goods between the colony and the interior states. The changes in the attitude of colonial officials emboldened Muslim merchants and clerics, such as the Fula, Soso, and Mandinka, who used their relations with their commercial partners in the colony to spread their religious faith. Not unlike the ways in which the Christian missionaries in the colony combined their evangelical activities with their agricultural and commercial ventures, the Muslim merchants exploited their religious solidarity with the Muslim community in Freetown to spread their faith. Muslim merchants frequently used their sojourn in the colony to engage in propagating Islamic scriptures among the colony population. They cultivated closer relations by giving favorable treatment to fellow Muslim merchants, such as making available to fellow Muslims trade items not otherwise available to non-Muslims in the colony.

As Allen Howard has shown, Muslims cooperated through interregional trade to move goods from the interior to Freetown.[23] Many stayed in groups in the Liberated African rural villages outside the colony, where the process of Islamic proselytizing had begun decades earlier among the population of ex-slaves and their progeny or, in the case of those who had been introduced to the faith prior to their being taken captive in their natal societies, to improve their knowledge of Islamic tenets and of the Qur'an. Many of the Muslims in the colony thus came to be introduced to the cattle, hide, kola, and ginger trade, while being integrated into the larger Islamic Ummah. In time, many of the older Muslims and the new converts would travel to the interior with their fellow Muslims, who assisted them in procuring trade goods or acted as agents for the major traders who stayed behind in the interior. Inhabitants from the Muslim Krio communities of Fourah Bay, Fula Town, and Aberdeen thus became heavily involved in the transporting of large volumes of kola nuts, ginger, shea butter, and other items from the interior to Freetown where they became a prominent part of the commercial and social life of the city.[24]

Thus, given their shared Islamic ethos, Muslim Krio merchants and their interior counterparts combined to have a major impact on colony-interior trade. Ultimately, their heavy involvement in trade contributed to the growth of Islam in the colony. By the late 1800s, immigrant Muslim families from the Guinea-Conakry area, such as the Tounkara and Sillah, were taking up residence in the Fourah Bay community.[25] While the bulk of immigrant groups from the Guinea-Conakry region usually stayed in the central part of Freetown, a few families elected to locate their domiciles of choice among the Muslims of Fourah Bay. The Tounkaras were among those who relocated to the Muslim community in the east of Freetown, where they established a Qur'an school in which they taught Arabic *sura* (verses) by rote to local children, while retaining their participation in trade. The Tounkara family would later lease land at Krojimi, in the Fourah Bay community, and sought to establish roots, even as they maintained a distinct cultural separateness from the larger Muslim Krio community.[26] Mandinka and other itinerant groups like the Marrka, Soso, and Fula invariably sought to preserve their ethnic identity in the colony by creating and maintaining their own identifiable communities. Nonetheless, some Mandinka families, such as the Jabbie, Kamara, Kallay, and others, many of which concentrated in the Magazine Cut area to the west of Fourah Bay, developed close ties with Muslim Krio through intermarriage and adoption of Yoruba cultural societies such as Ojeh and Odeh.

MUSLIMS AND THE MEAT AND FISH TRADE IN THE COLONY, 1870–1900

The large population of commercial diaspora communities in the colony provided an opportunity for Muslim Krio merchants to utilize their religious links with the Muslim merchants from the interior. Merchants from the communities of Fourah Bay, Fula Town, and Aberdeen sought to increase their business transactions in the Scarcies River, Bonthe Sherbro, and other parts of the hinterland. The Aberdeen merchants, in particular, saw their kola nut and cattle trade increase significantly during the mid-nineteenth to early twentieth centuries.[27] Cattle purchased in the interior were transported to the colony and subsequently relocated to *worreh* (cattle corrals) owned by Aberdeen merchants; such facilities were professionally managed by Fula cattle herders under whose care the herds multiplied, leading to increased profits for the Muslim Krio merchants. Cattle raised in the Aberdeen stockades were invariably sold to butchers at Fula Town, as well as to those in the Mandinka and Fula communities in the colony. Kola nuts bought by Krio merchants from the Sherbro and Temne country were sold in Freetown to the Muslim merchants at Fourah Bay, who usually moved their goods to the Gambia and Senegal where they used the profit from the kola trade to purchase sheep for sale in Sierra Leone.[28]

The kola business was clearly an important part of colony-interior commercial exchanges during the nineteenth century, perhaps for the same reasons it had been for much of the history of West African societies. Kola was very significant to the peoples of the region, and its value could hardly be overemphasized. As Walter Rodney observed, it was "associated with religious rites, initiation ceremonies, and property rights; it is used as a stimulant, a yellow dye, for medicinal purposes, as a symbol of hospitality, and in diplomatic relations between rulers; and it was particularly highly-regarded among Islamized peoples."[29] The colony merchants benefited from the movement of kola traders, who procured the item from other traders on the "important route that stretched from the upper valley of the St. Paul River through Kankan and Kissidougou." As Rodney maintained, "It is highly probable that from early times some kola was sent across the Niger from the area now held by the Koranko and Kono in the hinterland of Sierra Leone, since they both adjoined Kissidougou."[30] Merchants from the colony tapped into the kola trade, it may be argued, because of its availability; kola trees were ubiquitous along the Rokelle and Scarcies Rivers. As a result, Temne and Bullom traders were exploiting this important trade item long before the arrival of the Portuguese in the fifteenth century.

The Aberdeen merchants were perhaps the most successful of the Muslim Krio traders. They were quite cognizant of the need for diversified trade investments in the interior; they usually purchased kola nuts on a wholesale basis at Kambia, up the Scarcies to the north, and sold these items to retailers in Freetown.[31] Aberdeen merchants also exchanged items such as sugar and imported clothes for kola nuts in the Sherbro country of the Sierra Leone River to the south of the colony. Amadu Deen Cole, Adib Muctarr, Rahman Ben Othman, Muctarr Amadu, Ismaila Davies, and Hadhi Noah[32] were by this time among the leading Aberdeen merchants engaged in diverse trade activities involving cattle, palm kernels and palm oil, rubber, groundnuts, benniseed, shea butter, and other sundry goods. Their success would ultimately attract the attention of larger investors and businesses that would seek to squeeze them out of the colony-interior trade. Nonetheless, Aberdeen merchants resiliently continued their commercial ventures, even as they were being systematically edged out of the interior trade. Many resorted to farming, as had their counterparts from Fourah Bay; Muslim Krio farmers were soon producing such items as pepper, arrowroot, Indian corn, cassava, plantain, okro, guava, pineapple, pawpaw, lime, pomegranate, coconut, mangoes, and ginger for wholesale and retail trading.[33] Production of such items as chili peppers and ginger was found to be fairly profitable; even though the price of ginger had suffered a downturn in the 1880s, chili peppers "fetched 12s.6p a bushel in London."[34] Ginger prices experienced an upswing by the 1890s, even if for a short while. Muslim traders generally played an important role in the hinterland; however, nowhere was the centrality of these traders more evident than in the provision of sources of protein for the colony through the cattle and fish trade, facilitated by the connections between colony and hinterland Muslims.

The growing demand for meat in the colony was met by the raising of livestock by the cattle farmers at Aberdeen and Fula Town, who fared much better than their small-scale produce counterparts. As commerce in the colony intensified in the nineteenth century, Muslim Krio merchants in these communities also intensified their efforts to meet the demands of the market by diversifying their holdings; they sought to increase their herds of sheep and goats bought from the Fula and Mandinka traders. The latter often deposited their herds at the government abattoir, from which they subsequently sold them to the Krio merchants and butchers. Muslim Krio cattle farmers from Aberdeen and Fula Town would later resell their livestock to other farmers or keep them at their farms for the purpose of fattening them in order to maximize their profits.[35] Prominent butchers, including Aruna Cole, Rahimi Cole, and Alamiru Cole, often arranged to meet with the cattle merchants privately at their homes, during which they would engage in haggling behind closed doors in an attempt to secure favorable prices.

The close social and commercial linkages between Muslim Krio merchants and their coreligionists from the interior provided them access not otherwise available to non-Muslim Krio. They usually received notice of the impending arrival in the colony of Mandinka, Fula, and Soso cattle traders, and upon the arrival of these traders in Freetown, the Aberdeen and Fula Town merchants would call on them to place their bids on the newly arrived batch of cattle. The cattle trade thus became a very valuable source of revenue for the Muslims of Aberdeen and Fula Town. The revenue derived from this trade became a pivotal source of capital accumulation for the Muslim Krio in the colony. As was the practice of non-Muslim Krio merchants, capital amassed from the cattle trade was subsequently invested in real-estate holdings in the colony. Perceiving the acquisition of Western educations as essential to the progress of their community in the developing colonial environment, the leading merchants also invested much of their resources in the education of their progeny. A Western education was by this time also reflective of the willingness of Muslims to pursue avenues of accommodation with the colonial establishment. Many scions of enterprising Muslim merchant families were thus enrolled in Christian mission schools, with the products of these schools subsequently entering the colonial civil bureaucracy.

The Sierra Leone River and the available marine resources therein also provided a major source of revenue for the inhabitants of the colony. By the late nineteenth century, the *Sierra Leone Gazette* was advertising a quarterly list of license holders in the fishing industry. The majority of the licensed merchants in the April 1875 issue of the gazette were Muslim Krio,[36] the vast majority of whom were from Fourah Bay and Aberdeen. The natural harbor at Fourah Bay ensured a useful wharf from which fishing boats sailed across the river to the Bullom shores to the north. The mid-nineteenth century ushered in a period of changes in fishing technology along the West African Atlantic coastal littoral. Maritime fishing communities were experiencing the benefits of a "veritable technological revolution in sea fishing." Fishing communities along the Sierra Leone River began to make less use of the old cast nets and seemed to have adopted the drift nets that were already popular among the Fante of the Gold Coast region.[37] The impact of the new technology was almost immediately evident; the size of the nets enhanced the volume of catch for the local fishermen, as the nets were not only large but also required less skill in their operation, compared to the old cast nets. The wide expanse of the river provided abundant catches of a vast array of marine resources, including grupa, mackerel, bonga, oysters, *minna* (minnow), and *kuta* (barracuda).

The dominant fish traders of Fourah Bay, including the brothers John and James Macauley, Thomas "Seabreeze," and Maria Joaque,[38] controlled the retail trade at the local outlets at Cline Town wharf, Fourah Bay wharf, and Kissy Road and King Jimmy markets, all of which attracted large crowds from Freetown and the surrounding villages.[39] The fish trade at the retail level was mainly in the hands of women merchants. Krio women of nineteenth-century Freetown were noted for their entrepreneurial endeavors, a skill often frowned upon by the European Christian clergy, who vehemently disapproved of the Krio "predilection" for trading. The natural inclination toward trading for Oku women has been attributed to their Yoruba cultural background.[40] Enterprising women traders usually gathered at the local wharves at dusk before the fishing boats came ashore. Using their haggling skills, the women almost invariably succeeded in purchasing large volumes of fish that they subsequently sold on a retail basis at the local markets at fixed or negotiable prices. Some of the women who had been in the fish trade for an extended period often purchased fish on a credit or "trust system," while some of the fishermen kept the business in-house and turned over their catches to their wives or other female relatives who owned stalls at the local fish market.

The fishing industry in colonial Sierra Leone was not limited to the wholesale and retail distribution of raw fish in the local market. An ancillary industry involving the production and wide distribution of dried fish was also an integral part of the colonial economy in which the dominant players were women. Women from various parts of the colony and the surrounding villages were deeply involved in the dried fish business, which came to provide the women with a significant source of economic empowerment and independence within their local communities as well as in colonial society in general. Using oversized *banda* (grills), the scaled and thoroughly cleaned fish were salted and smoked over the grills, thereby preserving them for households in a society where the homes lacked the necessary means of food preservation. Following the smoking process, the fishmongers distributed their wares in the local markets; Muslim Krio fish traders also purchased dried fish from traders who arrived in the colony on large boats from the Bullom shores to the north, along with other prepared food items, including *agidi, fufu*, and dried oysters.[41]

The hub of the colony's retail trade activities in food items from places across the Sierra Leone River was King Jimmy Wharf, which, according to an August 1885 edition of the *Sierra Leone Weekly News*, had "always been frequented by a large number of women, both from the city as well as from the villages."[42] The *Weekly News* noted that these women "prosecuted their daily avocations according to the dictates of their creed and profession. No shops or stores of any kind are thereon erected, but an array of baskets, calabashes or other convenient receptacles for immediate traffic grace the hands of these earnest competitors." The boats from Bullom usually docked at dusk with a bountiful supply of foodstuffs and utensils that were quickly purchased by the colony women on a wholesale basis for subsequent retail trade. The *Weekly News* illustrated the scene at King Jimmy Market on a typical, albeit rainy, day thus: "What a sight does one behold during the wet season, when at the signal of a 'trading canoe,' and amidst a heavy downpour of rain, these 'busy women' in Babel-like confusion and in the indulgence of the vilest possible language strenuously competing with each other for that which supplies only their temporal wants and necessities."[43]

The *Weekly News* editorialized that the scene at King Jimmy Wharf was rather deplorable and called for the construction of permanent stalls or sheds not only at that location but also at such major centers as Cline Town Wharf, Sawpit Market, and other places in the colony. While the editors of the paper reflected a rather prudish attitude and cultural condescension vis-à-vis the local women, they nonetheless advocated that the women were deserving of better trading facilities "where traders might conveniently carry on their legitimate calling," with the caveat that "a competent officer [be] appointed to collect a nominal revenue from every canoe arriving at any of these places for trading purposes."[44] However, the editors of the paper were still very anxious about what they perceived as an influx of non-Christian peoples from the interior. The paper thus published an appeal from some "concerned citizens" who wanted the colony administration "to consider and deal with a serious social problem" engendered by "the excessive influx of the useless portion in our midst of these strangers."[45]

The opinion of the *Weekly News* was clearly reflective of the continued intolerance in the upper echelons of colonial society for religious pluralism and a lingering cultural prejudice toward the interior peoples; an intolerance that would continue for quite some time during the twentieth century. To its credit, however, the *Weekly News* went on to caution that it would not be humane to expel immigrants who had taken up residence in the colony. Indeed, it would have been very difficult, if not impossible, for the colony government to deport immigrants from the interior who had taken up residence in Freetown, especially the women. Perhaps the paper was simply cognizant of the practice of Krio traders in the hinterland to return to the colony with wives and offspring from cross-cultural intermarriages and romantic liaisons that had developed during their sojourns in the hinterland. Muslim and Christian Krio traders who took spouses from interior societies developed a habit of dropping the original names of their wives and replacing them with Yoruba, as well as Muslim and Christian names, such as Ayodele, Olabisi, Rakiatu, Nancy, Josephine, Mary, and so on.

By the late 1890s, Muslim Krio merchants began to engage in increasing trade activities with immigrant Syrian traders, who were fast becoming active in interior trade. The latter would ultimately displace Krio traders, as they and European merchant groups subsequently joined forces to dominate colony-interior trade. The impact of their displacement in interior trade may have been lessened ultimately by their investment in retail stores in hinterland towns, specializing in the sale of imported goods bought in Freetown.

Ironically, it was the success of the Muslim Krio merchants that may have attracted the attention of large European firms like Patterson Zochonis (PZ), Sociéte Commerciale de L'ouést Africain (SCOA), A. Genet, Compagnie Francaise de L'Afrique Occidentale (CFAO), and G. B. Ollivant. PZ was a Manchester-based firm formed by former employees of another Manchester company, Randall and Fisher, who teamed up with G. B. Zochonis, "a Greek from Sparta," who was the firm's representative in Freetown.[46] The European firms initially employed Krio traders as agents in the interior trade, only to replace them with Syrian immigrants later on. The large European firms also gradually moved from wholesale to retail trade, subverting Krio merchants, often through exclusive mail-boat contracts and customs duties levied by the colony government. A new commercial outfit, named Company of African Merchants, was incorporated in Liverpool in 1863, with an eye toward taking greater advantage of the growing commercial exchange with West Africa, especially at a time when a steamboat service had been inaugurated by the African Steamship Company to

provide regular service between Britain and the coast. The financial flexibility of the European firms, with the Company of African Merchants
serving as a sort of chamber of commerce, "raising and remitting money,"
allowed them to have a great advantage relative to their Krio trading rivals
in the produce business. Efforts by Krio merchants to ameliorate the financial challenge by instituting a bank in 1871 were quashed when the colony
government refused to grant official recognition to the bank. According
to Fyfe, British business interests, "foreseeing the end of their monopoly,
protested officially."[47]

By the early twentieth century, the European firms had virtually eliminated Krio merchants in general from the interior trade, with Muslim Krio
traders reduced to selling their merchandise to Syrian merchants and the
large European firms. However, such relations lasted but for a short period
of time, as the latter entities, with their huge capital resources, soon found
the Krio traders expendable. With the construction of roads and the introduction of the railway linking the colony and the hinterland, Europeans
no longer deemed necessary the services of the Krio merchants, who were
soon replaced with Syrian agents.[48]

EXTENSION OF BRITISH RULE INTO THE INTERIOR

Meanwhile, by the late nineteenth century, when the race for colonial pos-
sessions by European imperial powers was growing to a fever pitch, the
British Colonial Office in London was becoming increasingly concerned
about the persistence of French penetration into what Whitehall considered
its "sphere of influence" in the vicinity of Sierra Leone. Both the British and
the French had entertained designs in the immediate hinterland of Sierra
Leone as far back as the late eighteenth century, with both imperial powers claiming controlling influence. In 1881, due to French activities in Futa
Jallon, Governor Rowe asked the administrator to the Gambia, Dr. Valesius
Gouldsbury, to sign a formal treaty with the local ruler, Almamy Ibrahim
Sorie, in order to prevent the French from cutting off the hinterland to the
British. Gouldsbury's treaty was ultimately superseded by an earlier treaty
between the French and Ibrahim Sorie, a fact that was formally recognized
in the Anglo-French convention signed in 1889.[49] The British may have re-
gretted their earlier rebuff of Samori's overtures, and perhaps in an effort to
forestall any further loss of territory to the French, the colony government in
Freetown formally annexed the hinterland of the colony in 1896.

Each of the imperial powers was interested in securing control of local
trade and therefore interested in shutting out the other in their developing

protectionist impulses. The important trading centers of Futa, Dinguiraye, and others were already being overrun by the French, thus the British determined that such places as Timbo, Kabala, and other population centers to the north of the Sierra Leone Colony were very likely to be next. Meanwhile, the struggle between the French and Samori Touré continued, unabated. Samori was given an ultimatum by the French to shut down the Freetown-Falaba route,[50] a move that had clear economic and political implications. The French move was not only motivated by a desire to secure control of the interior trade, but was clearly aimed at depriving Samori of his very important arms pipeline to Freetown. This, of course, was deemed unacceptable to the Mandinka leader, who promptly rejected the French ultimatum and invited the British government to enter into a mutual pact. A very complex diplomatic and political issue thus ensued between the two major European imperial powers in the region.[51]

The British government sought to protect its economic and political interests in the interior by promulgating the Foreign Jurisdiction Act of 1890, which enabled the colony government to extend its jurisdiction into the hinterland. This was but a precursor to the formal declaration on 31 August 1896 of a protectorate over the hinterland of the colony of Sierra Leone. The Legislative Council of the colony was duly empowered to make laws for both the colony and the new, yet ill-defined, entity. The administrative machinery of the colony was transplanted to the protectorate with minor changes; the former hinterland was divided into five districts, each under the administrative control of a district commissioner. Theoretically, the latter was expected to share political authority with the sovereign monarchs of the interior states (who were now designated "paramount chiefs," since, to the British, there was only one recognized monarch, resident in London); however, the traditional rulers were effectively subordinated to the authority of the district commissioners. The traditional monarchs were henceforth restricted to hearing minor legal cases involving local subjects, in what came to be characterized as the Native Court System; their juridical authority did not extend to "British subjects" (i.e., the Krio merchants doing business in their jurisdictions). The implications of this arrangement would ultimately prove to be problematic for relations between the colony citizens and their counterparts in the protectorate. An uprising in 1898 (dubbed the Hut Tax War), ostensibly a consequence of the imposition of taxes by the colony government but in reality part of a widespread anticolonial resistance movement in the interior, resulted in the murder of many colony administration employees, Christian missionaries, and Krio traders.[52]

While the Krio traders and others who served as clerks and police constables, as well as in other capacities in the protectorate administration, came to be identified with the British imperial authority and were, consequently, targeted by the resistance forces in the south, many of the Muslim Krio traders in the north escaped the carnage virtually unharmed. This may have been due to the practice of these traders of sharing close living quarters with their trading contacts while doing business in these parts, rather than living in separate quarters, thereby demonstrating their capacity to integrate on multiple levels, with religion providing a clear indication of that demonstrated cultural identification with interior peoples. Unlike their Christian counterparts, the Muslim Krio were not deemed a threat to the traditional structures, thus they mostly continued to conduct trade missions as they had before the extension of colonial authority to the interior. The extension of the railway system to the interior by 1898 for the purposes of facilitating the effective exploitation of the natural resources of the land further allowed the Muslim Krio to continue their trade activities between Freetown and the main stations along the railway route. However, by the turn of the century, with the ascendancy of the large European firms in interior trade and the extension of British rule to the hinterland, the fortunes of the Muslim Krio traders as well as that of their Christian Krio counterparts were negatively affected. Many of the Krio merchants therefore turned their attention to the growing traffic along the West African coast, plying their wares and looking for profitable trade in the Gambia and Senegal.

MUSLIMS AND THE KOLA TRADE
IN THE SENEGAMBIA REGION

The movement of Krio traders along the West African coast during the late nineteenth to mid-twentieth centuries was momentous in the history of Krio society. An important part of this development was the phenomenon of female gender empowerment, due to the important role played by women who took a leading role in the movement of trade goods to such places as the Gambia, Senegal, Fernando Póo, and Nigeria. E. Frances White notes that even though many of these women traders lacked significant initial capital to launch their businesses outside the colony of Sierra Leone, this fact did not discourage them from venturing away from Freetown to try their luck outside familiar terrain. With dedication and tenacity, they soon became busily engaged in the kola trade connecting Sierra Leone to the Gambia and Senegal, and the Bight of Benin and Niger Delta region.[53]

Thus, toward the end of the nineteenth century, Krio women were well established in the transnational kola trade along the West African Atlantic coastal littoral. The availability of relatively inexpensive steamship fares between Freetown and the Gambia allowed these women to move their shipments of kola and other trade goods between the ports of Freetown and Bathurst.

From the mid-1800s onward, there was a constant movement of Krio traders, clergy, civil servants, and others between Freetown and various parts of coastal West Africa. The Krio diaspora across West Africa soon grew large enough to warrant the stationing of correspondents by a fledgling Freetown newspaper, the *Free Press*, in the major port cities in the region, including Bathurst, Cape Coast, Lagos, Abeokuta, Onitsha, and Fernando Póo,[54] to serve the growing migrant Krio population from the colony. While many were motivated by commercial reasons to venture out along the coast, others were on a quest for a reconnecting with long-lost kith and kin; the Atlantic slave trade had caused much cultural dislocation that had engendered a need among many Krio for a return to their natal communities, as it had been almost universally among those who had made the transatlantic voyages during the Atlantic trade.

Upon returning to the coastal communities of West Africa from whence they originated, many reestablished contact with kinsfolk, and most sought to improve their lives in their various chosen vocations. Those who had left Freetown for commercial reasons sought to accomplish their missions, while others sought gainful employment in the colonial civil service. Indeed, many of the African personnel of the civil administrations along the Atlantic coast were Krio, given their preponderance among the available educated elite of West Africa. Many civil service positions in the civil administration of the Gambia came to be ultimately filled by Krio; in fact, largely because of their education and their penchant for entrepreneurial endeavors, the adjacent French colony of Senegal also came to have a large community of immigrant Krio from Sierra Leone.[55] In both the Gambia and Senegal, they either joined established religious congregations or founded their own churches or set up their own Muslim jamaats.

By the 1890s, Muslim Krio merchants were an integral part of the trade along the Upper Senegal River, which was the base for the French colonial appropriation of land in the so-called Western Soudan. Even at the height of the competition for imperial control of territory between the British and the French, when they were viewed with suspicion by the latter, Muslim Krio traders continued their commercial activities, unfettered by the prevailing political circumstances. The French commandants in the area regularly reported on the activities of these traders to the governor at Dakar;[56] however, there is no evidence of any official action taken by the French to subvert or restrain their activities at this time. Traveling back and forth across the colonial borders between the Gambia and Senegal were traders including Hassani Thomas, Sidia Nichol, Mamadu Williams, and Yazid Fadlu-Deen,[57] all of whom were part of the strong contingent of traders from the Freetown Muslim communities of Fula Town and Fourah Bay. A large proportion of the traders from Fula Town concentrated their commercial activities in Saint-Louis and Dakar, unlike their counterparts from Fourah Bay, who cast their commercial nets far and wide.

By 1894, Muslim Krio traders had become quite prominent among the Freetown traders involved in the kola trade in the Gambia. The kola traders, foremost among whom was the Savage merchant family of Fourah Bay, would buy large quantities of kola from the Aberdeen merchants in Freetown and ship them to the Gambia.[58] Others purchased large quantities of trade items such as leather, palm oil, pepper, shea butter, beans, fufu, benniseed, dried fish, oyster, and bitter kola in Freetown, which, due to the facility provided by the new technology of the steamboat power, they were able to ship to the Gambia and Senegal. For the return trip to Freetown, items such as baskets, calabashes, country cloths, haberdashery, iron pots, goats, sheep, and other sundry goods were procured in the Gambia and Senegal for sale in Freetown and in the interior.[59] Trade figures such as Lamini Joaque, Abu Savage, Abu Bakarr Gillen, and Hassani Thomas all grew prosperous in the commerce between Freetown and the Senegambia region. Joaque maintained a big store at New Street in Freetown that served as a warehouse for storage of his merchandise prior to shipment to the Gambia and Senegal in the early 1900s. Thomas was reported to have developed a kola farm of his own in the Gambia that ultimately enabled him to amass enormous wealth and consequently obtain large tracts of real estate in the Gambia as well as in Sierra Leone. He eventually retired from active trade and returned to Freetown and subsequently became an active member of the Fula Town jamaat, rising eventually to the position of alkali (al-Qadi).[60]

Trade along the West African coast facilitated the quest for economic empowerment among Muslim Krio traders. The prosperity made possible by coastal and interior trade allowed for a noticeable material improvement in the lives of people in the Muslim communities. Fourah Bay and Fula Town became increasingly transformed by the growing wealth accrued from long-distance commerce. Large concrete and timber houses were constructed by merchant families, and "mud huts" were replaced by houses with sheet metal roofs. Others settled for more modest homes with bamboo-thatched roofs that were, nonetheless, an improvement on their earlier homes. Like their Christian trading counterparts, Muslim merchants sought to invest the profits from their trade activities in real estate. The relative inexpensiveness of building materials served to ensure a rapid proliferation of new constructions at both Fourah Bay and Fula Town.[61]

Martin Lynn has analyzed the impact of the steamship on the Krio diaspora, and on the growth of commerce along the Atlantic coast of West Africa in general during the nineteenth century.[62] Steamboats certainly allowed British traders to better exploit the commerce of the region during the period of the so-called legitimate trade after the Abolition Act of 1807. But the introduction of steamship service in regional trade also facilitated the fluid movement of goods and people along the coastal littoral as well. Lynn pointed to the enthusiasm of the local and expatriate business communities regarding the availability of the steamship, quoting the *African Times*' effusive praise for the steamship and the paper's crediting of the transportation service for the evident "new life and vigour for production, trade and commerce" in the region. As Lynn noted, the steamship was highly beneficial to "small-scale African traders, hitherto excluded from the trade by its high capital costs of entry."[63] Certainly, as the *African Times* had hoped, many of the Krio traders were "able to utilize the opportunities provided by steam to establish themselves at the heart of West Africa's seaborne trade." The steamship served to break the hold of the "old oligopoly" on regional and transatlantic trade and eliminated the need for chartered ships to transport goods by Krio traders doing business along the coast; but it also made for a more fluid and easier movement of goods and persons between coastal ports. There is little, if any, doubt as to the significance of the steamship in the efforts of Krio who had relocated to various points along the Atlantic coast to maintain family connections in Freetown. Thus, as Lynn observed, the steamship vessels facilitated the cohesiveness of the Krio diaspora in West Africa.

WOMEN TRADERS IN THE SENEGAMBIA

Prominent among the regular travelers on the steamships were the women traders, who were an integral part of coastal trade, even if outnumbered by the men. The business acumen of these women allowed them to recognize the opportunities provided by the steamship technology, especially for those involved in the kola trade. The kola trade dominated by women traders had grown significantly by the late 1890s when, based on official reports, "the value of kola exports grew from £40,866 in 1895 to £61,645 in 1899."[64] A significant proportion of the export of kola involving Muslim Krio women was bound for the Gambia during this period. The women traders proved to be quite flexible in commercial transactions, as well as in their other social relations in the region, fluidly interacting on multiple levels with the local communities in both the Gambia and Senegal. The Muslim Krio women unabashedly used their Islamic connections in the Wolof, Mandinka, and Sarakule communities to bolster their trade contacts. Prominent female figures such as Kalaytu N'jie and Asatu Savage became as much known for their independence as for their business acumen. Savage was generally referred to as "Tity Frock," given her habit of wearing long frocks.[65] While the latter was quite well known in Freetown, not much is known of N'jie, which may be a consequence of her having married into a local family, thereby reducing her movement between Bathurst and Freetown. Nonetheless, her name was among the prominent women traders of the Krio diaspora in the Senegambia valley at the turn of the century. Other less prominent women engaged in petty trade selling foodstuffs at the retail level, including agidi, ogi, lubi, *egusi* (melon), olele, ebe, *acara* and a host of small items.[66] The Muslim Krio traders formed a distinct community in the Gambia, even though a good number of them married into local families in Bathurst, MacCarthy Island, and such other places as Georgetown in the central part of the Gambia Colony. Muslim traders in these towns attained social prominence in the communities through marital and other social ties and many became involved in local politics.

As J. Lorand Matory has observed in discussing transatlantic traders plying the ocean between Brazil and West Africa, "Idioms of identity and sameness with other West Africans were also necessary" for Krio traders traversing the West African Atlantic coastal littoral in the late nineteenth and early twentieth centuries. Without taking anything for granted regarding the probability of reconnecting with "erstwhile kin," Muslim Krio traders, like their Afro-Brazilian and Afro-Cuban counterparts engaged in transnational commerce in the Atlantic world, "had a strong interest in creating idioms of identity and terms of cooperation across the borders that they traversed."[67] Again, as was the case with Afro-Brazilian and Afro-Cuban traders in West Africa, Muslim Krio traders were quite cognizant of, and promoted, "the value and sources of their imported products." While trade goods from West Africa, including those from Sierra Leone, came to be valorized by merchants from Brazil, Saro merchants also laid great emphasis on the authenticity of trade goods imported from places along the West African

Atlantic littoral, from Lagos in particular. Black "peppeh" (pepper), black soap, *Oku lappa*(*aso oke*/handwoven cloth), *ori* (shea butter), bitter kola, alligator pepper, and other products imported from the Bight of Benin were highly valued by merchants and among Krio and non-Krio consumers in the colony. These goods were thus distributed in the coastal communities, from Freetown to Bathurst (Gambia), and Saint-Louis and Dakar.

By the early twentieth century, Muslim Krio figures such as Umaru Torbieu aka Tibabu, Barakieu Thorpe, Abdul Salaam Coker, Suberu Thomas, and Madieu Thomas[68] were among the prominent traders in the Gambia and Senegal. The Oku-Marabou (as the Muslim Krio came to be referred to) community spawned by these traders from Freetown remains a prominent part of these societies up to this day, with Islam serving as its anchor. While they mostly speak Wolof and a few of the other local languages, the Krio language still serves as a lingua franca for the Krio diaspora, and is itself widely spoken among non-Krio youths at least in modern Banjul, the Gambia, in spite of the inverse proportion of those for whom the language serves as the primary mode of communication. But the Krio merchant presence in the Senegambia valley was only part of a larger Krio diaspora in West Africa, as a much larger concentration of Krio traders and others was found in the Bight of Benin and the Niger Delta.

The pivotal intersection of Islam and commerce in Sierra Leone and West Africa, which, as I have noted, was already under way and known to British officials long before the formal introduction of Crown colony rule in 1808, became glaringly clear by the end of the nineteenth century. While the colony administration had expended much time and energy seeking to undermine Islamic influences in the colony, mostly due to the lobbying efforts of the European evangelical groups, particularly the CMS and their influential backers in London, for the better part of the century, the economic imperatives of colonial rule ushered in a change in policy and attitudes both in the colonial office at Whitehall and on the ground in Sierra Leone. By the 1840s and 1850s, efforts were being made by colony administrators to effect a policy of accommodation vis-à-vis Islam and Muslims in the colony. Not only were capable Muslims recruited into the colonial bureaucracy, a policy of rapprochement with the Muslim community writ large was also being pursued with some vigor by colonial personnel. Muslim Krio merchants, along with their Christian kinsfolk, were subsequently to play a pivotal role in a much wider distribution of Krio merchants and bureaucrats along the Atlantic corridor of West Africa. With the introduction of steamship technology, female and male traders from Sierra Leone became a noticeable presence in the British-controlled Gambia, as well as the

French-controlled colony of Senegal and in such other places as Fernando Póo and the Congo. The Saro immigrants in Lagos and elsewhere in what became Nigeria were soon to become part of a transnational community of returnee groups, including Afro-Brazilians and Afro-Cubans, the commercial, political, and religious contributions of which were pivotal to the making of modern Nigeria.

4 ⮑ The Krio Diaspora in Nigeria

THE GREATEST PROPORTION OF THE KRIO DIASPORA in West Africa could be found in the Bight of Benin and Niger Delta region of what is today Nigeria, the destination of choice of many of the freed Africans and their progeny, whose motivations transcended strictly commercial factors. From the 1820s onward, when the outward migration of Liberated Africans took off, many were motivated not only by a desire to expand their trade ventures for purposes of profit maximization, but also by a long and burning desire to reestablish contact with their natal communities. Those who eventually left the Sierra Leone Colony were almost invariably propelled to do so due to a long-standing conviction that not only could they go back home again, as it were, they could also tap into what many had come to believe was a thriving economic landscape in that other British colony down the West African Atlantic coast. Some of the returnees could still speak the Yoruba language, and many identified Oyo as their ancestral land, while many others remembered their respective natal communities. The nineteenth century would thus usher in a period of expansion of Krio trade activities into the Bight of Benin, particularly in Abeokuta, Badagry, and Lagos. The commercial environment in these parts was influenced by the increasing demand for agricultural produce by the European imperial powers; Britain was by this time encouraging the creation of "economic enclaves" for its commercial and industrial interests in West Africa. Lagos and its environs in the Bight, as well as the Niger Delta, were a part of these enclaves and a resultant growth in trade in palm produce and other cultivable items would therefore attract many of those who set off from Sierra Leone by the mid-nineteenth century. The advent of the Saro (as immigrants from Freetown came to be called) in Nigeria had the effect of complicating the economic environment, particularly in relation to the European merchants who wanted to establish a dominant presence in commercial relations with the local peoples. In Abeokuta in the 1850s, for instance, the Saro merchants worked in concert with indigenous traders to call into question the business practices of their European counterparts who, left to their own devices, would rather do away with the middleman role played by the Africans in the so-called "legitimate" trade in cultivable goods. The Freetown merchants subsequently assisted the Egba people in developing a political and economic organization known as the Egba United Board of Management, the ultimate raison d'être of which was the protection of the "socio-economic and political interests" of the local people vis-à-vis the British and other European business groups; thus the Saro "disorganised the business activities of the European merchants" in Abeokuta.[1] A Krio, G. W. "Reversible" Johnson, served as the board's secretary as well as its director, which may suggest a political and economic motivation for Krio intervention in the divide between the Europeans and the local Egba.

Among the earliest of the Freetown traders to immigrate to what would later become the colony of Nigeria were Muslims from the Freetown communities of Fourah Bay and Fula Town. Like their Christian compatriots in Freetown, many of the Muslims had some knowledge of the specific areas in Yoruba country from whence they had been taken away into Atlantic slavery. Having experienced what many of them perceived as religious and political persecution in the Sierra Leone Colony in the decades before the 1840s, many were consequently quite anxious to return home and leave their bitter experiences behind. A significant proportion of the inhabitants of Fourah Bay, Fula Town, and Aberdeen spoke the Yoruba language, as a result of which the *qutba* (sermon) was delivered in that language during the Friday jumaat prayer services in those communities. Their yearning for a return to their land of provenance was therefore whetted when they began to hear stories of former captives and ex-slaves returning home in the 1820s. They received more substantive reports in 1836 when a couple of formerly enslaved Hausa stopped in Freetown en route to Badagry,[2] a trading center on the Bight of Benin from where many a Liberated African may have embarked for the transatlantic voyage before their relocation to Freetown.

The first major organized trip to Badagry left Freetown on 1 April 1839, on a retrofitted ship bought by a group of Liberated Africans, and their reception and experience in Badagry served to motivate others to make the journey themselves. As Fyfe noted, "Within a couple of years several hundred had gone back to the shores whence they had been carried in chains and were moving inland to their old homes."[3] One of these former captives, Osoba, purchased a condemned vessel, *Nancy*, and used it to relocate his family back home to Egba country. The main organizers of these initial trips to Badagry and elsewhere in the Niger Delta region were Christian traders and lay preachers of the Wesleyan and Anglican missions; the leader of the Liberated Africans in Freetown, Thomas Will, and the other owners of the ships subsequently agreed to provide free passage to Rev. Henry Townsend of the CMS to Badagry and to Abeokuta. Townsend later advised the Central Committee of the CMS in London to officially sponsor a mission of Liberated Africans to spread the Christian gospel in Nigeria.

Muslims from Fourah Bay and Fula Town were just as anxious to join the movement to Badagry and elsewhere in the Bight, some of them with perhaps a religious agenda as well. The Reverend Samuel Adjai Crowther, who had been tapped by the CMS to begin the mission in the delta, was contacted by Muslims to allow them to join in the movement to Nigeria; however, Crowther and the other Christian missionaries were less enthused about including non-Christians and therefore sought to discourage them from making the trip.[4] The Muslim traders were nonetheless resolute in their endeavor to join the exodus to Nigeria and therefore decided not to rely on the Christian missionaries and, consequently, pooled their resources to organize their own voyages. The acquisition of a ship by Alfa Mohammadu Savage,[5] Imam of Fourah Bay, encouraged many more to seek their fortunes in their ancestral land. In fact, many of the Muslims were inclined to travel on vessels owned by their own leaders rather than on those catering to the immigration of Christian converts to the Niger, especially at a time when they were deeply suspicious of efforts by the colony government to assist in the transporting of Liberated Africans to the West Indies.[6] Savage and another Liberated African leader, John Atakpa Macauley, had taken Gov. Arthur Kennedy to task for the colony administration's policy of facilitating the "transportation" of former slaves to replenish the labor force in the West Indies following the abolition of slavery. Thus they pooled their resources and organized their separate movement to Nigeria, mostly settling in Badagry. While many chose to resettle in Badagry, others moved into the interior in spite of the evident instability engendered by the military encounters between the forces of Ibadan and Ijebu. The Egba, under the leadership of Shodeke, eventually prevailed and brought some stability to the trade routes linking the region with Abeokuta. News of these developments may have motivated the immigrants from Sierra Leone, who were soon making the trek to Abeokuta. The Muslims among the immigrants became an important part of a fledgling community of merchants in the area.

By 1841, Reverend Crowther was reporting back to the CMS of the fluid movement of Sierra Leone Muslims in Abeokuta, who impressed him by their easy integration into the local culture and by their command of the Egba dialect. According to Crowther, some of the returning Muslims "found their children, others their brothers and sisters, by whom they were entreated not to return to Sierra Leone."[7] Indeed like everyone else, including Crowther, who had joined the exodus from Freetown, part of their motivation for embarking on the journey to Nigeria was to reestablish family connections in their native communities. Another prominent Muslim merchant, Salu Shitta,[8] also took his family along with other organized groups of Muslims who made the trip as well. Consequently, many Muslim traders and nontraders as well made the trip to Nigeria during the mid-1800s. Shitta was by the 1820s already a successful trader in the rural Liberated African village of Waterloo, from which he relocated to Fourah Bay in 1831. He became a leading figure in the community and later rose to the position of Imam of the jamaat. But, like many others, he still longed for his ancestral homeland, and thus in 1844 he joined the movement back to his ancestral land, settling his family, including his young son, Mohammed, in Badagry. The young Mohammed would later succeed his father, following the latter's death just five years after the family's arrival in Badagry, and would go on to become a successful and prominent personality in Nigeria.

Badagry was a popular choice of disembarkation for the Muslim returnees from Sierra Leone, partly because it was the point of embarkation for many taken across the Atlantic following their capture and subsequent sale into slavery, partly because of its reputation as a center of trade, and also because the town had an established Muslim community; the presence of a Muslim community was reported by British officials John and Richard Lander in 1830.[9] Following the initial voyages from Freetown in the 1830s, the selection of the town for the setting up of a mission station by the Christian evangelical societies in Sierra Leone provided much impetus to further embarkations from Freetown. The location of this coastal town was an additional factor for its becoming a historic place, not only in the return of ex-slaves and their progeny from Sierra Leone, but also in their initial distribution across the Atlantic, as noted earlier. The area adjoining the town consisted of lagoons, creeks, and rivers that served as transportation highways of sorts for the interior towns, as well as larger urban centers such as Lagos and Porto-Novo.[10] Its strategic location thus made it an important port of call for slave trading vessels plying the Atlantic Ocean and for large- as well as small-scale traders in the aftermath of the slave trade. Badagry itself had been a part of regional and long-distance trade going back to the trans-Saharan trade system, and its role in regional trade affected relations between the neighboring kingdom of Dahomey and the Oyo Empire during the seventeenth through nineteenth centuries. However, by the late eighteenth century, Badagry was slowly being superseded by Lagos in regional trade, a development attributed to the efforts of the then ruling entity, Oba Akinsemoyin, who sought to make the town the epicenter of commercial activities. As Adefuye notes, Badagry was ultimately reduced to a virtual "outpost of Lagos" as the latter grew in commercial importance, largely as a result of the natural advantages provided by a lagoon system that connected the town with its neighbors, including Badagry, Epe, and Porto-Novo.[11]

But before the town was superseded by Lagos, it was the premier port of call for the Krio dispersal in the 1830s and 1840s. Following the initial voyages from Freetown, the Sierra Leone immigrants were quite enthusiastic about the environment of Badagry to the extent that they petitioned the British government for permission to extend British jurisdiction to the town, with the immigrants as the nucleus of the proposed colony.[12] Notwithstanding the initial tepid response of the British government to the suggestion of the immigrants from Freetown, the decade of the 1840s opened with a growing presence of Sierra Leone traders and Christian missionaries in Badagry. The beginnings of the distribution of Saro traders across the town coincided with the establishment of a growing presence of British merchants in Badagry and Lagos, and the Sierra Leoneans found themselves without much support from the British government; indeed by 1886, the British Crown had granted the Royal Niger Company a royal charter to establish monopoly control over commercial transactions in the Niger Delta, at the expense of African and non-African rivals. The Niger Company went on to place restrictions on the participation of "foreigners" in commercial transactions in the delta in an effort to preclude competition to company trade. However, the Muslim traders would go on to make some headway in their new environs, due to the fact that Islam was already established in the area going back to the seventeenth century, albeit with limited distribution across Yoruba society in general. In Abeokuta as well, the Muslim population was experiencing some growth. As Gbadamosi notes, the Muslim population in the town moved in from Owu "and they formed in Abeokuta a predominantly Muslim quarter,"[13] which by 1848 was large enough to require two mosques and Qur'an schools of their own to accommodate the increasing congregations. Despite the social challenges posed by tensions between Islam and local traditionalists, the community persisted and continued to grow.

The growth of Islam in Badagry, Abeokuta, Lagos, and elsewhere in Yoruba society was greatly assisted by the arrival of emigrants from the Sierra Leone Colony in the 1840s, even though the vast majority of the emigrating population consisted of Christians. And it was in Lagos where a considerable number of the emigrants chose to settle for obvious reasons, the most important of which was the economic opportunities offered by the cosmopolitan environment of the city; added to that was the propensity of the Saro, like other Yoruba, to reside in large urban centers. Lagos was also the point of disembarkation for ex-slaves of Yoruba and Hausa ancestry from Brazil, as well as slaves of Cuban ancestry, who, like their counterparts from Sierra Leone, were relocating to Nigeria in the nineteenth century just a few years after the arrival of the initial groups from Freetown. Known as Aguda/Amaro, the Afro-Brazilian and Afro-Cuban returnee population also included Muslims who had experienced the challenges of life in a predominantly Christian society, as had their coreligionists from Sierra Leone. Robin Law notes that the moniker "Aguda" was used in Brazil as a referent for "Portuguese and Brazilians of European as well as African descent [while] an alternative term, 'Maro' [or, in Yoruba, 'Amaro'] seems to have been used more specifically of the African-born slaves."[14] Law further notes that the term *Maro* usually referred to communities of Muslim merchants in Brazil. These manumitted slaves from Brazil had participated in a large-scale resistance in 1835, a rebellion in which Islam was identified as an agency of resistance by the authorities. Consequently, Muslims of Yoruba provenance were subjected to further repressive measures, leading ultimately to the relocation of the Aguda to West Africa.[15] The population of Aguda would subsequently increase as others left Brazil for a variety of reasons, including commercial motivations.

Citing correspondence between Campbell, the British consul in Lagos, and London, Law notes that Aguda and Saro returnees may have been encouraged to settle in Lagos by the establishment of British influence in the city and the resultant "effective framework of security."[16] According to Gbadamosi, the Muslims from Sierra Leone settled in Olowogbowo and Isale Eko, two areas in which the descendants of such prominent traders as Abdullah Cole, Amodu Carew, Muhammad Savage, and Umar Williams can still be traced.[17] The most prominent of these still remain the descendants of Salu Shitta, whose son, Mohammed (about whom more will be said later), constructed the first stone mosque in the city. The growing population of Muslim emigrants from Sierra Leone necessitated the construction of a mosque, formally opened in 1861, which was named Jami'ul-Mubaraq. The Afro-Brazilian Aguda also constructed their own places of worship, including the Alagbayun mosque, the Tairu Eko mosque, and the Salvador mosque. Through intermarriage and other "social interaction[s]," Saro, Cuban, and Brazilian returnees managed to contribute to the emergence of Lagos as a center of "diasporic resettlement" in the nineteenth century.[18] The newcomers from overseas ultimately served to enhance the growth of Islam, both in terms of their numbers and in terms of their practical skills and talents; their numbers included not just traders but also tailors, carpenters, masons, bakers, and other sundry vocations.[19] Perhaps more importantly, the arrival of more Muslims in Lagos allowed adherents of Islam to worship openly without fear of persecution, as had been the case before the 1840s.

The Muslims from Sierra Leone and Brazil would also make significant contributions to the growth of Islamic scholarship and development of Western education in the Muslim community of Lagos. On 28 April 1894, the *Lagos Weekly Record* trumpeted the arrival in the city of a young Muslim Krio scholar, Harun al-Rashid, who had pursued advanced Islamic scholarship and Arabic in Fez, Morocco, as well as in his native Freetown. Rashid later taught Arabic at Fourah Bay College in Freetown and made enormous contributions, along with other notable Saro including Alfa Umar, to Islamic scholarship in Lagos. The contributions of these immigrant scholars would inspire local Muslims to seek further knowledge in Islamic literature. To further the spread of Islamic knowledge, local *mallams* (teachers) were given charge of young children by parents for tutoring in Arabic. These mallams provided lessons on the scriptures of the holy Qur'an by rote over a period of time, following which the young students would embark on advanced studies in the commentaries on the Qur'an, as well as the Sunna and Hadith.[20] Students almost invariably continued their studies in a variety of disciplines, including poetry, philosophy, mathematics, medicine, Islamic mysticism, and astronomy, among others.

IMPLICATIONS OF RELIGIOUS PLURALISM

The arrival of the Saro and Aguda Muslims in the Lagos area led to complications between Islam and Christianity not unlike the situation in Freetown in the decades before the 1840s. As in Sierra Leone, Muslim Saro in Lagos were perceived by the Christian missions as constituting a major impediment to their evangelical agenda. The task of the CMS, Wesleyans, and others in "the battle to win pagan souls" was further complicated by the fact that Islam had a wider distribution in Lagos than it may have had in the colony of Freetown. Also, and perhaps more significantly, the Islamic faith was deeply embedded in the political, administrative, and military strata of traditional Yoruba society. Thus the Christian missions were in a relatively weaker position than they were in Freetown, where the support of the colonial establishment had been pivotal to their success vis-à-vis the Muslims before the 1830s. The Muslim Saro immigrants were also not incognizant of their shared religious and social relations with the traditional elite in Lagos and elsewhere in Yorubaland. It was therefore not surprising that they sought to subvert the efforts of CMS missionaries such as Townsend and Bowen among the Yoruba in the 1850s.[21] However, the Yoruba people demonstrated great tolerance for religious diversity and, consequently, the efforts of the Muslim hard-liners were not always successful; this was the case in 1859, for instance, when Muslims in the Ibadan town council unsuccessfully sought to prevail on a Saro Muslim, Atere, to block the Reverend Hinderer (a CMS missionary) from engaging in evangelical activities in the town.[22]

The evident clout of the Muslims may have been of grave concern to Christian missionaries, especially the CMS. To counter the perceived Muslim clout, it was suggested by the Reverend James Johnson that several Christian clergy be trained in Arabic and Islamic knowledge at Fourah Bay College in Freetown; Johnson was clearly aware that the prevalent perception among church officials of Muslims being uneducated was largely responsible for the limited progress made in converting Yoruba Muslims to the Christian faith. Indeed, Johnson was quite aware of the inherent respect Muslims harbored for the knowledge base of adherents of the Christian faith, whom they referred to as the "people of the book." He therefore communicated with the CMS Central Committee in London the need for proficiency in Arabic and Islamic literature on the part of CMS missionaries.[23] The Christian clergy saw their role in this context as a fundamental part of their "civilizing" mission among the natives, as they would be utilizing their knowledge of Arabic and Islamic literature in the mission schools in which the children of Muslims would be enrolled and acculturated in European Christian morality and values. The Muslim Saro, according to Titilola Euba, "also felt the obligation to convert their 'infidel' brothers to a better way of life. They too could therefore be considered as 'agents of civilization.'"[24] Euba believes that the socially elevated position thus enjoyed by the Saro Muslims allowed them to "more easily maintain equilibrium in a changing African society." She suggests that the Muslim emigrants from Freetown demonstrated an evident disinclination toward the "acquisitive tendencies of the West," in spite of their success in commerce and their Western education. Both Gbadamosi and Euba are in agreement that the Saro Muslims straddled the cultural line between traditionalism and the dominant culture of colonial society. As Euba notes, "By virtue of being Muslims, they could discard the objectionable aspects of traditional customs while retaining the more beneficial ones. By virtue of being Saro, they could partake of those aspects of western culture that did not conflict with the Muslim way of life."[25] The Saro Muslims could certainly not be confused with their culturally ambiguous Christian counterparts from Freetown, whom the locals identified as Oyimbo, due to their penchant for European cultural preferences.[26]

The development of their religious community through Islamic knowledge and rituals paralleled the trading activities of the Muslim Saro, as was the case with their Christian counterparts in Lagos and elsewhere in Nigeria. Trade in the 1840s and after saw Saro traders heavily involved in local trade and regional commerce. Several became immersed in the internal exchange of trade items with which they were already involved in Sierra Leone, such as kola nuts and shea butter. But they also expanded their interests in local trade in Badagry and Abeokuta, as well as in Lagos, to include such foodstuff items as *ogiri* (fermented melon), *egusi* (melon), and *gari* (farina); these goods were also often exported to Sierra Leone, along with other items like shea butter and *Oku lappa* (Oyo handwoven cotton cloth); the trade in Oku lappa was mostly in the hands of women. The women traders from Sierra Leone joined their counterparts in the Bight to maintain a large share of the local marketplace. Saro women traders concentrated on foodstuffs, textiles, household goods, and sundry items at the local level; however, they also sought to export their trade wares to Sierra Leone whenever they could.[27] Other Saro sought an expanded commercial venue in the growing colonial trade system of West Africa. Among the most successful of the emigrant Saro traders was Mohammed Shitta, son of the former Imam of the Fourah Bay community, Salu Shitta, one of the earliest immigrants to Badagry.

MOHAMMED SHITTA BEY

By the late nineteenth century, the name of Mohammed Shitta Bey was being identified with the entrepreneurial success of the immigrant Saro community of Lagos, and across Nigeria in general. However, much more significantly, he was increasingly identified with religious piety, primarily because of his role in single-handedly financing the construction of the first modern mosque in Lagos, which was opened with great fanfare in 1894. Aside from his renowned religious piety, Shitta also demonstrated great political dexterity and cultural flexibility to the extent that he came to exemplify the capacity of the Saro to not only fit into their new surroundings but also to exercise great social and political clout in the Nigeria. While the Saro may have been considered ill-equipped by the dominant British colonial establishment to act as a civilizing agency in church and state, they nonetheless emerged as a force to be reckoned with in the sociopolitical environment of late nineteenth-century Lagos.

Following the cession of Lagos in 1861, with the political state of affairs complicated by the ill-defined status of the Oba of Lagos, the Saro emigrants, particularly the Muslims, found themselves in a state of colonial limbo as "subjects" of the British Crown who also exhibited fealty to the traditional Yoruba sovereign. The arrival of Saro Muslims had contributed to the numerical strength of adherents of the Islamic faith by mid-century, thereby elevating the morale of the Muslim community of Lagos at a time when their position was tenuous at best, before gaining significant support from the Yoruba prince Kosoko, who eventually assumed political authority. Several of the Saro supporters of the new Yoruba sovereign thus felt obliged to follow their leader into exile when Kosoko was expelled by the British in 1851;[28] however, the presence of the Saro Muslims and those from Brazil had transformed the social and political dynamics of Lagos, and served to further the entrenchment of Islam in the city. Those Muslims who had elected to stay in Lagos nurtured close political relations with Akitoye and his successor, Dosunmu, whom the British sought to protect. Muslim Saro thus managed to establish and maintain a beneficial relationship with the political locus of power within the traditional society. Ironically, they would also come to play a significant role in the promotion of Western culture among all Muslims due to their advocacy in favor of the establishment of Western education schools.

As Gbadamosi notes, there had been a strong chorus of opposition to the opening of schools in the Yoruba Muslim community, not unlike the situation with the Muslim Krio in Sierra Leone.[29] As was the case in Freetown, the Lagos Muslims were suspicious of what they perceived as a proselytizing agenda on the part of the Christian missionaries who controlled the schools. But just as was the case in Sierra Leone, many of the Muslim Saro in Lagos took the stance that education was the most assured route to "a better way of life," and thus assumed the role of an agency of modernity in advocating the establishment of schools in their community. Mohammed Shitta, who himself had obtained Western education, joined in promoting the benefits of education for the younger generation as well as posterity. But he was steadfastly opposed to placing the education of Muslim children in the hands of Christian evangelists whose agenda remained suspect to Shitta and other Muslim conservatives.

Mohammed Shitta was a teenager when his father, Sallu, decided to relocate the family from Freetown to Badagry in 1844. He was a little over a year old when the elder Shitta took him and the other members of the family from his birthplace in the Liberated African village of Waterloo to settle at Fourah Bay in Freetown, about twenty-five miles away. Sallu Shitta experienced some success in trade in the colony and later rose, as noted earlier, to serve as Imam of the Fourah Bay community before relocating to Badagry. The family patriarch did not survive long in his new environs, dying just five years later in 1849.[30] By all indications the young Shitta was motivated by the early demise of his father to assume control of the family business in Badagry, while simultaneously honing his business skills in the import-export world by serving as an agent for the European firm of Pinnock B. Co.[31] His employment with Pinnock allowed him to travel widely in the interior and thus he became quite familiar with the social and cultural landscapes of the communities of the region, a knowledge that he put to use in furthering his fledgling commercial enterprise; along with his trade in kola nuts he bought and sold various other commodities, including hides, cotton cloth, *egusie* (melon), and gum copal. The growth of his business investments and the commercial experience he garnered in the process enabled him by 1864 to broaden his base of operations from Badagry to Lagos, and the Upper Niger region to Sierra Leone. By 1869, with much of his time consumed by his detailed attention to the Upper Niger end of his business, Shitta placed his brother, Yusufu, in charge of the Lagos branch of the family business.[32]

The growing success of his business enterprise ultimately provided Shitta with the resources to help in furthering the growth of Islam in Badagry, Lagos, and Freetown. Indeed, between 1869 and his death in 1895, he devoted a good portion of his time to the affairs of the Islamic Ummah, both in Nigeria and in Sierra Leone, in addition to his active participation in the politics of Yoruba society in Lagos. As Euba notes, because of his enormous wealth, "his connection with the Christian sector of society and his ability to speak English, [he] was able to assume in time the leadership of the Muslim community in secular matters." He was elevated to the position of Seriki Musulumi in 1894, in which position he served as the secular equivalent of the Imam of the mosque, who remained the spiritual leader of the community.[33] Perhaps because of his social ascendancy in the Lagos community, he had, for all intents and purposes, replaced the chief Imam as adviser to Oba Oyekan I. Indeed, Shitta's relations with Oyekan I transcended his advisory role. According to Euba, "He was his personal friend as he was of his predecessor, Dosunmu." He was also one of Oyekan's chief supporters as candidate to the throne, financing him personally for a year until the government approved the succession in 1885.[34]

Shitta's growing social and political clout in Lagos had also become manifestly clear in 1893, when acting Governor Denton identified him as "the principal opponent to the government proposal to introduce the elements of western education into Muslim schools and to place some of those schools under the Board of Education."[35] His stance may have appeared as rather contradictory, given his earlier criticism of the colonial government for its failure to extend financial support to schools attended by Muslim children. However, it was subsequently pointed out by no less a personality than Edward Blyden that the likes of Shitta and other Muslim leaders were not necessarily against Western education per se, but were merely apprehensive of the proselytizing agenda of the school authorities.

In 1893, there were 412 Muslim students officially enrolled in the government-assisted mission schools in Lagos, which are said to have accounted for about "12 per cent of the total number of children in these schools." The limited number of Muslim children in mission schools was merely reflective of the concerns of the Muslim population regarding the potential for use of the schools for purposes of conversion of their offspring to Christianity. They would rather have their children obtain their education in Muslim schools, in which most of the children were enrolled even as late as the 1890s, primarily because of widespread fears in the Muslim communities that the Christian schools were "a mirage designed to lure Muslim children from the straight path" (or *sirat al-mustaqim*).[36] The fears of the Muslims were not unfounded, as the mission schools required their students to attend church services and Sunday school, as well as to participate in other religious activities of the Christian faith. As such, Shitta and many other Muslims remained adamant about placing their offspring under the supervision of Christian missionaries. In an attempt to assuage the fears and suspicions of the Muslim communities, the colonial government instituted a legal proviso in the Education Ordinance of 1887, essentially requiring the government-assisted schools to refrain from imposing mandatory attendance on Muslim children in classes for scriptural instruction. However, this proviso was hardly known in the Muslim communities, a fact that the mission schools exploited by continuing to impart religious instruction to the students enrolled in the schools, regardless of religious affiliation.[37]

Thus, to many of the Muslim adherents, it was imperative that they retained control of their own schools, which they considered the last bastion against the intrusion of European Christendom. Shitta, it was observed, may have simply "wanted government aid without government control." But, as was the case in Sierra Leone, Shitta and his fellow resisters to Christian mission schools experienced a growing chorus of doubters within the Muslim communities. An increasingly equally strident voice appeared in the younger generation of Muslims, who preferred a "path of accommodation" with the colonial establishment and welcomed the opportunity to share in the positive attributes of Western education. The position of the "Young Turks" within the Muslim community would later be provided with an added impetus by the April 1894 arrival in Lagos of the Muslim Saro scholar Harun al-Rashid; in a series of meetings with young Muslims, Rashid stressed the importance of education in the modern world and the need for a more broadly based education for Muslim children. The emergent progressive stance of the younger generation eventually won the day following the death of Shitta, who was by then developing a strong identification with a Pan-Islamist worldview championed by the sultan of Turkey; his brother, Yusufu, ultimately acquiesced when the sultan of the Ottoman Empire, in a July 1894 letter, urged the Muslims to embrace Western education for the betterment of the younger generation.[38]

THE SHITTA BEY MOSQUE

Shitta did live long enough to see the completion of a mosque in Lagos that still bears his name to this day. The completion of the mosque remains the singularly most important testament to his contribution to the development of Islam in Nigeria, and for that matter in Sierra Leone, where he made significant financial contributions to the construction of the mosque in the Fourah Bay community; he made an even larger financial contribution to the construction of the Jami' ul-Salaam mosque at Fula Town. The construction of the Lagos mosque began in 1891, and upon its completion three years later it became the largest place of Islamic worship in Lagos, with a distinctly Brazilian architectural style. It also had the distinction of having a separate residential quarter for the Imam and the muezzin. The completion of the mosque was also interpreted as "a manifestation of the rapid development of Islam in Yorubaland," a fact that was underscored by the formal recognition of the Lagos Islamic community by the Ottoman sultan, Abdul Hamid II, whom the *Lagos Weekly Record* of 16 June 1894 characterized as the recognized secular head of the Muslim world.[39] The formal letter of recognition of the Islamic Ummah in Lagos was hand-delivered to the official opening of the mosque by a special representative of the sultan, Mr. Abdullah Quilliam, Esq., the president of the Liverpool Muslim Association. Quilliam was also given the task of conferring the Order of the Medjidiye of the third category, and the title of "Bey" of the Ottoman Empire on the person of Mohammed Shitta.[40]

The formal opening of the mosque on 4 July 1894 was a momentous occasion for the Muslims of Lagos, especially the Saro immigrants. The opening ceremony was attended by colonial government officials, including the governor, Sir G. T. Carter, traditional rulers of Yorubaland, Muslim ulema from various parts of West Africa, and Dr. Edward Wilmot Blyden, who attended as a special guest of Shitta's, as well as throngs of Muslims, Christians, and devotees of traditional religions from across Lagos and its environs. In his opening remarks, Governor Carter touched on the need for religious tolerance in society, but also called on the Christian missions to take cognizance of the sensibilities of non-Christians in their relations with them. He drew the ire of the Christians in attendance when he sought to draw a distinction between Muslims, who can openly marry up to four wives, and "a professed Christian with one nominal wife and several irregular ones in the background." The governor's remarks drew scorn from readers of the *Lagos Weekly Record*, including a note of "sad disappointment" from one reader.[41] The special representative of the Ottoman sultan, Quilliam, commended the Christians in attendance for having graced the occasion by their presence and their tacit acknowledgment of the need for better religious understanding. Quilliam also commended the governor, whose presence and speech he considered useful in solidifying the loyalty of the Muslims to the British Crown. His acknowledgment of the governor was given weight by several Saro Christians, one of whom was reported to have observed that the governor spoke in his capacity as a secular official, without the pretense of the Christian missionaries, noting that "it must not be forgotten that His Excellency is not a missionary although some missionaries would be governors."[42]

The Shitta Bey mosque remained a prominent part of historical Lagos Island, with its distinctive Brazilian architecture, which is itself reflective of the religious and social solidarity of the Saro and Aguda communities of Lagos. The opening of the mosque served as the epochal end of an important period in the growth of Islam in Nigeria; but it also was a manifestation of the conjunction of commerce and religion in the Krio diaspora in West Africa, as well as reflective of the pivotal role of immigrants from the Atlantic world, ex-slaves and their progeny as the case may be, in the evolution of modern Nigeria. Mohammed Shitta Bey, as the Saro emigrant came to be known after the conferment of the title by the Turkish sultan, was a personification of the social preeminence and success of the Saro immigrant community in the Bight of Benin and the Niger Delta. The founding of Krio diasporan communities in the Gambia, Senegal, and Nigeria were but a representative cross section of the wide distribution of peoples who sought to take advantage of the opportunities created by the flourishing commercial environment of nineteenth-century West Africa.

The movement of peoples between Sierra Leone and the other locations along the West African coastal littoral led to the establishment of consanguineous ties between peoples across these societies as a result of intermarriages. By 1910, Muslims, Christians, and those who still adhered to traditional religious practices, or became enmeshed in religious syncretism or dualism, found common ground in their shared cultural commonality, and the existential realities of commercial self-interest. Islam had not only made an enormous impact on the social and economic growth of the Muslim communities of Sierra Leone and the Krio diaspora in West Africa, it had facilitated a cultural integration of the Muslim Krio and their coreligionists in the so-called protectorate of the hinterland. Furthermore, trade also engendered a transparent change in colonial policy toward Islam, not only in Sierra Leone but also across West Africa.

5 ⤚ Piety and Praxis
Religion in Daily Life

EVEN AS THEY STRIVED TO ESTABLISH their freedom to worship freely and participate extensively in the economic life of the Sierra Leone Colony and West Africa, the Muslim Krio were also engaged in the reconstitution of community life that balanced their religious and cultural heritages. The mosque became the spatial, spiritual, and political center of Muslim Krio life in the colony. Notwithstanding the centrality of Islam in the lives of the Muslim communities of Aberdeen, Fourah Bay, and Fula Town, Yoruba-derived and other African cultural practices, especially those relating to the rites of passage of birth, circumcision, marriage, and death, continued to be pervasive. Equally influential among significant sections of these communities were the esoteric societies like Ojeh (Egugu), Egunuko, Keri-Keri, Gelledeh, Géréfé, and Akpansa, which were linked to Yoruba divinities. Religious and cultural syncretism was not new or peculiar to the Muslim Krio; various West African groups had historically incorporated indigenous beliefs with the teachings of the Bible and the Qur'an. As both religions grew, syncretism (or a dual/parallel engagement with two or more religious/cultural forms) created great anxieties among the Christian and Muslim clergies and would ultimately become a great "source of tension," leading to a confrontation between piety and praxis in nineteenth-century colonial Sierra Leone. Within the Freetown Muslim communities, these tensions developed not so much over the cultural practices, but over

Muslim membership and participation in the Yoruba, and Yoruba-inspired esoteric societies. These tensions would inevitably lead to an open conflict between an orthodox Islamic leadership and Yoruba, and Yoruba-inspired cultural groups.

Leaders of the mosque, schooled in a more puritanical Islam, perceived these African cultural elements among Muslims at Foulah Town, Fourah Bay, and Aberdeen as obstacles to the expansion of the religion. Thus what ensued was not so much an interfaith but an intrafaith struggle among Muslims who disagreed on the relationship between elements of African culture and the *adini* (faith). As in the case of Muslim communities in late nineteenth-century Lagos, the disagreement developed between what could be loosely described as the orthodox group, which desired more puritanical Islam, and their less doctrinaire-oriented counterparts, who did not see any contradictions between Islam and their African cultural heritage. The introduction of a "new set of values" by Islamic purists would gradually undermine the long-established clout enjoyed by the leaders of the Yoruba-influenced cultural organizations in Freetown.

It is a paradox that Muslims in Krio society who had experienced an extended period of religious persecution by Christian missionaries and the colonial administration had to contend with religious purists in their own community who perceived elements of African culture as anathema to Islam. Thus the schism that developed at Fourah Bay, one of the three Muslim Krio communities in Freetown, was born out of a fundamental difference between those who did not believe there was a place for indigenous African customs in a community defined by its Islamic values, on the one hand, and on the other, Muslims who asserted their right to uphold these customs. The latter did not perceive their communities as theocratic, and did not see any fundamental discordance between being good Muslims while simultaneously embracing customary practices. They did not deem Islamic Shari'a to be an overwhelming force in daily life, even if they recognized its significance in some aspects of daily life, such as marriage, personal and communal disputes, births and deaths, and inheritance matters. For this group, which perhaps constituted the majority of the people in the community, there was little, if any, difference between piety and praxis. Whether they had a doctrinaire devotion to Islam or perceived themselves as merely just cultural Muslims, the inhabitants of the identifiable Muslim communities of Fourah Bay, Fula Town, and Aberdeen all recognized the mosque as the religious and cultural epicenter of the community.

By the mid-nineteenth century, the mosque (*masjid*) had become the religious and cultural heart of the community among the Muslim Krio. In the various Muslim Krio enclaves in the colony, it provided the space for the community to observe one of the central tenets of the Islamic faith, namely the *salaat* (or *namaaz*), encompassing five daily and Friday (*juma'a*) prayers to Allah. While salaat could be performed individually, Muslim clerics encouraged believers to do so in congregation, preferably in the mosque. The mosque was the preferred sanctuary in which Muslim Krio could, to borrow Robinson's formulation, "celebrate the faith, show devotion, and give Islam roots in the local society."[1] Thus, by the 1880s, the communities of Fourah Bay and Foulah Town had constructed places of worship (the Jami ul-Atiq and Jami ul-Salaam, respectively). The mosque enabled the community (or Ummah) to come together for religious worship and to develop social cohesion. It came to constitute a central and powerful force in colonial Freetown, a development that was not unanticipated by the colonial state. Indeed, it was precisely the manifest fear of the mosque as a competing or parallel influence and social force that primarily accounted for the protracted struggle between Islam, the Christian evangelical missions, and the colonial state in the early nineteenth century.

The mosque was more than a place of religious worship for the Foulah Town, Fourah Bay, and Aberdeen communities. It was also the location of the political structure that directed the lives of members of these communities and that represented communal interests to the colonial state. After relocating to Freetown in the early nineteenth century, the Liberated African Muslims (not yet Krio) created various offices—Imam masjid (or Limomu Ratibou), Imam gharyat, alkali (or al-Qadi), naib, and ladani—to provide leadership for their respective jamaats, drawing from the examples of other Muslim communities and their own historical experiences. Holders of these offices drew on the counsel of other leading scholars in the community who possessed a depth of knowledge and clout within their respective communities.[2] They also received the support of older members of the mosque and community who served in sundry capacities, such as leading occasional prayers and providing counsel to the leadership. The ability of the various clerics and older male Muslims to lead the daily ritual prayers was particularly important, especially given the pivotal role of the salaat in the lives of Muslims; after the profession of belief (*shahada*), a "deceptively simple affirmation" that "there is no deity but Allah and Muhammad is the messenger of God," the five daily prayers were emphasized by the leaders of the mosque as essential to the construction of Muslim identity.[3]

In the hierarchy of the mosque, the Imam masjid was the acknowledged leading religious authority, while the Imam gharyat was the secular leader, with the occupants of both offices working in a complementary and cooperative relationship. The position of Imam gharyat, which was not common in Muslim communities, and remained almost exclusive to the Muslim Krio, was in many ways subordinate to that of the Imam masjid, and was usually given to a respected personality who, more often than not, was not necessarily the intellectual equal of the head of the mosque. The position of Imam gharyat eventually served as a convenient political football for the colonial government when the latter sought to equate it with the leadership of emigrants from the interior, thereby attempting to "tribalize" the Muslim Krio with the enactment of the so-called Tribal Administrative System ordinance of 1905. The Imam masjid, however, was hardly an all-powerful authority, and his position could be described as primus inter pares, for he did not possess an overwhelming legal or political power over the other clerics and elders of the community. His authority, like that of clerics in other Muslim societies, was not derived from any sacred birthright but simply from his detailed knowledge of the Holy Scriptures of the Islamic faith and his personal piety toward Allah.[4] The various jamaats required that the person appointed to the position possessed piety and the requisite knowledge of the Qura'n, in addition to a personal ability to maintain the confidence and respect of the community. He was not expected to be affluent, but "rich in health and strength, and above all in knowledge . . . a sound mind in a sound body."[5] He was without doubt someone who possessed significant "moral capital."

Below the position of Imam masjid was that of the naib, who served as deputy to the spiritual leader and was in many instances the individual deemed most likely to succeed the Imam; he was in effect the Imam-in-waiting. Thus he was regularly called upon to officiate in the Friday juma'a prayers whenever the Imam was unavailable. Below the naib was the ladani, who served as the official interpreter for the Imam at juma'a prayers and in other community events, including *sara'a* (*fidau*; prayer) ceremonies. The ladani was especially useful to the community during the nineteenth century, and remained so well past the turn of the century, because the Yoruba language was the primary mode of communication for a significant proportion of the inhabitants of Aberdeen, Fourah Bay, and Foulah Town. Consequently, the *qutba* (sermon) delivered in the original Arabic by the Imam required the ladani to not only render an interpretation of the Qur'anic verses, but to translate such verses to Yoruba and subsequently to Krio, the language spoken by the majority of the congregants.

The next important position in the administrative structure of the mosque was that of the alkali (al-Qadi). Disputes of a religious or secular nature were brought before the court of the alkali, who was recognized as the leading interpreter of the Shari'a. Between the 1830s and the late 1870s, the alkali was the official responsible for adjudication of civil disputes in the Muslim communities and the person who was most relied upon for the settling of personal, family, and communal conflicts. He adjudicated disputes ranging from trade disagreements and marital relations, to inheritance issues in accordance with the Shari'a. Conflicts of a theological nature within the jamaat were settled by a group of clerics sitting as a court presided by the alkali. By 1893, however, the court of the alkali was experiencing a decline in stature, primarily because of the hegemonic position of British common law vis-à-vis Islamic Shari'a. The colony government succeeded in undercutting the efficacy and applicability of the Shari'a, especially in cases involving non-Muslims and Europeans in the colony.

MOSQUE LEADERSHIP, YORUBA CULTURE, AND THE RISE OF ISLAMIC PURITANISM

The first spiritual leader of the fledgling Fourah Bay jamaat was Muhammad Yadalieu (or Alfa Yada, as he was fondly known to his congregants).[6] Prior to his formal installation as Imam masjid, Alfa Yada had provided spiritual and political guidance to the Muslims in the constricted social environment of the Liberated African village settlements located on the outskirts of the colony. He led the first group of Muslims from the village of Waterloo to Freetown and went on to establish a permanent community in the east end of the city. However, upon their relocation to the colony, the community faced the challenge of finding an available structure in which they would be able to offer the ritual prayers required of the faithful. Not to be discouraged, Alfa Yada led prayer sessions known as "arootas"[7] until the congregation was able to finally construct a mosque. He went on to serve as Imam of the jamaat from 1836 till 1849; his period of stewardship of the community at Fourah Bay actually began when he built a *zawia* (Islamic center) in his compound in order to provide a place of instruction on Islamic scriptures, as well as a center of worship for the people.[8] Alfa Yadalieu had "moral capital," and therefore commanded enormous respect and significant political clout within the community, and was thus seen as the one person who ensured the cohesion of the community during a period of uncertainty in a colonial society that still frowned on any creed other than Christianity.

By the 1840s, when the communities of Fourah Bay and Fula Town had gained some stability, the religious leaders turned their attention to further developing and consolidating the social and religious structures of their respective communities.[9] This effort was also crucially related to the shaping and development of the emergent Muslim identities of that segment of Liberated Africans who had elected to uphold the Islamic faith; it was also very much reflective of the resolute assertion of independence by the Muslims in the face of religious and political marginalization following a period of social persecution at the hands of church and colonial officials. Perceiving a clear need for more institutionalized religious and Qur'anic training, especially for the younger members of their communities, the Imams of Fourah Bay and Fula Town decided on the founding of educational institutions known as Ile Kewu, a progression from the lonely zawia established earlier on by Alfa Yadalieu. There was, however, a conspicuous dearth of educated scholars in the Liberated African community capable of providing instruction in the newly established madrassas. Many of the inhabitants of Fourah Bay and Fula Town had themselves been converted to Islam in their native Yoruba society during the Islamic jihads engendered by the teachings and leadership of the Fulani scholar Uthman dan Fodio in the early nineteenth century. Islamic praxis, as it obtained in Freetown before the mid-nineteenth century, could thus be hardly characterized as orthodox. It was therefore necessary to turn to the Fula, Mandinka, and Soso Muslim scholars in the colony, who represented a more orthodox Islamic culture, for religious and Qur'anic tutelage. The Mandinka, Fula, and Soso also had a long experience in providing Islamic education in their own institutions known as Karanthe. The use of immigrant Muslim scholars in the colony madrassas was initially deemed by Liberated African Muslim leaders as but a temporary necessity, and envisaged a time when well-qualified Muslim Krio would replace the scholars from the interior. With an eye toward this outcome, elders of Fourah Bay and Fula Town decided to send some of their young and promising students to Islamic centers of learning at Timbo, Labe, and Dinguiraye.[10]

In 1842 a delegation of young Muslim students and community leaders from Fourah Bay and Fula Town, led by Alfa Yadalieu, left Freetown for Dinguiraye. The group, which mostly traveled overland by way of the Northern Rivers, also included such prominent clerics as Alfa Kassim, Mohammed Sanusi, Alieu Thomas, Sumanu Othman Ajibodeh, Alfa Amara, Alfa Aliyu Badara, and Alfa Dowdu.[11] The latter two clerics would go on to become Imams of Fula Town and Aberdeen communities. Alfa Yadalieu and his fellow clerics were intent not only on paying homage to Al-Hajj Umar Taal, the leader of the Tijaniyya *tariqa* (brotherhood), but also on obtaining Islamic knowledge. They were equally motivated by the need to further expose the young students to the teachings of the Qur'an and Islamic philosophy and jurisprudence, and Tijaniyya Sufi traditions. Along with instructions on the concept of the *Dar al-Islam* (abode of Islam) that they received at Dinguiraye, the students from Freetown also were exposed to and became increasingly absorbed into the community of the faithful in Dar al Hijra. It was in that climate of reformist zeal that the Sufi traditions of the Tijaniyya tariqa came to exercise a profound influence on the Muslims from Freetown.[12]

During the visit to Dinguiraye, the leader of the Freetown delegation, Alfa Yadalieu, received a major boost in status when Al-Hajj Umar anointed him "muqaddam," leader of the Sufi community in Sierra Leone. This was clearly an adroit move on the part of Al-Hajj Umar, who had assumed the title of "Kalifat Khatim al-Awiyya" (successor of the seal of the saints; i.e., Ahmad al-Tijani, founder of the Tijaniyya order) and was very much interested in expanding his political base beyond the Senegambia River valley.[13] Al-Hajj Umar himself had been inducted into the Tijaniyya order by one of his early teachers, Sheikh Abdul Karim, a scholar from Futa Jallon. The Sufi tariqa was at the time just beginning to spread its influence in the Western Sudan, and was rapidly gaining ground in southern Mauretania and the Senegambia valley, areas where the tariqa had been introduced from North Africa.[14] Umar's form of Sufism was quite revolutionary, and he was able to inculcate in his coreligionists from Sierra Leone the Islamic orthodoxy that would ultimately have an enormous impact on the internal dynamics of the Freetown Muslim community. The Tijaniyya order introduced the Freetown Muslims to the concept and practice of dhikr, or wird (*wiridu* in Freetown), which became a central part of the rituals of prayer for Muslim Krio, and remains so to this day. *Dhikr* (or remembrance of God) "effects personal integration and balances the tension between power and powerlessness, hope and despair, knowledge and ignorance, freedom and determinism." This concept came to be spread in Lagos by Saro Muslims in the late nineteenth century.[15] Imam Yadalieu and some of his fellow clerics from Fourah Bay would attempt a second trip to Dinguiraye, following the successful jihad of Al-Hajj Umar. However, on a stopover visit to Forekaria and Melakhori, the Fourah Bay Imam took ill and eventually died in Forekharia in 1849.

The integration of the Muslim delegation from Freetown into the Tijaniyya movement would subsequently have the effect of introducing orthodox Islamic ideas into the practices of the Muslim communities in the colony, thereby solidifying relations with the more orthodox Fula, Mandinka, and Soso. But the evident centrality of the Futa Jallon nexus in the experiences of the Muslim recaptives would have profound social implications for the Muslim communities in the colony, particularly those of Fourah Bay. The growing religious reformist tendencies that emerged in the Muslim community following the return of the visitors to Dinguiraye, especially the young students who spent an extended period of time in the Senegambia valley, would have the effect of engendering a religious schism, the impact of which virtually tore the community apart and resulted in the formation of two distinct and competing jamaats. Tijaniyya orthodoxy, it could be argued, may have led the returning students from Futa Toro to question the legitimacy of the leadership role in the mosque of members of traditional secret societies, such as the Egugu, Ordeh, Egunuko, Gelede, Keri-Keri, Akpansa, and others.

The 1850s thus saw a creeping encroachment of Islamic orthodoxy into the social and political structures of the Freetown Muslim communities, especially at Fourah Bay, where the office of Imam was being gradually radicalized. It is suggested that this orthodoxy could be dated to 1856, with the visit to Sierra Leone of a brother of Al-Hajj Umar, who subsequently returned home accompanied by some members of the Freetown community, including a young Ligaly Savage, a future Imam of Fourah Bay, to be educated at Dinguiraye.[16] Savage eventually returned home in the 1870s, and as an assistant Imam of the jamaat became a leading force in the interlocking struggle between piety and praxis. Due to his influence, the *qutba*, sermons delivered during the Friday juma'a prayers, soon began to address more than the usual issues, such as the obligations of Muslims to the faith and to the Ummah. The sermons increasingly reflected a clear concern on the part of the leading clerics regarding the daily lives of members of the community. Savage openly questioned the customary practices of some of the leading members of the jamaat, who became perplexed by his perception of an essential conflict between daily praxis and religious piety. Many congregants interpreted the Friday sermon as an attack on their fidelity to the faith. The most politically charged portions of the juma'a sermons following the elevation of Alfa Ligaly were aimed at the role and place of the esoteric societies in the Muslim community. To the members of these societies, such as the Egugu, Egunuko,Ordeh, and others, the attacks of the clergy were unwarranted, precisely because they did not perceive their customs and traditions as incompatible with their fidelity to Islam. To them, the Egugu and other traditional societies were just that, traditional organizations that they believed were part and parcel of their Yoruba heritage and identity. However, to Alfa Ligaly and the more conservative clerics, the traditional societies were but pagan elements that predated Islam, which the Muslim community ought to be rid of. The line, as it were, was drawn in the sand between the older elements of Fourah Bay and the younger, but orthodox, faction.[17]

AFRICAN RITES OF PASSAGE AND CULTURAL LIFE AMONGST THE MUSLIM KRIO

The Krio, as do peoples of many other cultures, attach a great deal of significance to birth, marriage, and death, among other rites of passage. These events also constituted a significant part of the worldview of Muslim Krio, who, conscious of their obligation to continue the ritual practices related to such events in much the same way as their ancestors, sought to appropriate Islam while emphasizing ritual features grounded in Yoruba traditional ceremonies. Yoruba rituals were, and still continue to be, emphasized on the occasion of a birth, marriage, or death, albeit with adaptations to fit into the cultural and religious landscapes of colonial Freetown society; the komojade (or pul nar doe; child-naming ceremony), put kola (or put stop/engagement) and fidau, were all commemorated in the awujoh ritual. The latter term, awujoh, was generally used to refer to the large cookout gathering held in commemoration of deceased members of the community, but gradually came to be used in reference to any such cookout gathering on the occasion of a birth, marriage, or other social event.

The rites of passage celebrated by Muslim Krio were crucial to communal and social identity formation among a group of people who had experienced a long period of religious and cultural persecution and marginalization in the colony. These rites also constituted ways in which the Muslim Krio community as a whole sought to reproduce itself in the larger Krio society. Indeed, the reproduction of community life and identity formation was itself fraught with controversy, as members of the identifiable

Muslim communities grappled with the questions of what kind of Islam should be practiced, and what role African-derived culture ought to be assigned in such communities. Rituals related to rites of passage such as komojade, bondo, gej, and forty-day, which respectively dealt with birth, female circumcision, marriage, and death, were deemed acceptable by the Islamic clerics, while the esoteric societies were not. The former were considered to be acceptable forms of African/Yoruba cultural retentions, and were in no way perceived as antithetical to or constituting a threat to Islamic precepts, quite unlike the esoteric societies, whose ceremonial rituals, known only to the initiated, were presumed to be contradictory to fundamental tenets of Islam. The struggle that ensued at Fourah Bay was essentially a struggle to prune out what a faction of the congregation perceived as idolatory and un-Islamic.

Circumcision of both male and female members of society was a practice that predated the advent of Islam in many of the African cultural groups in the colony, and was not necessarily considered to be un-Islamic. Among Muslim Krio, boys were normally circumcised on the third day after birth, while young girls were initiated into the bondo society during puberty, beginning in the nineteenth century.[18] The adoption of bondo by Muslim Krio was probably the result of sharing close physical/social space with Muslim immigrants from the hinterland, and other non-Yoruba Liberated African groups, particularly the Mende at Kossoh Town. The bondo secret society was reportedly introduced in the village of Hastings in 1858.[19] Its introduction in colonial society gained impetus as a result of the outbreak of diseases such as smallpox among the Liberated African population during this period. An African lay preacher, the Reverend Joseph May, credited the success of the propagators of the new phenomenon to its leaders, who were able to convince the women of the rural villages of the efficacy of circumcision in combating the feared epidemic of diseases afflicting the colony population.[20] The success in recruiting the women of Hastings was followed by successful recruitment at Wellington and subsequently in the Muslim communities of Freetown. Adolescent young girls were secluded in a confined backyard enclosure, known as a "bondo bush," for an extended period of time after circumcision (a surgical process of clitoridectomy), during which they were "ritually introduced into the art of communal living."[21] The clerics of Muslim Krio communities tolerated the circumcision of young girls, and rationalized the circumcision rites as essentially an obligation required of them by the Islamic Sunna.

Having been instructed in "the art of communal living" by the *sowei* (leader of the bondo or sande society) and her assistants on such diverse existential matters as procreation, sexual independence, and personal responsibility, young women were deemed eligible for marriage, the next logical rite of passage. The process of marriage in the Muslim Krio communities has not undergone much change since the 1870s; Yoruba cultural influences have remained central to the rituals. Young men were usually discouraged from getting married before they reached their (presumably matured) twenties. However, young women who had graduated from the bondo society were often encouraged to marry before they reached their twenties.[22] The need for evidence of mastery of a trade or vocation on the part of a young male suitor, presumably to ensure financial support for himself and his potential family, may have been the rationale for the seeming unevenness regarding the question of age appropriateness between the male and the female genders.

The late nineteenth century saw an increasing integration of Western conventions into what had hitherto been a two-prong wholly African traditional ritual ceremony involving the solemnization of the bonds between a would-be groom and his bride-to-be and their two families. The *gej* (engagement) ceremony, which became an important part of the marriage rites of the Muslim Krio, was actually appropriated by the latter from Christian Krio practices in the early 1900s. It was quite similar to the initial put kola ritual, only much more elaborate, with many invited guests present. The ritual involved readings from the Qur'an, followed by general celebrations. For all intents and purposes, this concluded the marriage as required by Yoruba-derived and Islamic traditions, because the gej ritual ceremony was essentially the *nika'u* (Arabic *nikka*), as prescribed by Islamic tenet. However, by the end of the first decade of the twentieth century, Muslim Krio began to have formal wedding ceremonies at the home of the Imam masjid, and subsequently at the mosque. This development was again quite likely due to the modernist influences of colonial society, and the fact that Christian Krio also increasingly had elaborate formal wedding ceremonies in church. As they were by the Christian clergy in church wedding ceremonies, Muslim clerics, in their *dua'u* (*al-dua*; prayer of supplication), often exhorted both the *yawo* and the *okoh yawo* (bride and groom) to adhere to traditional and religious values instilled in them by their respective families, as well as lectured them on the holy institution of matrimony and the expectations of married couples to exercise restraint and exhibit self- and mutual respect "till death."

The requirement to stay married till death was emphasized because Muslim Krios were generally disinclined to entertain the notion of divorce for married couples. In order to preclude, or at least reduce, the probability of such an eventuality as much as possible, the jamaat established a complicated structure in the event of a decision by one party or the other to seek a divorce. For instance, the party seeking separation was required to first apply for a hearing and judgment in front of the jamaat through the Imam, who may or may not transfer the case to the court of the alkali for final arbitration.[23] It was generally believed that the Imam's role was to unite and not facilitate separation between married couples, thus he usually assumed a mediating role. Women were often the initiators of divorce proceedings when they did occur, since the men, under Shari'a, could have as many as four wives. In the event of the death of a husband, his widowed wife was required to be in a state of mourning for a period of 130 days, and was restricted to her room for at least the first forty days during that period, all the while dressed in white, attended by in-laws and other immediate family members.

The notion of death, as in virtually all African societies (and across the world, for that matter), was a rite of passage of great significance. The demise of an individual was a momentous event in the family of the deceased and the community as a whole. Indeed, the death of any one person was considered to be a community-wide event and, as such, the expression "we all osh o" (an expression of shared communal grieving, of condolences) was the common refrain exchanged among the sympathizers. This common grieving was an ambiguous phenomenon, for the deceased person was not necessarily perceived as having been completely removed from the community. As in most African societies, the dead were perceived as having simply departed to join the ancestors and continued to be a part of the community, presumably maintaining links with surviving relatives.[24]

The Krio generally maintained the Yoruba customary awujoh ritual to celebrate and memorialized the dead in the nineteenth century, and continue to do so to this day. As Wyse noted, the awujoh is a social and spiritual symbolic ritual in the "Krio calendar of customs," and it was normally held to commemorate the very important three-day, seven-day, and forty-day anniversaries of the death of a member of the family.[25] The next important commemoration was the wan-year sara (the first anniversary of the passing), a traditional custom largely informed by Islamic principles and rituals. The three-day sara was particularly significant to the Oku, whose pre-Islamic traditions held that it was on the third day after death that the dead realized their transition from the temporal world of the living (the marketplace in traditional Yoruba worldview) to the world hereafter; thus tradition required that the dead be acknowledged on the third day after passing away, in order to avoid alienating the ancestors and the potential for misfortunes afflicting the community. The practice assumed Islamic proportions when the three-day became a ritual acknowledging the ascension to heaven of the dead with a fidau, during which the Imam offered prayers of supplication in Arabic and Yoruba, imploring Allah to forgive the deceased person for any transgression that he or she may have committed, knowingly or unknowingly, while on earth.[26] The same ritual was repeated for the seven-day sara, albeit on a smaller scale. On the fortieth day after the burial of the deceased, a more elaborate forty-day sara ritual was performed, commemorating the final departure of the dead to the hereafter. On the first anniversary of the death of a member of the community, the cultural requirement for a wan-year sara was usually strictly adhered to with prayers and offerings of traditional foodstuff (such as fura, acara, beans, etc.) in the customary awujoh setting.

Indeed, Islam had a very strong influence on the understanding of death in the Muslim Krio communities in colonial Freetown. Nonetheless, Yoruba cultural precepts continued to play a crucial role, resulting in what amounted to a religious and cultural syncretism/dualism that eventually contributed to the chasm at Fourah Bay. On the death of a member of the community, the corpse was cleansed and wrapped in a white shroud, following which the Imam and other clerics, who had been called to the home, offered prayers for the deceased. The dead was required to be buried within twenty-four hours, in keeping with Islamic tenets; while the soul was recognized as having the ability to linger around the community, the body of a dead person was required to be returned to the earth almost immediately.[27] But such a belief may also have been necessitated by the clear lack of a means of refrigeration to preserve corpses in colonial Freetown, since Muslims in contemporary Sierra Leone have increasingly allowed for corpses to be kept past the hitherto strictly adhered-to twenty-four-hour burial requirement.

From about the late 1800s, the Muslim Krio communities began clamoring for a separate cemetery in colonial Freetown, in a bid to ensure that their religious requirements with regard to funeral rites be respected and adhered to. By 1885, a three-acre tract of land, which the colony government later dubbed the Aku Muhammedan Cemetery, had been reserved at Kennedy Street in Fourah Bay in order to accommodate the needs of the Muslim Krio communities in Freetown.[28] The decision to provide a separate cemetery for Muslim Krio was not without its critics, however; in the 16 September 1885, issue of the *Sierra Leone Church Times*, the editorial board of the paper roundly criticized the decision of the colonial administration, which drew attention to the Islamic mode of burial, as reprehensible. The editorial cited the "normal mode of burial at the cemetery," where the Islamic interment process was carried out "without a regularly made coffin" and restricted the participation of women. The editorial was perceived as yet another attempt by the mostly European board members of the *Church Times* to subvert the cultural and religious freedom of Muslim Krio. In a rejoinder column published in the *Methodist Herald* of 23 September 1885, the Christian Krio columnist castigated the local correspondents of the *Church Times* (presumably Christian Krio) for allowing "themselves to be deceived by . . . foreigners [i.e., Europeans]."[29] *The Church Times*, however, had the last word when it responded that its editorial board was merely concerned with enforcement of "the laws of a Christian country."

AFRICAN (YORUBA) ESOTERIC SOCIETIES AND RELIGIOUS PIETY

The unfavorable reaction of conservative sections of colonial society to the religious tendencies and cultural praxis of Muslim Krio was particularly resonant vis-à-vis esoteric societies, and in some cases popular masquerade groups. In a rather paradoxical way, the growth of Islamic orthodoxy in colonial Freetown and the antipathy of the Christian clergy toward cultural praxis combined to resist the continued existence of Yoruba-derived cultural societies, such as the Egugu, Egunuko, Keri-Keri, Gelledeh, Akpansa, Géréfay, and Ordeh "devils" (as the costumed figures were derisively referred to by Christian missionaries). John Nunley has shown how Yoruba tradition was effectively utilized as an instrument of resistance to the cultural imperialism of European missionaries and colonial officials in Freetown during the period of British colonial rule.[30] However, this cultural resistance was not limited to the European clergy and missionaries, as the Muslim clerics were equally interested in stamping out many forms of pre-Islamic cultural practices in the colony. Thus an uneasy relationship existed between the mosque and the traditionalists with regard to popular and esoteric societies, which culminated in the schism at Fourah Bay in the 1870s.

Yoruba culture found expression in the open societies and dance groups, as well as in those societies in which membership was tightly controlled and restricted to those who had undergone the requisite rituals that were known only to the initiated; the disclosure of the nature of the elaborate rituals by members was strictly prohibited by the secret societies, and failure to comply could result in severe penalties, including death. Because of the coercive powers of these organizations, the members almost invariably maintained high moral and social discipline and were usually feared, if not respected, in the community at large. These groups, including the ones mentioned above, were accessible by Muslims and Christians alike, thus both the church and the mosque were equally dedicated to their elimination. Both world religions saw the traditional societies as representatives or "manifestations of idolatry and as part of Satan's plan," and as such both the church and the mosque considered it imperative that the Egugu, Egunuko, Keri-Keri, Géréfay, and other such societies be permanently removed from the colony. However, the Christian clergy and Muslim clerics failed to comprehend the depth of the reservoir of allegiance to traditional Yoruba cultural praxis in the Liberated African society, and subsequently in the emergent Krio society of Freetown.

As was the case in Yorubaland, the growth of Islam in Freetown reflected a challenging situation for traditionalists and the Muslim clerics. Unlike the situation in Nigeria, where Muslims were subject to physical attacks as they attempted to worship openly,[31] the challenge for the mosque in colonial Freetown consisted of the strength and resiliency of Yoruba culture and customary practices. However, as in the old country, continued membership in the jamaat of Muslims who were also prominent or "eminently placed" in the traditional secret societies led to a growing discord between the cultures of Islam and Yoruba and the emergence of a schism in the mosque and a fissure that threatened to tear the very fabric of the community. The conflict between Islam and traditional forms of worship in Yoruba societies in Nigeria could also be compared to the situation in nineteenth-century Freetown, in that, as Gbadamosi notes with reference to Nigeria, the expansion and growth of Islam brought the faith into direct conflict with the secret societies, thereby creating a "source of tension between the votaries of the new and the traditional [societies]." In the case of late nineteenth- and early twentieth-century Freetown, it was a resultant discordance not so much between a perceived paganism and Islam, but between Islam and Yoruba culture, represented in the secret societies. At least that was the stance taken by many members of the latter groups who did not perceive their membership in these organizations as necessarily reflective of traditional religious forms. To them, the Egugu, Egunuko, and the other organizations were but reflective of the deep roots of Yoruba traditional culture in Krio society.

The most resilient of the secret societies was that of the Egugu. Among the earliest chapters (known as *ojeh*) were Awodi and Oke Muri, of Fourah Bay and Fula Town, respectively, both of which had been part of Liberated African society since the early nineteenth century, and had been subjected to sustained attacks by European missionaries and African lay preachers. Secret societies had been part of the cultural landscape in the villages of Hastings, Waterloo, and, to a lesser extent, Benguema.[32] Hastings had the reputation of being the center of Egugu activities during the early nineteenth century in spite of the sustained intolerance of the European clergy; the groups emerged in Freetown in mid-century and were soon confronted by clergymen who were not shy about visiting the masked figures with physical violence, as was the case in 1833 when an Anglican clergyman, Rev. James Beale, attacked an Egugu.[33] Consequently, it would take several decades before these groups could venture into the open; Awodie and Oke Muri emerged openly in Freetown in the 1880s, but only after securing an assurance of safety from the colony administration.

Like the other esoteric societies of nineteenth-century Freetown, the Egugu was introduced by Yoruba recaptives who were resettled in the colony after the promulgation of the Abolition Act of 1807. According to Bishop Samuel Adjai Crowther, who was vehemently opposed to the influence of the group in the colony, the reputation of the Egugu had its roots in Yoruba politics when the society exerted its influence over the king and his subjects.[34] By 1844, Crowther's personal journal was reflecting the Anglican Church viewpoint, which maintained that the society constituted an insidious force in the colony, and the clergyman sought to position himself as the leading expert in the colony on the Egugu, and Yoruba culture in general. He traced the origins of the society to "the time of Awijoh, a king of Yoruba who also entitled himself Oba mi Igbogi," the king of Igbogi.[35] Crowther maintained that the Nupe, who had introduced the society to Yorubaland, had succeeded in persuading the latter that the Egugu "was an inhabitant of an invisible world, that he was [the] spirit of a dead man which had made its appearance again on earth as a heavenly messenger, whose dress must not be touched or the delinquent will be punished with immediate death by a supernatural power of the Egung."[36]

Thus the Egugu was a feared and respected entity among Yoruba Liberated Africans who transplanted the secret society to the village settlements of Hastings and Waterloo. The society was simultaneously re-spected and feared, primarily due to the reputation of its members' capacity to inflict great bodily harm to perceived transgressors of the society's socio-cultural space. The Egugu itself, as well as its *atokun* (guide), were believed to carry powerful *merecine* (charms or potions) of a benign and malignant nature. The practitioners of this culture thus had the ability to cure and inflict grave bodily harm on individuals, particularly the uninitiated, across the community. The most feared of these, probably only because it was the most commonly known, was allay, which was widely believed to be a toxin. By the late nineteenth century, Orjeh had become a powerful institution in Krio society, with the social structures of Muslim Krio communities in particular largely influenced by it, not unlike the ways in which the villag-ers of Hastings and Waterloo and, for that matter, their ancestors in Yoruba country, had been influenced by the Egungun.

As Peterson noted, "The Agugu in Hastings was the virtual power behind the throne."[37] And as it had exerted considerable influence at Hastings, the society sought to flex its powerful political muscles in the colony Muslim Krio communities. Its ability to influence the inhabitants of these communities could be easily discerned in the cementing of social structures and social relations that transcended religious boundaries. The common ancestral ties and Yoruba lineages of Freetown Krio who hailed from Hastings, Waterloo, Benguema, and the other rural villages popu-lated by Yoruba-speaking Liberated Africans were defined and solidified by membership in the Egugu society. The efforts of the Christian clergy to eliminate what they characterized as "devil societies" were often met with derision and ultimately proved unsuccessful across the colony. But if the church had effectively given up on trying to get rid of the esoteric society, the Muslim clerics, at least at Fourah Bay, were prepared to con-tinue with their reformist efforts, even if it meant a resultant chasm in the community. Indeed, to many of the clerics at Fourah Bay, the continued existence of the Egugu constituted, for all intents and purposes, a religious and cultural schism.

CONFLICTING COMMUNITIES: THE TAMBA AND JAMA FACTIONAL STRUGGLE AT FOURAH BAY

A prelude to the division in Fourah Bay occurred at Fula Town in the 1840s, when a dispute arose over the question of community leadership in the ab-sence of some of the elders who were part of the delegation to Dinguiraye.

Those who were charged with stewardship of the town soon started jockeying for power, leading to a fissure in the jamaat into the Tamba and Jama factions. Fortunately for the Fula Town congregation, the dispute was short-lived, thanks to the intervention of leading Fula and Mandinka clerics in the colony, who peaceably settled the dispute. Upon the return of the Fula Town leaders, the alkali was asked to mediate in the dispute between the two factions, a responsibility that he reportedly carried out "according to rules laid down in the Holy Koran." However, the holy Qura'n, it appears, was not enough to satisfy the reservations of some of the disputing parties. Thus, those who were left unsatisfied elected to relocate to Aberdeen village on the Atlantic coast. The effectiveness and perhaps relevance of the office of alkali reached its nadir in the 1890s, when the local occupant of the office failed to settle the factional dispute at Fourah Bay.[38]

The case of "Sulaiman Johnson and Others vs. Gheirawanieu George and Others," as reported in the *Sierra Leone Weekly News* editions of 1 and 8 April 1899, respectively, commenced in the civil division of the Supreme Court of the Colony on 15 October 1898. According to the *Weekly News*, the plaintiffs were represented by one of the colony's finest legal minds, Sir Samuel Lewis, while the defendants retained the counseling of the equally reputable team of Messrs. A. J. and J. C. Shorunkeh-Sawyerr. This case was the culmination of a protracted religiocultural schism in the community of Fourah Bay that had been simmering for decades before finally entering the public consciousness in the 1870s; it centered, as the contending parties appearing before the Honorable Chief Justice George Stallard argued, on the competing claims of the rival factions for control of the jamaat and the "Trust Deed" to the land on which the community's mosque was constructed. Specifically, the plaintiffs were seeking "an Injunction restraining the Defendants and their servants and followers from interfering with plaintiffs" in, inter alia, the conduct of their clerical roles in the mosque, acting as trustees, and in the appointing of other clerics to official positions in the mosque.[39] While the arguments of opposing counsels hinged on the specific issues mentioned above, the ultimate factors accounting for the fissure could be traced to a developing rejectionist attitude emerging in a group of clerics who were determined to curtail the pervasive influences of traditional organizations, such as the Egugu, Egunuko, Keri-Keri, Akpansa, and Odeh, as well as the remnants of suspected orisha adherents, in a community that was being increasingly impacted by an Islamic orthodoxy emanating from conservative forces in West Africa, particularly in the Tijaniyya *tariqa* (brotherhood) stronghold of Dinguiraye. It was in essence the consequence of a fundamental conflict between piety and praxis. Certainly the most immediate factor that precipitated the case in the colony Supreme Court was concerned with the question of political control of the Fourah Bay mosque, occasioned by the death in 1892 of the then Imam of the jamaat, Alfa Haruna. The son of the deceased Imam, Gheirawanieu George, was chosen to succeed his father, a decision that was immediately challenged by a faction of the congregation that questioned his youth and modernist attitude, particularly his tolerance for Western education. The opposing faction backed the election of Sulaiman Johnson, a much older member of the jamaat.[40] The contending parties soon began to worship in separate quarters, thereby creating and solidifying a schism within the community.

The Fourah Bay factional dispute emerged in the public consciousness of colonial society as essentially a conflict over ownership of the land on which the community's mosque was situated. The arguments propounded by counsels for the plaintiffs and defendants to the dispute occasioned an inevitable encounter between British common law and Islamic Shari'a. As the Honorable Chief Justice George Stallard perceived the issue, the Sierra Leone Supreme Court was ultimately required to determine whether "Mohammedan Law . . . though made in Arabia to Muslims independent of locality," could be properly considered "local customs," and whether such law could coexist with the colonial "Order-in-Council of 3rd September 1844," which required that "officers shall observe until further orders such of the local customs of the said countries and places as may be compatible with the principles of the Law of England."[41] In his address to the court before delivering final judgment, Justice Stallard seemed inclined to uphold the primacy of British law over Shari'a, in spite of efforts by many in the Muslim community to have the case judged according to the "law and usages of their faith." In response to a suggestion by counsel that Muslims may be unfamiliar with English law, Justice Stallard noted that the parties in the case "are old residents in the colony and I see no reason why they should be more ignorant of the law of their residence than their neighbours of the same descent and origin who happen to be Churchmen or Wesleyans."[42]

The case before the Supreme Court was itself partly a product of the growing importance of Shari'a precepts and of an orthodox "Islamic consciousness" in the colony of Freetown, ultimately culminating in the fissure that affected the internal cohesion of the Fourah Bay community in the late nineteenth century. To many in the community, the actual tangible reasons that precipitated the crisis in the years before the 1870s have long been shrouded in mystery.[43] However, certain discernible factors accounting for the schism became evident in the 1880s, including an increasingly acrimonious land dispute, Islamic orthodoxy, the continued existence of secret societies, and, finally, personality conflicts within the leadership of the community. While the land dispute was adjudicated in the colony Supreme Court in 1898, the struggle between adherents of doctrinaire Islam and cultural conservatives who were determined to maintain their Yoruba-derived customary practices remained the most significant issue threatening the social stability and cohesion of the community. This inherent struggle between cultural traditionalists and defenders of Islamic dogma continued to be played out in lawsuits filed with the colony courts, and those of Independent Sierra Leone, over ownership of the land on which the mosque was situated in the years after a judgment was delivered by Justice Stallard on 23 March 1899, in effect becoming the pivot on which the schism revolved.

The dispute over ownership of the land on which the mosque Jami ul-Atiq was built is instructive, if only because it became the symbol for a cultural fissure, the accounting factors of which could not otherwise be addressed openly, as much of the underlying issues had to do with the role and place of members of the jamaat who were also active in the esoteric societies that resulted from Yoruba cultural diffusion in the post–slave trade settlement in Sierra Leone. Societies such as the aforementioned Egugu, Egunuko, Keri-Keri, Akpansa, and Odeh (Untin) constituted a central part of the social structure of Krio society by the 1870s and as such became problematic for the growth of Islam in colonial Freetown. Consequently, as Islamic orthodoxy began to take root in the Muslim communities, particularly at Fourah Bay, the struggle between Islamic piety and cultural praxis became heightened. If the issues concerning the secret societies, intelligible only to the initiated, could not be addressed openly, then a struggle over control of the mosque became inevitable. Two groups emerged from this fissure, namely the Tamba (or Trust) and Jama (or Mass). Each claimed exclusive ownership of the physical structure of the mosque and the land on which it stood. The actual breakup itself arose out of a political disagreement regarding the position of the Imam, a conflict that had been simmering since the 1850s.[44]

In 1857, a struggle over succession to the office of Imam masjid that had been going on outside the public view became an open and divisive issue. The death of the first undisputed Imam, Alfa Yadalieu, created a religious and political vacuum that would go on to have a lasting impact on the community. No one personality within the jamaat emerged to muster enough support among the elders to secure the position of Imam. As the succession struggle was going on, the mosque came to be controlled by satellite groups, with each taking turns in securing temporary leadership for one of their own. Consequently, several Imams were appointed and replaced in quick succession for well over a decade after the demise of Yadalieu.[45] Among those appointed to the position during this volatile period were Alfa Ali (also known as Daddy Limamu) and Alfa Yunusa. The latter is said to have been forcibly removed from the mosque while delivering the qutba during Friday Jumaat prayer. Hisphysical expulsion was justified on grounds of incompetence; however, the event alienated a significant faction of the congregation.[46] The ongoing drama in the mosque, however, failed to attract much community-wide interest, thereby allowing some of the leading clerics to install a son of the late Imam Yadalieu as the de facto Imam. The new Imam, Sulaiman, who had studied Arabic and Islamic philosophy in Dinguiraye, is acknowledged as having brought some semblance of social tranquillity to the community.

Sulaiman seemed to have been aware of the political challenges of the office leading up to his installation and was, therefore, reportedly reluctant to accept the position of Imam immediately after the death of his father. Apparently chagrined by the conflict in the mosque, Alfaqa (as Sulaiman was commonly referred to) removed himself from Fourah Bay and relocated to Lungi, in Kafu Bullom, across the Sierra Leone River.[47] He secured a parcel of land and devoted his attention to farming and trade, and to teaching the Qura'n. The ruler of Kafu Bullom, Almami Sanusi, and the people of the district became concerned about reports of his imminent departure when word reached the local leaders that Sulaiman's services might be needed in his native Fourah Bay community, and sought to convince him to stay permanently in his adopted community. Realizing that it would be almost impossible to get Sulaiman to voluntarily return home to Fourah Bay, a group of community elders decided to kidnap him during the night and return him to Freetown. Having declined the position of Imam in the past, the elders determined to prevail on him, albeit in a quite untraditional manner, to take up the mantle of leadership.

But in spite of the success of the elders to relocate him to his natal community, Sulaiman remained steadfastly reluctant to lead prayers in what, from his perspective, was a dysfunctional situation in the mosque. He was evidently acutely aware of the difficulty of commanding popular support in the prevailing circumstances in which the religiocultural fissures had left the community in a state of total disharmony and had, consequently, made it virtually impossible for any one person to bring the contentious parties together. M. S. Alharazim, writing in the 1930s, contended that Sulaiman was also much influenced by his mother, Hassanatu, who had grown disenchanted by the quarrelsome divide in the mosque and the community at large.[48] Hassanatu had herself played a leading role earlier in the decision of the family to send the young Sulaiman to the Senegambia region for further Islamic studies, and may have wanted her son to maintain his intellectual and personal integrity by insisting that he stay out of the politics of the mosque. In the end, Sulaiman agreed to accept the position of Imam, with the caveat that he would restrict himself to Islamic studies and not be involved in the internal politics of the jamaat. Meanwhile, the struggle over ownership of the land continued to simmer.

While Alfa Sulaiman's tenure as Imam served to ensure some social tranquillity in the community, the deed to the land on which the mosque was constructed was transferred from one person or group of persons to another. Until his death in 1849, control of the land was in the hands of Alfa Yadalieu, who acted as if he actually owned the property and later gave up part of it for the purpose of constructing the Jami ul-Atiq mosque in 1839, after years of leading prayers in his compound.[49] His death subsequently served as a catalyst for the succession dispute in the jamaat and, in essence, over the land and mosque.

Interestingly, even before the late Imam's death in 1849, the land on which the Fourah Bay community itself was located had been a source of conflict within the family of William Henry Savage, the one-time attorney for the Liberated African Muslims. Following the death of Savage, a dispute arose between his heirs, Henry Garel and Mary Savage, for exclusive control of the vast real-estate holdings of the former lawyer and merchant. According to court documents, both offspring of William Savage laid competing claims to, and dealt with, the land as if each had exclusive control of the title deed to the property; both Henry G. and Mary Savage "claimed and dealt with the land as if [they] had a good title, claiming rent, among other things" between 1849 and 1859.[50] Henry Savage subsequently transferred ownership of part of the land to E. A. Bell on 4 August 1860, with the other part finally transferred on 12 May 1862. It was after the latter conveyance was completed that a series of dealings and counterdealings regarding the land started. As the *Weekly News* noted in its 1 April 1899 edition, the transfer of ownership in 1862 "began a series of apparently regular dealings with the land," with the property being mortgaged on 13 February 1864 to Ann Bell, who in turn sold it to Theodore Amadeus Rosenbush, a British merchant-banker originally from Hamburg. Rosenbush then transferred the mortgage on January 1865 to William Rainy, who sold the land on which the mosque was built to William Cole of the Fourah Bay jamaat on 14 July 1865.[51] On 26 June 1876, Cole transferred ownership of the land to the trustees of the jamaat. The deed in question constituted the basis of what became a celebrated case in the Fourah Bay community and the colony.

The transfer of ownership in 1865 of the land in question did not have a legal conveyance to support the claim of ownership by William Cole. This was at least the stance taken by a section of the jamaat.[52] The uncertainty over the lawful conveyance continued until 1876 when a trust deed was drawn transferring the property to the Fourah Bay community. The deed was laid claim to by the two contending parties, the Tamba and the Jama factions. Both claimed that their respective membership was responsible for the collection of money used to purchase the land.[53] But while the Jama faction claimed the land on behalf of the whole community, the Tamba asserted that the land rightfully should be under the control of the family of the late Imam Yadalieu (i.e., the Savage family). Chief Justice Stallard, who presided over the proceedings of the case in 1898, seemed to agree with the stance taken by the Jama faction when he noted that the transfer of the land to the trustees of the jamaat in 1876 could have been carried out only for the benefit of the whole community. The presiding judge faulted the negotiator of the conveyance, William Cole, only for unscrupulously "being paid the purchase money twice over."[54]

The chief justice was also able to ferret out enough information during the proceedings to understand the nuanced nature of the case and thus made it crystal clear to the contending parties that the land dispute was certainly not the sole basis for the conflict and lawsuit. Justice Stallard observed that the doctrinal divide within the mosque was the real reason for the lawsuit. Stallard was actually only partly correct in his observation, since the conflict transcended merely doctrinal issues that existed among the clerics. Personal and family conflicts also accounted for the fissure at Fourah Bay. In 1890, Ligaly Savage, in his capacity as assistant Imam, officiated at the wedding of a woman whom he believed was the former wife of Gheirawanieu George, one of the leaders of the Jama faction. The bride in the marriage ceremony, as it turned out, had only been estranged from George, not completely divorced. The legitimacy of the marriage was thus contested by George and his supporters on grounds that the assistant Imam had "improperly performed the ceremony of marriage over a woman who had not been properly divorced," and that the assistant Imam, furthermore, had no legitimate authority to officiate in said ceremony. Both Ligaly Savage and Sulaiman Johnson were consequently forced out of their respective offices of assistant Imam and Imam; Savage for having performed the ceremony and Johnson for having allowed the ceremony under the prevailing circumstances. The situation was further complicated by the fact that the two religious leaders were forced out of office by the Imam gharyat, Alfa Haruna George, who happened to be the father of Gheirawanieu George. Chief Justice Satallard noted that the dismissal was "ex parte," the accused not being called upon for explanation or defense. Even though Johnson attempted to regain his position in the jamaat, he was disallowed from ever setting foot in the mosque again, in effect excommunicated.[55]

Consequently, in December 1891, Johnson went on the offensive, seeking a legal injunction against Haruna George, Momodu Langley, and Baylu Savage, the leaders of the Jama faction, "restraining them from preventing him acting as Imam according to the terms of the Trust Deed of 1876." On 3 December 1896, the lawyers for the disputing factions reached an agreement that allowed Johnson to resume his duties as Imam masjid, with Ligaly Savage as his assistant.[56] However, just two weeks following his reinstatement, Johnson was forced to leave the mosque by the Jama faction. His return happened to have taken place just after a new structure had been built to replace the old mosque. Thus he was leading prayers in a brand-new mosque, much to the chagrin of the Jama group, which claimed to have been largely responsible for the construction of the new structure.

Chief Justice Stallard finally rendered his decision on the case on Thursday, 23 February 1899. On the question of the dismissal of Johnson and Savage as Imam and assistant Imam, respectively, the chief justice decided in favor of the latter, on grounds that both were dismissed without being given the opportunity to provide a legitimate defense of their actions. This, Justice Stallard concluded, was contrary to British common law ideas and "utterly inconsistent with any notion of justice or propriety." The chief justice had earlier drawn the court's attention to the question of whether the Shari'a could be deemed applicable in deciding the final outcome of the case and whether Islamic jurisprudence was in fact applicable in the courts of the colony. He concluded that English law was already in force in the colony "for more than seventy years when the deed was executed and was well known by many as no less than 2,419 conveyances and 315 mortgages were registered between 1865 and 1876."[57] The Supreme Court decision regarding the land, for the most part, went in favor of the Tamba faction. However, Stallard did not acknowledge the group's claim of outright ownership. He merely decided that the deed of trust drawn up in 1876 was not prepared with the intent of depriving the other faction of ownership or legitimate claim to the land and mosque. The court finally implored the elders of the congregation to select some respectable and credible members of the Muslim community in the colony, with the requisite "moral capital," who would pursue an amicable accord between the two factions. That decision merely postponed the fight for a future date, as the competing parties continued to file legal suits well into the 1970s.

GHEIRAWANIEU GEORGE

The conflict at Fourah Bay may have been exacerbated by the political ambitions of Gheirawanieu George. Even though he occupied a very prominent position in the community, George may have harbored far more ambitions than the position of Imam gharyat could satisfy. Being the singularly most important leader of his community would have given him the kind of exposure and recognition in the colony that being a mere agent of a European-owned firm (which he was) could not possibly provide. It is important to note that while Johnson and Savage were his superiors in the jamaat and more knowledgeable in Islamic studies, George was clearly the more advanced in Western education and had a more modernist outlook. At a time when the Muslim Krio were suspicious of mission-run schools in the colony, given the latter's record of evangelization in Freetown, the father of young Gheirawanieu was unafraid to enroll him at the CMS Grammar School. Upon completion of his secondary school education, George enrolled at the CMS-run Fourah Bay College. It was not difficult for him to attend the Christian institution even though he was a Muslim, because he was officially enrolled as Thomas G. George.[58]

In 1892, George managed to persuade some of the leading clerics to install him as Imam masjid following the death of his father, Alfa Haruna;[59] and in 1895 he combined the two offices of Imam masjid and Imam gharyat.[60] This was the period when Johnson and Savage had been removed from their positions as Imam and assistant Imam, respectively. Upon his assumption of the headship of the mosque, George came under vehement opposition by many among the older generation of the jamaat. But he and his followers seemed to have concluded that with his Western education and modernist views, and his having nurtured close relations with officials in the colonial bureaucracy, he would ultimately prevail. They proved to have made an adroit political calculation, because his ascendancy was immediately given official recognition by the colonial state, which evidently wanted someone like George to take over the leadership of the largest Muslim Krio community in Freetown. With the help of Governor King Harman, George was invited to pay an official visit to the United Kingdom in 1901–1902. On 4 July 1902, he led juma'a prayers in the central mosque in London, and was inducted into the Ancient Order of the Zuzumites, a Sufi mystical group, three days later.[61]

ISLAM AND TRADITIONAL CULTURE

In the meantime, an even more troublesome development in the social and cultural landscapes was taking place. A strong undercurrent of antagonism between traditionalists and advocates of orthodox Islamic practices in the Muslim Krio communities had been a fact of life at Fourah Bay, Fula Town, and Aberdeen. This undercurrent was less evident among the Christian Krio; nonetheless, church clerics were just as concerned about what they considered uncomfortable encroachments by "pagan" institutions. Krio society in general has long attached a great deal of significance to the beliefs and customs passed on from one generation to the next. However, the customs and traditional practices that had come to distinguish the Krio from other groups in the colony were much more represented and celebrated in the Muslim communities than in the Christian sector, especially due to the long-standing efforts of church officials to discourage the retention and consolidation of African cultural traditions. Muslim Krio communities reflected an overwhelmingly African cultural outlook, save for the Islamic traditions of the mosque. However, by the 1870s, some leading Muslim clerics, particularly at Fourah Bay, were beginning to question the legitimacy of some traditional and customary practices. As Robinson notes, "Islamic law and theology did not create an obvious space and time for Muslims outside of the Hijaz."[62] The world, to Islamic jurists and theologians, was simply divided into the abode of Islam (Dar al-Islam) and that of the unbelievers, Dar al-Kufr. While Muslims in the colony of Freetown recognized this bifurcated space in the context of Islamic theology, their appropriation of

Islamic tenets was much more nuanced, as they were rather cognizant of the significance of pre-Islamic customary practices that they did not necessarily construe as antithetical to their faith, and as such sought to adapt the faith to existing cultural praxis.

EGUGU AND SCHISM AT FOURAH BAY

Bishop Adjai Crowther and his fellow Anglican clergymen who had been vehemently opposed to the continued existence and widespread social and political influence of the Egugu were not the only ones concerned with what they perceived as the corrupting influences of the society and its un-Christian essence. At Aberdeen, Fourah Bay, and Fula Town, the religious clerics were just as adamant about the need to separate the mosque from what many of them also considered an un-Islamic institution. Many of the leaders of the jamaat often admonished the congregation on the need to ensure some social and physical separation between the mosque and the Egugu society, and pronounced the holding of official positions simultaneously in both the mosque and the society as a conflict of interest. The subject would consequently become a fundamental source of friction in the community.[63] From the perspective of the clerics, one cannot continue to be a practicing Muslim and a devotee of the Egugu simultaneously, for Islam and the latter were mutually exclusive. However, the people of Aberdeen and Fula Town assumed a more liberal attitude toward the Egugu and sought to accommodate the members of the society, thereby allowing for what could be described as an amicable, if uneasy, coexistence between the mosque and the esoteric society. This was possible because Aberdeen and Fula Town were relatively small communities, and many of the younger nonclerical members of the jamaat failed to see any fundamental problem in participating in what they perceived as strictly cultural groups, devoid of religious undertones, and in effect upholding their Yoruba cultural heritage, while also maintaining their *adini* (Islamic faith). The situation at Fourah Bay was not as easily resolved. Here, simultaneous membership in the Egugu and the holding of official positions in the jamaat became a pivotal and incendiary issue in the social and religious landscapes and thus a source of internal fissure. By the 1870s and 1880s, the conflict over the role and place of the secret society within the community had become a major factor in the feud that culminated in the breakup of the congregation into two factions. This divide ultimately led to the civil suit of 1898.

The influence of the Tijaniyya brotherhood, especially its requirement of an enforced adherence to strict Islamic principles, already discussed, clearly contributed to the resultant cultural cleft at Fourah Bay in the late nineteenth century. The successors of Alfa Yadalieu, and their conservative Tamba faction, advocated a much more doctrinaire Islam and questioned the legitimacy of the leadership role played by members of the congregation, who, in spite of such increasingly important positions in the jamaat, continued to play key roles in the Egugu and other secret societies, the rituals and initiation requirements of which were declared to be *haram* (heresy) and therefore in complete contravention of Islamic tenets and utterly untenable.[64] The tension within the Fourah Bay jamaat was at a fever pitch by the late 1880s, and even though there was hardly any open violence in the community, relations between members of the community, including kinsfolk on opposing sides, deteriorated significantly. The social atmosphere surrounding the role and place of the Egugu society in the community was only compounded by the defiant attitude of its members, who sought to enforce a constricted environment during certain periods of the year when they performed their ceremonial rituals. For instance, the society restricted the *igberi* (the uninitiated) to their homes during the night when the *Oro* (spirit), which was not supposed to be seen by the uninitiated, traversed the streets of the community. This situation was not unlike that in Yorubaland in Nigeria, when the Egungun, the Aborisa, and the Elegugun of Ado-Ekiti alienated the Muslim community by insisting that the uninitiated, particularly women, be confined to their homes "during festivals involving certain rituals that women were forbidden to see."[65] The conservative Muslims at Fourah Bay took umbrage over the fact that the period of curfew during such festivals and ritual ceremonies often coincided with the required early dawn prayers; as a result, the chasm created by the dissonance between piety and praxis only grew wider. Ultimately, the chasm could not be amicably resolved, thereby leading to a permanent breakup of the congregation, with the conservative Tamba (or Trust) faction retaining control of the mosque following the decision of the colony Supreme Court in 1899.[66] The liberal Mass faction opted to found an alternate jamaat and commenced praying at another mosque.

The leaders of the Mass sector of Fourah Bay seemed to have entertained a rather nuanced approach to the notion of piety and praxis. It appears that while they recognized and appreciated the concept of a bifurcated world of Dar al-Islam and Dar al-Kufr, they were reluctant to accept the argument of the conservative clerics that the simultaneous embracing of the traditional practices and customs of their Yoruba heritage and devotion to the *adini* (faith) were mutually exclusive. Many of the clerics in the Mass faction seemed to have concluded that the substitution of Arabic culture for their inherited Yoruba way of life would be much more inimical to their community than the founding of an alternate jamaat, thus they opted for the latter rather than acquiesce in the face of the Supreme Court decision of 1899. They were also quite conscious of the fact that the Yoruba had an array of orishas, including Sango and Ogun, both of whom had quite a significant following among Liberated Africans settled in Freetown following the Abolition Act of 1807. However, they were prepared to accommodate the Orjeh men (members of the Egugu) in the jamaat, with the caveat that the latter did not hold such important positions as Imam, naib, or alkali.

The "clash of values" evident in the Muslim Krio community in the late nineteenth century would continue to have significant social implications for Muslims well into the twentieth century, and still do so. The more conservative adherents of Islam still disapprove of the continued observance of many of the cultural trappings of Yoruba praxis; many of the young clerics trained in Middle Eastern countries such as Saudi Arabia and Iran, as well as many of their locally trained counterparts, have recently raised eyebrows by advocating the discontinuation of the use of such food items as kola nut, acara, and fura in traditional ritual ceremonies with Islamic appropriations.

ISLAM AND POPULAR CULTURE IN LATE NINETEENTH-CENTURY FREETOWN

The divisive struggles for leadership, land, and the definition of Islam within the Muslim communities (or more precisely, Fourah Bay community) did not stop Muslim Krio from contributing to the development of urban popular culture. Beginning in the late nineteenth century, the Fourah Bay and Fula Town communities began concluding the holy month of Ramadan with lantern parades. The lantern parade subsequently became a central part of the "visual culture" of Freetown Muslims, and remains so to this day. It remains not only a unique contribution of Muslim Krio to Freetown urban life, but distinguishes the urban culture of the city from that of the entire West African subregion. The clerics and leaders of the jamaats in the colony gave their blessing to the various lantern groups, and the practice soon became a much anticipated aspect of the monthlong period of fasting, in spite of the fact that the occasion itself lay outside any prescribed "Islamic canon."[67] The parades started in the 1840s, when Muslims in the

Liberated African community marched in groups along the streets of East Freetown in celebration of the conclusion of the Ramadan period of fasting, and often ended the procession at Government House.[68] By the 1890s, the processions were marked by the inclusion of small handheld candlelit lanterns, but now held during Lail at ul-qadr, the "night of power" (when Muhammad is believed to have received the first revelation), on the twenty-sixth of Ramadan. The procession reverted back to the end of Ramadan, on the eve of Eid ul-Fitr, in the early 1900s, probably due to concerns on the part of leading clerics about the propriety of such a celebration on what was considered one of the holiest nights of the Islamic calendar. By this time, the annual procession had expanded to include the Mandinka community and other Muslim Krio residing in Murray Town and Aberdeen. The celebratory groups sang and danced to songs that incorporated Islamic verses into the Yoruba and Krio languages. By 1910, the songs performed during the lantern parades took on special meaning when they began to reflect the prevailing social and political mood of the colony.[69]

The practice of building lanterns may have started with small lantern displays arranged by one Daddy Maggay, an emigrant from the Gambia.[70] The inclusion of small lanterns, mostly replicas of the mosque, provided an added touch to the procession, thereby serving to attract larger and larger crowds to the parades. To avoid injury, parade participants began wearing "heavy marching boots," which also provided "a means of coordinating their steps into rhythmical patterns." The group most identified with this rhythmic style was Bubu Gegn from Fourah Bay, which is said to have been founded by a young lady known simply as Rokie Bulli; she had a pet baboon, which became the group's mascot and was often depicted in its lantern floats.[71] The Bubu Gegn became the foremost lantern club in the colony and subsequently expanded its repertoire to include "a bugle player," as well as *bata* (drums) and other assorted musical instruments, thereby allowing it to consistently attract the largest crowds on the eve of the Feast of Eid ul-Fitr. Not to be outdone, the communities of Fula Town, Magazine Cut, Kossoh Town, and others in the colony began the building of more elaborate lantern floats, over and above the initial simple handheld candlelit items introduced by Daddy Maggay.

EID UL-FITR AND OTHER ISLAMIC EVENTS

The lantern parades ushered in the Feast of Eid ul-Fitr, marking the completion of the Ramadan fast. Notwithstanding the challenges of rising up very early in the morning for the Eid prayers, following the all-night festivities, the Muslim communities in the colony usually turned out en masse to attend prayers at the various mosques. The mosques ultimately became inadequate to accommodate the throng of believers, thus making the streets in the immediate vicinity an extension of the mosque. The Eid prayers served as the culmination of the monthlong period of fasting and spiritual cleansing, and was considered one of the foremost events in the Islamic calendar when many adherents of the faith usually hoped to receive *baraka* (spiritual blessing) from Allah.

The Eid prayers, however, became more than an expression of religious obligations; they became reflective of the larger process of Africanization, or more precisely the *Yorubaization*, of Islam by the Muslim Krio of Freetown in the late nineteenth and early twentieth centuries. An unmistakable expression of Yoruba visual culture during the Eid prayers was evident in the mode of dress preferred by the celebrants; the women were often dressed in elaborate long-flowing kabaslot, buba, and lappa, while the men demonstrated a preference for the agbada.[72] They also substituted Yoruba for the traditional Arabic greetings following the ritual prayers; rather than the Arabic Eid ul-Mubarak, most of the people greeted one another with Eku Yedu (or Eku Odun). Similar trends could be discerned during the Feast of Eid ul-Adha (or Greater Bhairam), which marked the end of the hajj, or pilgrimage to the Muslim Holy Land of Mecca. And in keeping with the required *zakat* (charity), the Krio Muslims distributed *jaka'a*, consisting of rice, kola, meat from sacrificed sheep (in symbolic commemoration of the attempted sacrifice of Isaac by his father, Abraham), and other assorted food items, as well as money to neighbors and the poor and destitute. Indeed, the Muslim Krio also appropriated Islam through the rendering of mostly Yoruba songs, interspersed with Arabic words and phrases, by neighborhood youth groups in the early dawn hours during the period of fasting. These singing groups were inspired to render beautiful, melodic traditional songs not only to mark the holy month of Ramadan, but for the more practical purpose of waking up the faithful to partake of their pre-fast meal (*saree*).[73]

The Africanization of Islam by Muslim Krio was not lost on non-Muslim observers in the colony. In 1893, the *Weekly News* commented on the adaptation of Islamic events and holy days to a typically African cultural setting within the Muslim Krio communities.[74] The newspaper reported that the 'end of Ramadan was ushered in by "the beating of drums and the firing of guns," as well as with "music and dancing in true African style." The *Weekly News*, on yet another occasion, observed that the Islamic celebrations were quite unique in a Christian colony, noting furthermore that "there was nothing in these dances resembling the European style" so clearly notice-able in the Christian gatherings of colonial Freetown.[75] According to the journal, the celebrations by the Muslim Krio reflected "an authentic ab-original setting with the females exhibiting their African finesse," and "the sexes, as is usual in uncontaminated Africa, danced separately to the strains of the most exhilarating music by native performers on native [musical] in-struments." The *Weekly News* further editorialized on that occasion by con-tinuing on the theme of African authenticity in what can be described only as evidence of a resistance to the cultural imperialism of the colonial estab-lishment, by drawing a clear contrast with the ballroom dances frequented by the educated elite of the Christian Krio community. It pronounced the Muslim gatherings as "cheerful, regular and decorous," and observed that "though there were three or four hundred men and women in attendance, there was nothing like disorder, nothing like those irregularities which arise from the unfortunate proclivities introduced by the use of stronger bever-ages than tea, lemonade, and water."[76]

Acknowledging the growing importance of the Muslim Krio in the col-ony and the resultant accommodation policy of the colony government may have served as the motivating factor for Governor Sir John Pope Hennessy's attendance at the Eid prayers in the Cline Town section of Fourah Bay in 1872. The governor was accompanied by the Second West India Regiment, which provided a guard-of-honor for the Imam, Alfa Sulaiman.[77] In 1879, Governor Samuel Rowe sought to include all Muslims in the colony in his administration's efforts to recognize the increasingly significant role of Islam in the colony by inviting the leaders of the Muslim Krio communities to Government House for a cocktail gathering, careful enough to note that only nonalcoholic beverages would be served.[78] Rowe was also politically astute enough to invite the leaders of immigrant Muslim groups, such as the Mandinka and the Fula, to his official residence on a separate day to observe the important religious occasion.

The conflict at Fourah Bay may have been engendered by religious and cultural factors internal to the Muslim community; however, Western education and issues relative to modernity and Euro-African relations in the Atlantic World were particularly relevant to an understanding of what contributed to the developments that culminated in the landmark case of 1898. While conversion to Islam did not require any period of study of Islamic scriptures, conversion to Christianity did, relative to biblical scrip-tures. Thus the CMS and other evangelical groups founded schools and other educational institutions in Sierra Leone and elsewhere in West Africa for the express purpose of instructing children and adults in the tenets of the Christian faith. The extension of mission-controlled education to the Muslim community would also come to play a meaningful role in the fissure at Fourah Bay. Nonetheless, while Western education became somewhat controversial in the Muslim community, local modernist forces ultimately prevailed, and their efforts helped usher in a period of construction of schools that had the effect of breaking down social boundaries in the colony.

6 ↢ Education and Educational Reform within the Muslim Community

THE KRIO DIASPORA IN THE ATLANTIC COMMUNITIES of West Africa is largely reflective of the positive impact of Western education on developments in the post–slave trade social environment of Sierra Leone and, for that matter, in West Africa as a whole. It is a paradox that some of the people most identified with the development of Western education in the colonial environment of the subregion, such as Dr. Edward Wilmot Blyden and Rev. James Johnson, were also among its most vociferous and ardent critics. These men were advocates for the promotion of Western education and at the same time critical of the nature of the education provided by the Christian missions. From their perspective, colony government–assisted schools superintended by the European evangelical missions were promoting an educational system that was geared toward the production of educated Africans who were but caricatures of Europeans; of Anglo-Saxon Europeans, to be precise. Blyden, in particular, steadfastly believed that the European mission schools were endeavoring to inculcate in children under their supervision a rejection of their African heritage and the cultural attributes of their native societies. Inherent in this agenda was a pervasive attitude and assumption of European racial and cultural superiority vis-à-vis the Africans.

Thus critics such as Blyden maintained that evangelical and colonial officials sought to promote a values-laden educational curriculum that, from their perspective, was not in consonance with the developmental interests of the native societies. The critical assessment of Western education was indeed reflected in the appearance of a society that was thoroughly acculturated in Victorian English mores when, by the mid-nineteenth century, Krio society was being identified by some as "a Westernized African society." While the society as a whole was anything but a collection of "Black Englishmen," the educated elites and their Victorian English cultural proclivities gave credence to the inherent cultural assumptions of the educational agenda of mission-controlled schools in the colony. British colonial officials and the European clergy proactively sought to create an educated elite who would "identify with Europeans culturally and politically." However, outside the upper echelons of Krio society, anglophiles with an evident propensity to identify with the empire were categorized as Oyimbo. By reserving a cultural referent for such Anglophiles, the rest of Krio society was somewhat reflective of a rejectionist attitude toward Western culture, in spite of the entreaties of the evangelical and colonial establishment.

Edward Blyden was representative of the school of thought in colonial West Africa that did not subscribe to the wholesale appropriation of Western culture by the "subjects" of the British Crown; a contrasting figure in this context, it could be argued, was the Rev. Samuel Adjai Crowther, who advocated a wholesale embracing of the values of European Christendom, even up to that point in his life when he was being subjected to the most humiliating forms of racial discrimination at the hands of the European clergy of the CMS in the late nineteenth century. Crowther uncritically accepted the teachings of the church, including the rejecting of all things African. He assumed a rather condescending attitude, like his European fellow clergymen, toward the cultural and social institutions of the various ethnicities in the colony of Freetown, and later in the Niger Delta pastorate. He identified the Egungun, Egunuko, and other cultural organizations as "pagan" institutions with as much passion as he equated Islam with paganism. As Ayandele observes, Crowther was uninterested in developing an intellectual understanding of African institutions and traditional religion; "Rather, he had the worst epithets for these institutions and the Delta peoples."[1] Perhaps, the clergyman who could be said to have had one of the most significantly nuanced points of view regarding the role of Western education and its relation to African culture was the Reverend James Johnson. Like Blyden, Johnson did not necessarily advocate a wholesale rejection of Western cultural attributes; however, he was not prepared to propose an abandonment of African cultural institutions, as Crowther seemed willing to do. As Jean Herskovits notes, Johnson saw, as Crowther did not, that elements in African culture not only need not be destroyed, but should not be destroyed! Indeed, Johnson strongly believed that they should even be reasserted in the face of the Western challenge. African names, African dress, and other such continuities did not interfere with the practice of Christianity, and Johnson saw no reason why they should be discarded.[2] It was this shared need to preserve, rather than emasculate, African culture that largely defined the advocacy of Western education in Sierra Leone and West Africa in general by critics such as Blyden, Johnson, Mohammed Sanusie, Mohammed Shitta Bey, and others.

Based on a self-conscious perception of racial and cultural superiority, European missions could be said to have perceived it their "manifest destiny" to lead the Africans along the road to "civilization" through the auspices of the church, with the mission schools not only emphasizing the three R's, but also consciously inculcating in the minds of young students enrolled in their schools the benefits of Victorian English values. The so-called three Cs—Christianity, commerce, and civilization—were therefore seen as the essential program that would ultimately transform and usher in the regeneration of the African peoples. African critics clearly understood this European mind-set, and it thus became the lifelong mission of Blyden and like-minded thinkers to seek the "vindication of the African race." Part of that mission was to restore the confidence, self-respect, and pride of the African following several centuries of the slave trade and slavery; and these critics, chief among whom was Blyden, were also committed to debunking the notion that the African race was inferior to that of Europeans and therefore intellectually less than equal. To successfully refute European misconceptions of Africans, Blyden became a prolific scholar, dedicated to the production of knowledge geared toward what can be described as an Africa-centered interpretation of the history and cultures of the continent and its peoples; an interpretation that took close cognizance of historical continuity,[3] with the objective of subverting the prevalent nineteenth-century Hegelian misrepresentation of Africa as an entity with no history it could call its own.

To Blyden, not only did Africa have a past, the African personality was indeed reflective of that worthy past. Thus, in a May 1893 lecture titled "Study and Race," he cautioned an audience of the Young Men's Literary Association of Sierra Leone not to "do away with our African personality and be lost, if possible, in another race,"[4] lest Africans risked losing their humanity. It is in this context that Blyden's vehement denunciation of the curriculum of mission schools can be better understood. He seems to have steadfastly believed that the European clergy who ran these schools were equally steadfastly devoted to a program of cultural alienation, which would be ultimately detrimental to the interest of Krio society and other subject peoples in Africa. While he was just as committed to the spread of the Christian faith in West Africa, he nonetheless advocated the dissemination of the scriptures in ways that would not be inimical to the development of the "African personality," but instead would take cognizance of the cultural characteristics of the native societies among whom Christian morality was being disseminated. He was convinced that European Christian morality, as it was being propagated by the clergy, was incapable of contributing to the developmental needs of local societies, as the mission schools, and the church, seemed dedicated to producing educated Africans who would have been disabused of their capacity to retain pride in their history, customs, and institutions.

Blyden in particular sought to contrast the failure of Christianity to engender racial and cultural pride in the products of mission schools with the teachings of that other agency of "civilization" in Africa, Islam. To Blyden, the teaching of the Qur'an by the Islamic ulema was evidence of the capacity of Islam to inculcate the benefits of a major world civilization without the cultural subversiveness of European Christendom. He noted in the preface to the second edition of his magisterial work *Christianity, Islam and the Negro Race* that the work had been "originally written with a view of instructing Negro youth in Christian lands eager to study the history, character and destiny of their race"; he had been frustrated prior to the publication of the book by "what the white man had said in his own way and for his own purposes" about Africa and Africans.[5]

Before Blyden's arrival in Sierra Leone, relations between the Christian missions, particularly the CMS, and the non-Christian factions within colonial society had been quite fractious during the early decades of the nineteenth century. With the providing of Western education being utilized as an essential instrument of religious conversion by the evangelical missions, as well as a means of creating a social dichotomy between Christians and non-Christians, Blyden came to recognize the urgency of extending the benefits of Western education to those inhabitants of the colony who had elected to retain their allegiance to non-Christian faiths, particularly Islam. Upon his assuming the role of champion of Muslim interests in colonial

Freetown in the late nineteenth and early twentieth centuries, the providing of education to Muslim Krio consequently helped in transforming the socio-religious dynamics within the colony. It also had the effect of rendering him susceptible to political diatribes from his detractors within the political and religious establishment as well as, paradoxically, in the Muslim community in Freetown. Muslims in Krio society often wondered why, in spite of his consistency in defending the rights of Muslims and the appropriateness and need for cultural self-consciousness and expression by Africans, Blyden was always garbed like a Victorian English dandy. By all indications he was as enigmatic a figure in Liberia, where he had initially settled, as he was after relocating to Sierra Leone, and would remain so for much of his life. Nonetheless, in spite of the evident personal challenges engendered by his growing engagement with the religious and cultural debates in the colony, Edward Blyden ultimately played an invaluable role in the development of Western education in the history of Sierra Leone.

EDUCATION IN FREETOWN BEFORE THE MID-NINETEENTH CENTURY

In an article in which he sought to trace the evolution of theological studies in Sierra Leone, Canon Harry Sawyerr notes that when a settlement for freed slaves was established in 1787, the patrons of what was to become a haven for manumitted slaves, and captives en route to the New World, were very clear about the relevance of education, inter alia, in the new community and therefore gave specific instructions "that a church, a fort and a school are to be built." Sawyer observes that the Church Missionary Society was charged with providing "the means necessary to the religious improvement" of the colonists, a charge that the CMS interpreted to require a theological curriculum in so far as the educational needs of the colonists were concerned.[6] Thus from the very early stages of the colony of Sierra Leone, education was not only provided by Christian missions, but was also perceived and utilized as an essential instrument of evangelicalism in Sierra Leone as well as across the African continental in general. This may be attributed to the efforts at social and cultural engineering undertaken by the commercial oligarchy of London and the established Church of England who were instrumental in the founding of the settlement.

Thus, from the late eighteenth century, the CMS emphasized a theological curriculum in the mission schools, with the latter becoming the conduit through which the evangelical agenda of the established Church of England was effected, thereby converting the vast majority of Liberated Africans to Christianity. Consequently, the European missions, including the CMS, Wesleyans, Methodists, and others, were able to create an educated elite of mostly Christian converts. Only a handful of Muslims had succeeded in obtaining Western education prior to the mid-nineteenth century. However, the dearth of Muslim Krio among the emergent educated elite was due less to any evident policy to restrict admission to Christian converts than to a conscious decision by parents of Muslim children to keep their offspring from enrolling in mission schools.

The reluctance of Muslim Krio to enroll their children in Christian schools was due to a pervasive suspicion in the colony Muslim communities of the intentions of Christian missionaries, whose teaching methods did not recognize and/or establish a fundamental difference between literary and denominational instructions. The Christian missions in Sierra Leone, as elsewhere in Africa, were certainly aware of the potent instrumentality of schools as magnets for conversion and were therefore reluctant to separate literary and scriptural teaching. As a result, while Muslim parents were increasingly aware of the material benefits of Western education, they remained reluctant to enroll their children in the mission schools. The reluctance of Muslims to send their children to Christian schools was also due to a need to ensure the growth of Islamic education in the Muslim communities. The elders of these communities were concerned that the enrollment of Muslim children in Christian schools would lead to a loss of the important knowledge base provided by the Qur'an madrassas in the colony. In fact, some believed the Christian schools represented a systematic threat to the availability of Qur'anic knowledge in the colony. Therefore, rather than sending their children to mission schools, many simply opted to enroll their offspring in the local madrassa, known as Ile Kewu, where the young pupils were instructed by Muslim scholars from the immigrant Mandinka, Fula, and Soso communities in the colony.

The use of Muslim instructors from the interior for the purposes of Arabic education among the Muslim Krio was also motivated by a decision made by the colony administration in the early nineteenth century to provide official support to schools under the supervision of the CMS.[7] The decision of the general superintendent of schools in 1827 expressly required an adherence to what the Office of the Superintendent characterized as the "moral and religious conduct" clause by teachers and students alike. The CMS was charged with the mandate of selecting only those students deemed appropriate for admission to the colony schools; the criteria for admittance to these schools were henceforth to be determined by such moral and religious conduct and the "inclinations" of children whose religious predispositions were shaped by their family settings. Thus children whose parents were either Muslims or worshippers of Sango and Ogun were deemed unsuitable for enrollment in the schools, and the office of the general superintendent of schools decreed that such students "will cease to be maintained at the expense of the government."[8]

Furthermore, the CMS adopted what amounted to a class- and gender-based policy in its recruitment of students in the mid-1800s, as admission records evidenced a preponderance of students from families belonging to the upper strata of colonial society.[9] The official pamphlet of the CMS Grammar School, for instance, even boasted of providing "an education of a higher character than that given in the ordinary schools." The Fourah Bay Institution, also founded by the CMS, emphasized its objective of educating "a certain number of young men for the Christian ministry in order to enable them to proceed as missionaries into the interior of the country."[10] The emphatic objective of providing education to young males, who would subsequently be dispatched across West Africa to spread Christian scriptures, was universally shared by the evangelical missions, including the Anglicans, Wesleyans, Lutherans, Methodists, and Baptists.

Consequently, educational policy was geared toward the creation of a hierarchical structure in colonial Freetown. The ultimate objective of this policy was reflected in a dispatch sent to the colonial office in London by Governor Neil Campbell in 1827, in which the governor suggested that the period of schooling for some colony children be limited to three years (i.e., for children ages nine, ten, and eleven years), as these children were to be trained with a modicum of educational instruction so that "a considerable expense would be saved and the pupils would be much happier and fitter for cultivating the soil or other labour, for which a long residence at school is in a great degree injurious." Insofar as Governor Campbell was evidently concerned, three years of schooling was "fully sufficient for the moral and religious impressions necessary for them in the situation inevitably destined for them."[11] The prescribed destiny of these students was clearly that of tillers of the soil, while a select few would become teachers and preachers. It was under these circumstances that Muslims in the Liberated African communities of the colony seemed to have determined very early on to keep their children out of the colony mission schools, and opted instead for an alternative educational system of Arabic instruction in the neighborhood Ile-Kewu, or sending them off to Arabic madrassas in interior centers

of culture and learning such as Futa Toro, Futa Jallon, and even as far away
as Fez, Morocco.

ILE-KEWU (QUR'ANIC SCHOOLS)

The debate over the usefulness and/or insidious nature of Western education provided by the evangelical missions was predated by the institution
known as Ile-Kewu, which was the primary venue for the dissemination of
Islamic education in the colony; it was the equivalent of the primary school
system run by the evangelical missions. Muslim children were introduced
to the Qur'an scriptures at the Ile-Kewu at an early age, and were tutored
on scriptural *sura* (verses) that they learned by rote on wooden tablets
(*wala'a*). They were required to memorize each chapter of the Qur'an, but
the young students were also introduced to the obligations of practitioners
of the faith, including the fundamental pillars of Islam. Primary education in these schools also stressed the history of the Islamic faith, as well
as the cultural environment of Bedouin Arab society of Mecca, in which
the prophet Muhammad experienced his awakening to the existence of an
omnipotent, omniscient, and omnipresent God (or Allah) in his encounter
with the archangel Gabriel (*malaikat-ul Gibril*). The Ile-Kewu was also
the institution in which the young pupils were introduced to Islamic culture outside the immediate environs of their family settings, the environment where it could be said that their lives as cultural Muslims actually
got started. The alfas (*ulema*) of these schools presided over what has been
described as "an important seminal institution" that served as the locus for
the distribution of Islamic literature, but they also served to ensure the sustainability of the nascent Muslim community in colonial Freetown.

By the 1840s, following a prolonged period of religious persecution, the
people of Fourah Bay, Fula Town, and Aberdeen began to devote their
attention to the establishment of these Islamic madrassas in their localities. As noted above, the teachers in these schools were almost invariably
recruited from the immigrant Muslim scholarly community from the interior who had played a primary role in Islamic missionary activity in the
colony and in the rural villages on the outskirts of Freetown. In several
instances, some Muslim families opted to have their children enrolled in
the Islamic educational institutions (or *Karanthe*) of the interior to study
under more renowned Muslim scholars, rather than sending them to the
local Ile-kewu following their initial period of study in the colony. Many
Muslim Krio traders involved in the colony-interior trade often took their

sons and entrusted them to the care of the leading clerics "upcountry" for tutelage.[12] The upcountry Karanthe institutions were far removed from the Christian institutions of the colony and thus may have been perceived as being more conducive to proper Islamic instruction by some of the Muslim Krio, mostly because of the prestige of the scholars who supervised the interior institutions.

Many of the Muslim Krio had made a calculated decision to adhere to Islam and pursue Islamic knowledge for themselves and their children, clearly because they seem to have identified with the shared outlook of Blyden and Sir Samuel Lewis, one of the prominent Krio luminaries of the nineteenth century, that the ulema who supervised the madrassas were part of a religion that was providing a crucial service, in terms of scholarship, as well as liturgically, to their society in ways that the rival Christian evangelical groups could not. Lewis, a Christian, pointedly denounced those Europeans who sought to cast aspersions on Islam by suggesting that the spread of the religion in the colony was attributable "to its sensualism." He asserted that "such an explanation is, at once, unworthy of a great religion and insulting to the Negro race, although it is one to which some European travelers of recent date—more qualified to traduce an unfortunate people than to engage in the philosophical investigation of their character and history—have not been ashamed to attribute its rapid spread and its influence."[13] The respect harbored by the Muslim Krio for the scholars of the interior was not unfounded. Blyden was himself highly impressed by the intellectual rigors of Islamic education in the institutions of the interior; he subsequently noted that the scholars of the interior were not only highly learned in the scriptures, they were also exposed to a vast array of Islamic literature in the hinterland, which he had seen firsthand during his travels after 1872 when he was designated the colony government's agent to the interior. He observed that Muslim scholars located in interior centers were quite conversant with the debate on Islam and Christianity in the global context and noted, as well, their capacity to read and comment on the works of some of the leading scholars of the Islamic world. He reported a personal encounter with a Muslim scholar in the interior who engaged his coreligionists on works by leading Muslim scholars such as Rahmat Allah's review of the *Mizzan al-Haqq* (Balance of Truth) by Carl Pfander, a nineteenth-century work then known for its attack against Islam (*CIN*, 4).[14]

The Muslim Krio preference for the educational environment of the interior can also be attributed to the social organization of the Islamized societies. Blyden's travels in the interior gave him the opportunity to observe and comment on the social organization of the various societies he visited, and to compare and contrast these societies based on their religious and social mores. According to him, there was an unmistakable "difference in the methods of government [as well as] in the general regulations of society" in the localities he visited. He noted the disciplined adherence of the faithful in Muslim communities to the "devotional exercises" of praying five times a day. "After the labours of the day they assemble in groups near the mosque to hear the Koran recited, or the Traditions [Hadith] or some other book read." He further observed:

> In traversing the region of country between Sierra Leone and Futah Jallo in 1873, we passed through populous Pagan towns; and the transition from these to Mohammedan districts was striking. When we left a Pagan and entered a Mohammedan community, we at once noticed that we had entered a moral atmosphere widely separated from, and loftier far than, the one we had left. We discovered that the character, feelings, and conditions of the people were profoundly altered and improved. (CIN, 7)

The impressions made on Blyden by the social organization of the Islamized societies of the interior had a profound impact on his thinking regarding the efficacy of the two world religions in West Africa. He developed a thesis in this regard that would ultimately alienate him from his fellow CMS missionaries, especially his assertion that Islam had a more progressive impact on the African than did Christianity. While he had what can be characterized as a nuanced perspective, he asserted that

> the Mohammedan Negro is a much better Mohammedan than the Christian Negro is a Christian, because the Muslim Negro, as a learner, is a disciple, not an imitator. A disciple, when freed from leading-strings, may become a producer; an imitator never rises above a mere copyist. With the disciple progress is from within; the imitator grows by accretion from without. The learning acquired by a disciple gives him capacity; that gained by an imitator terminates in itself. The one becomes a capable man; the other is a mere sciolist. This explains the difference between the Mohammedan and the Christian Negro. (CIN, 44)

Blyden's point of view was clearly engendered by his close observation of relations between the European clergy and their African counterparts and the general congregation. Moreover, he was clearly impressed by the knowledge base and intellectual integrity of the Muslim scholars. In January 1873, he accompanied Governor John Pope Hennessy to Gbile, a town located on the banks of the Great Scarcies about sixty miles northeast of the colony, and a center of Islamic learning and culture. He was profoundly impressed by what he labeled the Mohammedan Literary Institution and the head of the institution, "the venerable" Sheikh Fodé Tarawally, whose immense library must have had a tremendous impact on the visitors from Freetown. Governor Pope Hennessy asked the government Arabic writer to make a list of the principal works in the library and, according to Blyden, the colonial official listed eighty-nine volumes, including the "*Commentary of Jelaladdin on the Koran, Commentary of Beidhawi, Traditions of Bukhari; Law Book*, by Khalil Ishaq (2 vols.); *Rizalat of Imam, Malik,* ... *Makamat of Hariri, Ancient* History ... written by Arabs," and "volumes of Prayers, Poetry, Rhetoric, History, composed by Mandingo and Foulah authors" (*CIN*, 72). Such a knowledge base located in the Muslim societies of the interior may have accounted for the inclination of many of the Muslim Krio in the colony to send their children to these places for educational instruction.

Blyden was more positively inclined toward the Islamic faith and believed that the religion, unlike Christianity (or more precisely, European Christendom), was not aimed at politically subjugating the African. To him, "Mohammedan conquests mean subjugation to the Koran, and not to Arab or Turk" (*CIN*, v). On the contrary, he perceived the church as an instrument of political repression, which the colonial and evangelical missions utilized to "produce absolute outward submission" (*CIN*, 38). Blyden may well have been equally impressed by the inclinations of the Muslim Krio toward cultural inclusivity vis-à-vis the peoples of the interior states, quite unlike their Christian kinsfolk in the colony. They were certainly even more inclined toward cultural integration with their fellow Muslims from the hinterland. For them, the Islamic values shared in common with the emigrants from the interior transcended ethnic identity. Indeed, it is in terms of Freetown-interior education that I interpret David Skinner's observation that "Muslim education developed in a context of extensive economic, social and political interaction which produced an interlocking network of indigenous and assimilated élite."[15] Muslim Krio parents were less concerned about their children imbibing the values of the interior peoples, since the elders of Fula Town, Fourah Bay, and Aberdeen shared a common agenda of facilitating Islamic knowledge among the younger generation of Muslim Krio.[16]

The decision of Muslim Krio to restrict their children to the Arabic schools ultimately served to increase the number of local clerics within the Muslim communities of the colony. Thus by the 1860s and 1870s, the Fula, Mandinka, and Soso Islamic teachers were no longer needed by the Freetown Muslims to provide instruction in the local madrassas. Young Muslim Krio students who had been sent away to study in such far-off centers of learning, culture, and trade as Futa Toro, Futa Jallon, and elsewhere in the interior returned home to take up prominent positions within their local communities in the colony. Thus, by 1872, one of these former students, Mohammed Sanusie, who had studied in Futa Jallon, had such an impressive command of the Arabic language, in addition to his fluency in English, that his services were deemed essential to the colonial administration's civil bureaucracy. He was, as already discussed, consequently appointed to the position of government Arabic eriter and interpreter in the Native Affairs Department. Another former student, Alfa Amara, who had received his tutelage at Dinguiraye, was by 1875 installed as Imam masjid of the Fula Town jamaat.[17] Sanusie and Amara of Fula Town and Gheirawanieu George of Fourah Bay subsequently gained considerable social and political prominence in the colony in the late nineteenth century, with Sanusie later securing an appointment as lecturer of Arabic and Islamic studies at Fourah Bay College in the 1870s. Given their integration into the colonial civil bureaucracy, it was hardly surprising that these men were becoming quite amenable to the idea of extending Western education to the Muslim Krio community. The arrival of Dr. Blyden in Sierra Leone during this period would open a new chapter in the history of Western education in the colony.

EDWARD BLYDEN AND WESTERN EDUCATION

Blyden's arrival in Freetown in 1871 was nothing less than a watershed in the history of Krio society, particularly that of the Muslim Krio. In the two decades following his relocation to Freetown from Liberia, he played a pivotal role, alongside the likes of Alfa Amara, Mohammed Sanusie, and Gheirawanieu George, in propelling the movement for the inclusion of non-Christians in the government-assisted schools of Freetown. As noted earlier, until his arrival in Sierra Leone, only a handful of Muslim Krio had been able to obtain a Western education. Even though he encountered enormous challenges in his efforts to assuage the fears of the older generation of Muslim Krio who were steadfastly reluctant to enroll their children in the colony schools, as well as in his dealings with entrenched forces within the colony administration and the evangelical groups who were not particularly enthused about the inclusion of Muslim children in the educational institutions, Blyden and others remained indefatigable and unrestrained in their mission of extending Western education to the younger generation of Muslim Krio. The ultimate success of this advocacy served to bring about a gradual change in attitudes and assumptions across the religious divide at the official level, and served to usher in a period of cooperation between Muslim Krio and the colony administration in Freetown.[18]

Blyden's role and place in the discourse on colonialism, Christian evangelicalism, and Islam in Africa was rather complex. His championing of the education of Muslims in what was deemed a Christian colony should not be construed as an effort to promote Islam at the expense of Christianity. Indeed, and quite the contrary, his initial efforts were geared toward utilizing Islam as a conduit through which the Christian faith could be established in the African continent without compromising the integrity of an essentially African cultural landscape. Unlike his fellow clergymen in the European missions, Blyden perceived Islam and Arabic as "unifying agencies" that would assist his grand proposition of synthesizing "the values of the Western Sudan and those of the Christian West."[19] He was quite cognizant of the anxieties of the Christian missionaries who may have perceived his efforts and his writings as having had the effect of undermining the church in West Africa, and, therefore, he sought to reassure his European Christian counterparts of his loyalty to the church. In his preface to the second edition of *Christianity, Islam and the Negro Race*, Blyden expressed his regret that a reviewer of his work in the *Church Missionary Intelligencer* "proceed[ed] upon the assumption that Mohammedanism is eulogised in this volume to the disparagement of Christianity" (*CIN*, iii). However, he was also quick to point out what he perceived as the cultural condescension and ultimate inefficacy of the efforts of European evangelists, whom he perceived as treating their potential converts as constituting a "*tabula rasa*"; he therefore instructed his Christian counterparts on the need for "a careful consideration of the elements in the methods of foreign Christian workers in Africa which prevent wider and more permanent results" (iii).

His criticisms were aimed at the pedagogical methods of the evangelical missionaries, not at Christianity writ large. Indeed, as he put it, his work simply constituted a "serious arraignment of the methods of the Christian teachers" (*CIN*, iii), who demonstrated an attitude of racial condescension toward the people whom they wished to convert. Blyden's immediate challenge was to convince his European colleagues of the need to emulate the flexibility of Islam in African societies. From his perspective, it was clearly the "more elastic social and political system" of Islam that was enabling the Muslims to make inroads into African societies. Thus he advocated the need for European clergy to recognize the basic humanity of African converts to Christianity and to allow the latter the freedom and space that will facilitate "social as well as spiritual advancement." He was afraid that church and colonial officials were incapable of recognizing the "inherent energies" of the African people and thus would seek to "[make] the Negro what they think he ought to be, by the plastic hand of European religious organisations and the moulding force of European laws" (CIN, iv).

Blyden evidently realized that until evangelical and colonial officials made a conscious and conscientious effort to rethink their attitudes and assumptions vis-à-vis the African peoples, Islam would continue to outpace Christianity, because the African peoples clearly resented the European "regulations and laws," which they viewed as "not only despotic but absurd" (CIN, iv). He was equally worried about the writings and pronouncements of evangelical groups and missionaries regarding the prophet Muhammad, who was being denounced as a "false prophet" (vi). He cautioned that until such denunciations, and what he characterized as "the unchastened conceptions of the Middle Ages," were abandoned by the European clergy, the teachings of the church would continue to face significant challenges (vi). Blyden was also quite eager to instruct his European counterparts on the common ancestral origins of the two monotheistic world religions, as well as other shared commonalities of the two faiths. He noted that just as "Christians speak of Abraham as 'the Father of the Faithful,'" Muslims also believe Islam to be "a revival of the Abrahamic faith and worship" (ix). He further noted that the Qur'an acknowledges "the Divine authority of the Scriptures of the Old and New Testaments" (ix).

Thus, unlike many of his fellow clergymen, Blyden did not believe the two world religions were mutually exclusive. He therefore maintained that it would ultimately be to the advantage of Christianity if the followers of the faith, especially the evangelical groups, would "give up their bitter hostility and study Islam . . . with greater sympathy and liberality" (CIN, vi). He recognized the implicit connections between the teachings of the church and the civilizing mission of the colonial state, an agenda Blyden did not necessarily share in common with his fellow clergymen. Consequently, he called for a cessation of the "indiscriminate Europeanising" efforts of the evangelical and colonial officials, which he rightly perceived as an obstacle to the successful spread of the Christian faith among the local peoples. He advised that when the cultures of the local peoples were respected by the missionaries, there would be "nothing to prevent Christianity from spreading among the Pagan tribes, and from eventually uprooting the imperfect Mohammedanism which so extensively prevails" (26). Islam, in Blyden's view, was to serve as but a conduit for the ultimate triumph of Christianity. This viewpoint would not be lost on some members of the Muslim Krio community of colonial Freetown, who would later challenge his efforts to extend Western education to Muslims in the colony.

In a meeting with Muslim Krio leaders following his arrival in the colony, Blyden informed them that he was relocating to Freetown in order to help spread the Word of God across the African continent. He informed the elders that "good men in England [i.e., the CMS] had sent me to reside in Sierra Leone that I might teach the Arabic language to young men who are to be the future leaders and missionaries, that they may be able to understand the Muslim *ulema* and carry the Word of God to Futa, Jenne and Timbuktu."[20] Blyden further informed the Muslim leaders of his intention of establishing Muslim schools in the hinterland. He subsequently shared his impressions of his meeting with the Muslim leaders in an 1871 letter to his close friend and CMS confidant, Rev. Henry Venn, noting that he quoted "several passages of the Quran showing the testimony which their own book bear to the divine origin of the Christian scriptures."[21]

Blyden was clearly aware of the negative attitude of the European and African clergy toward Islam and Muslims in Freetown. He observed in his correspondence with Venn that the Christian missionaries were hardly cognizant of the intellectual depth of such Muslim scholars as Mohammed Sanusie of Fula Town. He noted that not only was Sanusie a very liberal Muslim, but that the latter was quite versed in Christian literature and was desirous of seeing the gospel conveyed to the peoples of the hinterland. While this may or may not have been entirely accurate, Blyden suggested that the European and African clergy were unaware of Sanusie's stance. He lamented that the "missionaries here, native and European, excepting such men as Bishops Vidal and Bowen and Mr. Reichardt, have been accustomed to look with contempt upon the Mohammedans, and classing them with the pagan tribes have thus regarded their literary pretensions as unworthy of examination."[22] He noted that such an unfortunate attitude on the part of the missionaries had merely served to undercut the credibility and therefore the effectiveness of their proselytizing efforts among the

Muslim Krio. Blyden recalled that the Reverend Reichardt had intimated to him during a personal conversation he had with the CMS evangelist in England that his (Reichardt's) efforts to reach out to Muslims had been subverted by some of his fellow clergy in Freetown.

It was therefore not surprising that Blyden was determined to employ a different method of spreading the Christian faith in Freetown. His method of choice following his growing acquaintance with the leading Muslim Alfas in Freetown, especially those at Fula Town, was to extend Western education to not only the Muslim Krio but to the entire Muslim population of the colony and hinterland of Sierra Leone. He proposed to utilize the opportunity to educate, as it were, the adherents of both Islam and Christianity on the essential qualities of each faith. He committed himself to disabusing the European and African Christian clergy of their long-held contemptuous attitude toward Islam and adherents of the faith. He seemed to have concluded that by aligning himself with the modernist forces in the Muslim Krio community, he would simultaneously enhance the mission of spreading Christianity and Western education.

This method ultimately proved effective, but it initially engendered significant opposition to Blyden's efforts in the community of Fourah Bay. Some Muslim leaders, such as Ligaly Savage, were vehemently opposed to his efforts at extending Western education in the community. Savage had spent about two decades pursuing advanced studies in the Qur'an and the Arabic language in Dinguiraye, and he returned home in the 1870s to assume the position of assistant Imam at the Fourah Bay mosque.[23] His sojourn in Dinguiraye had the effect of exposing him to the ideological views of orthodox Muslims who had been exposed to the Umarian revolution, and thus he sought to introduce more stringent Islamic mores in his community upon his return home. The situation in Freetown could be compared to Saint-Louis in Senegal, where cooperation between French officials and Muslim leaders like Hamat Ndiaye Anne (1813–1879) engendered a division within the Muslim community. As Robinson notes of the situation in Saint-Louis, "Muslims attracted to the preaching of Al-Hajj Umar criticized Hamat for his close association with the administration."[24] The reactions to Hamat's accommodating of the French administration in Senegal was similar to that of Ligaly Savage and others in the Fourah Bay community who became suspicious of Muslims in Freetown inclined to cooperate with the colony administration in Sierra Leone. Ligaly Savage was even more suspicious of Blyden, who, while championing the cause of Islam nonetheless remained reluctant to renounce his Christian faith.

Savage was particularly vociferous in his opposition to Blyden when the latter started teaching a group of Muslim students at the local mosque; since Blyden was a Christian, this was anathema to Savage and other orthodox Muslims, and the class was soon suspended.[25] But Savage's was fast becoming a minority point of view, while Blyden was becoming firmly embraced by the majority faction in the community, and it was not long before he would become the undisputed champion of the cause of political and educational advancement of the Muslim Krio in the colony. Blyden's social and political activism was, however, not limited to the Muslim Krio community. His advocacy transcended local issues; he was passionately concerned about the limitations of the education provided by the European missions and had begun advocating for an institution of higher learning, with particular emphasis on the need for the establishment of a region-wide West African university as early as 1872.

Blyden's quest for an institution of higher learning under the control of West Africans received much impetus following his visit to the Muslim institute at Gbile on the Great Scarcies. Following his travels in the interior, Blyden began editing the *Negro*, an outlet that he used quite effectively in furthering his Pan-Africanist ideas as well as a forum for the airing of the grievances and frustrations of the colony population. The newspaper also reflected the aspirations and demands of the peoples of both the colony and the hinterland; Blyden unhesitatingly voiced his displeasure about the inadequacy of mission education in meeting the needs of the peoples of Sierra Leone. He pointedly compared the education provided by Muslim scholars to that offered in the Christian mission schools, maintaining that the pedagogical methods of the mission teachers essentially served to undermine the integrity of African cultures, rather than enhance them.[26] Hence his advocacy for a West African university, effectively a Pan-African educational institution, under the direct control of African scholars, which would serve to facilitate the educational development of West African societies and simultaneously enhance the cultures of the local peoples. Blyden envisaged such an institution to benefit from the scholarly expertise of Africans on the continent as well as from others in the diaspora in the Atlantic World. He made it quite clear that missionary education, unlike Islamic education, lacked the capacity to foster self-reliance and originality in the local students. Rather than uncritically imbibing European "civilizing" values, he called on colony students to look inward to the interior for educational inspiration.

Clearly, Blyden was far from advocating a wholesale abandonment of Western education. In fact, he was simply calling for a modification of the educational structure and curriculum offered by the mission schools, and advocating for one that reflected a tacit recognition of the characteristics of the local populations and a de-emphasis of Victorian English values in its instruction. The education curriculum he advocated had at its core such essential subjects as mathematics and the sciences. Additionally, he pointed out that the curriculum should also include Arabic "and some of the principal native languages—by means of which we may have intelligent intercourse with the millions accessible to us in the interior, and learn more of our own country" (*CIN*, 101). Blyden's rationale for the new curriculum was a rather farsighted one; he adroitly pointed out that the products of the mission schools were much more familiar with the geography and customs of foreign countries (i.e., European and American), and "can talk glibly of London, Berlin, Paris and Washington; know all about Gladstone, Bismarck, Gambetta, and Hayes; [but hardly] anything about Musahdu, Medina, Kankan, or Segu—only a few hundred miles from us." He therefore dismissed this reality as "disgraceful." Blyden was equally cognizant of the gender inequity of the education provided by the colony schools. Thus he called for the inclusion of young girls in the educational institutions; he observed that he could not envisage "why our sisters should not receive exactly the same general culture as we do," meaning his male gender (101–2). He was also careful to point out that the inclusion of female students in the proposed college would have profound implications for the progress of African society at large.

On the whole, Blyden manifested a profound understanding of the need for a rethinking of the philosophical and pedagogical methods adopted by the mission schools in West Africa; behind the emphasis on the three R's—reading, (w)riting, and (a)rithmetic—by the European educators was the colonial agenda of the three C's, as noted earlier. No West African colony better exemplified this educational agenda than Freetown. It was in the pursuit of fulfilling this agenda that the mission schools placed great emphasis on inculcating in the students the importance of Victorian English values and cultural mores, and the outright exclusion of indigenous cultural values and social mores. The academic disciplines offered were taught in the context of Christian scriptural values, laden with Anglo-Saxon morality. The schools also sought to disabuse the students of their cultures and customs, including an imposition of English as the only language allowed on school campuses. The biblical stricture of "Spare the rod and spoil the child" was constantly put into practical use, not only to ensure the avoidance of patois by students on campus, but also to encourage them to adopt European ways. Blyden was acutely aware of the prevalence of this practice and therefore sought to change "the method." As he noted,

> What is needed in the education of the Negro on this continent is not so much a change in the subjects ... but a change in the whole method is required. In our contact with the Christian world, our teachers have of necessity been Europeans, and they have taught us books too much, and things too little—forms of expression, and very little the importance of thought. The notion, still common among Negroes—educated Negroes I mean—is, that the most important part of knowledge consists in knowing what other men—foreigners—have said about things, and even about Africa and about themselves. ... Very few among us have got past this step. Hence, some of us are found repeating things against ourselves, which are thoroughly false and injurious to us, and only because we read them in books, or have heard them from foreign teachers. (CIN, 253)

Thus Blyden believed it was imperative that a rethinking of the pedagogical and philosophical methods adopted in the mission schools be undertaken. He urged the authorities, and educated Africans in particular, to consider the need for an inclusion in the school curricula of "subjects of enquiry ... about which the truth is yet to be found out—peoples and customs and systems about which correct ideas are to be formed" (CIN, 253–54).

BLYDEN AS CMS AGENT

Born on the island of St. Thomas in the West Indies in 1832, Edward Wilmot Blyden relocated to West Africa in 1851, initially settling in Liberia. He would go on to play a pivotal and historic role in the affairs of West African societies for the next half century, beginning with his editing of the *Liberia Herald* in the mid-1850s.[27] Thus, by the time he arrived in Sierra Leone, his reputation was already well established. His writings and speeches were widely distributed in the colony, and he was much admired by Christians and Muslims alike. His reputation was further enhanced by his continued advocacy for the uplift of the "African personality." He dismissed educationists who stressed what he perceived as the "foreign

educational philosophy" that placed undue emphasis on European historical personalities and on the "examination of alien biology or geography."[28]
Instead, as has been indicated, Blyden advocated the establishment of educational institutions that would be geared toward instilling in the African a
sense of cultural self-awareness and racial pride. He called for the teaching
of not just Islamic philosophy and Arabic but African history as well, at a
time when the prevailing European school of thought was dismissive of an
African consciousness of history. To Blyden, an educational curriculum
that emphasized African history would provide evidence of the significance
of the African past, thereby enhancing "the dignity of the African race," and
finally debunking the Hegelian notion of a lack of contribution by Africa
to world history.

Blyden's relocation to Sierra Leone in 1871 marked the beginning of his
tenure as a missionary of the CMS. Having run afoul of the Liberian political establishment due to political and personal differences, he was assisted
by Rev. Henry Venn in obtaining the evangelical position from the CMS
Executive Central Committee in London.[29] On 24 August 1871, Blyden informed Venn of his safe arrival in Sierra Leone from Liverpool, where he
had spent a brief sojourn following his departure from Liberia. In his letter
to Venn, Blyden informed his friend of the warm reception he received
in Freetown after a thirteen-day trip on the high seas. He noted that the
people of the colony were not unaware of the political challenges he had
experienced in Liberia and had extended their sympathies while welcom-
ing him to Freetown. He also reported that some of the Muslim clerics of
the colony had paid him a courtesy call, and others who had not been able
to do so had sent him "kindly messages."[30]

Blyden's knowledge of Arabic and his familiarity with Islamic literature
served to motivate him to engage the Muslim Krio scholars in Freetown.
But he was even more motivated to extend his evangelical activities to the
interior states, where there were much larger Muslim populations. He
therefore informed Venn that he had been in correspondence with the
Fula and others who wished to receive Arabic instruction from him, and
made known his intention to learn Pular, the language of the Fula, presumably in order to better communicate with his potential students and fellow
scholars and, to use his formulation, "to strive to establish Christian schools
in the great Mohammedan centres."[31]

As Fyfe observed, Blyden wanted to preach to Muslims "not to destroy
Islam but [to] purify it as a foundation for Christianity." He subsequently
traveled to the interior and succeeded in learning to speak the language

of the Fula, following which he proceeded to translate the Bible into Pular using the Arabic alphabet. His rationale for the latter endeavor, as he informed Venn, was based on his conviction that Muslims would be less enthusiastic about reading Roman letters, noting that "a strange language is always repulsive."[32] His initial request to be assigned to the interior for the purpose of preaching among the Fula and others was received with reticence by his CMS superiors. Consequently, he betrayed his frustrations with the CMS mission, and what he sensed to be a deeply entrenched and pervasive anti-Islamic sentiment within the mission, by vehemently denouncing the denominational and sectarian policies of not just the CMS, but also all the other Christian missions in the colony. He castigated the missions for policies that he believed would have the ultimate effect of transplanting "European ecclesiastical cleavages in West Africa."[33] His unconventional approach was clearly alarming to the CMS.

Blyden's evangelical method of preaching to the Muslims and other non-Christians in the colony in less doctrinaire fashion was clearly quite unorthodox and different from that of the missionary establishment in Africa. Being a proponent of the notion of the African personality, he was not prepared to participate in what he construed as efforts by the European evangelists to transform their converts into caricatures of Europeans. He was quite impressed by what he perceived as the natural disinclination of the Muslim Krio toward inculcating English Victorian values. As a result of his increasingly close relations with the leading scholars of the Muslim community in the colony, Blyden came to appreciate the evident cultural self-awareness of Muslim Krio leaders, most of whom evinced a disdain for the class-consciousness and the embracing of Victorian English values evidenced in the attitudes and assumptions of upper-middle-class Christian Krio. His time spent with the scholars at Fourah Bay and Fula Town allowed him to develop a better understanding of the "recognizable social system and values" of the communities. His close interaction with the Muslim Krio scholars also resulted in his rethinking of the use of education as a means of spreading the gospel.[34]

Blyden was quite impressed with the scholars, who demonstrated a profound knowledge of Islamic philosophy and Western commentaries on Islam. In his correspondence with Venn, he allowed that the Fula Town Muslim scholars had visited and inspected his library of Arabic works and demonstrated great familiarity with "the commentary [on the Qur'an] of Zamakshari, the Makamat of Hariri with De Sacy's notes, a work they did not suppose to exist in print—but with which they were thoroughly familiar, and Hugel's concordance to the Koran."[35] He observed that while the Fula Town scholars "had never before seen as extensive a commentary on the Koran as that of Zamakshari," they were nonetheless quite conversant with the commentaries of other contemporary scholars, such as Jelal al-Din. Blyden subsequently became part and parcel of the Fula Town community where he spent much of his time, and was soon given the name of Muktarr (meaning "the chosen one").[36]

On 25 October 1871, Blyden attended a meeting of the CMS Church Conference held at the grammar school. The major item on the agenda was the "duty of the church in relation to the Mohammedan and heathen population."[37] After an introduction by the Reverend James Johnson, the meeting heard presentations from members of the clergy and lay preachers. All confessed to what they described as "past neglect on the part of the church towards the Mohammedan population." Blyden noted with regret that notwithstanding such confessions, the conference adjourned without deciding on a meaningful and comprehensive method of dealing with relations between the church and the Muslim community. He complained to Venn that "no method was suggested which appeared to me likely to meet the necessities of the case." Instead, the clergy urged that the status quo be maintained; according to Blyden, some of the clergy were downright disdainful of the Muslims in the colony. The Reverend Knodler, for instance, suggested somewhat dismissively that few of the Muslims had any understanding of Arabic "better than the generality of Roman Catholics understand Latin." Blyden was consequently very disappointed with the performance of the European clergy toward the Muslim Krio. He thus deemed it incumbent upon himself to correct the myopic and ignorant attitude and assumptions of his fellow clergymen by pointing out that "not only do many of the Mohammedans understand the Arabic they read, they [also] speak, write and compose in it" as well.[38]

By this time, he had become quite alienated from the European clergy and later complained to Venn that he was made to endure discriminatory treatment by his fellow clergymen. On 17 November 1871, the Executive Committee of the CMS in London terminated the services of Blyden and sent him a severance "allowance of £50.0s.0d to save my family from inconvenience while I may be finding employment."[39] Shortly after receiving his notice of termination from the CMS, Blyden received an invitation from a personality he described as "an Arab Shereef" who had been visiting the colony; the Muslim emissary wanted Blyden to accompany him on a tour of the interior. Blyden therefore contacted the office of the governor, Sir Arthur Kennedy, indicating his willingness to accompany the visitor from Arabia. Kennedy subsequently gave his approval and offered Blyden any assistance he might need.

ESTABLISHMENT OF MUSLIM SCHOOLS

Upon returning from his travels in the interior, which took him to Falaba and other Muslim centers of learning and trade, Blyden assumed the editorship of the Negro, a fledgling Krio newspaper. The paper gave him the forum for publicly advocating the views he had long voiced in private settings. While he maintained that the paper's columns would be "devoid of disputes or quarrels," he was soon lambasting the European clergy for teachings that tended to undermine, instead of enhance, the "African personality."[40] He once again called for the establishment of a West African University, for which he envisioned an African leadership that would provide an education that would be emblematic of the African capacity for originality. From his perspective, this would at least serve as a counterweight to the Christian missionary education that he believed only copied European models.[41] However, even as he was advocating the institutionalizing of an Afrocentric curriculum, Blyden was not exactly calling for a wholesale overhauling of the educational curriculum in the colony schools; he was fully cognizant of the indispensability of such pivotal subjects as mathematics and the sciences. He envisaged his educational plan as a means of providing equal opportunity to study English and other traditional Western education subjects, as well as Arabic and African history.[42] Nevertheless, he did not shy away from his oft-stated stance of imbuing the curriculum, and therefore the students, with a strong sense of racial identity.

By 1876, when the CMS Mohammedan School was opened, many of the Muslim Krio were ready to enroll their children in the colony schools. While the number of parents who were so inclined was quite significant, many more continued to harbor fears of Christian motives, primarily a perceived hidden evangelical agenda on the part of the missionaries who supervised the schools. Yet the majority of the community elders were by now acutely aware of the need for Western education if their children were to make any meaningful progress in the political economy of the fast-growing colony.[43] Muslim Krio leaders had become aware of the limited capacity of Arabic and Islamic education to facilitate social advancement in the colony; they were by now firmly convinced that it was only by enrolling in the colony schools and obtaining Western education that their offspring would be able to gain meaningful employment in the colonial establishment. Nonetheless, they remained adamant that the schools be locally situated, a development that for all practical purposes rendered the CMS Mohammedan School impractical.

In 1889, the Reverend Metcalf Sunter, colony inspector of schools, released a report on the state of education for the Muslim population of the colony.[44] According to the Sunter Report, the Islamic education system consisted of about twenty schools where instruction was limited to the study of the Qur'an. The inspector of schools also noted a significant aspect of Islamic education, namely the gender inequity in student enrolment; the Ile Kewu had a limited number of girls in the student population. Though his report did not indicate what actions ought to be taken to rectify the prevailing situation, Reverend Sunter made it clear that Muslim Krio would welcome the colony government's help in constructing schools in their communities. However, Sunter did not mention the fact that Blyden had long pointed out the reported limitations of Islamic education in the colony and was already running a small private school at Fourah Bay, with the cooperation of the local jamaat.[45] Blyden was already "teaching English and Arabic to children and adults from the three Aku Muslim settlements." However, the school lasted only for a limited period, due to Blyden's departure for Liberia in 1889.

After a year away, Blyden returned to Sierra Leone in 1890 and almost immediately went to work trying to convince the Muslim Krio leaders to solicit the colony government's assistance in the construction of schools for the children of their communities. In 1891, Governor James Hay, who had been communicating with the secretary of state for the colonies in London on the need for elementary schools for Muslim children, initiated a scheme to accomplish that objective. Hay's educational program included the establishment of a school at Fourah Bay and another one at Fula Town.[46] Upon receiving the approval of the Colonial Office at Whitehall [a departure from colonial policy], the governor ordered the construction of an elementary school on crown land at Fourah Bay in 1891. The Hay administration not only provided the land on which the school was to be built, it also made available "a grant towards teachers' salaries and inspecting."[47] Ghairawanieu George, a graduate of Fourah Bay College, was placed in charge of the school in fulfillment of the caveat required by the community leaders in approving the school, and continued receiving government grants until 1901.

The fact that George was placed in charge of the school may have been a political miscalculation on the part of the Hay administration, precisely because George was a leader of one of the two opposing factions in a simmering sectarian dispute at Fourah Bay. His opponent, Ligaly Savage, was consequently opposed to the establishment of a school for Western education. As already noted, being an advocate of a strict adherence to Islamic tenets, Savage would not consent to what was perceived to be a Christian education for Muslim children. However, sensing the swing of popular opinion in favor of Western education in the Muslim community, Savage proved to be an astute politician and soon consented to the founding of a separate school for his own Tamba faction.

FOUNDING OF AMARAIA SCHOOL

The colony government was by this time quite convinced that the establishment of schools was of colony-wide concern and not necessarily a parochial issue. The administration therefore determined that it was politically imperative that schools be established in the Muslim Krio communities in order to secure the political loyalty of the local inhabitants, and to socialize Muslims into colonial culture. On 22 May 1899, Governor Frederick Cardew met with the leaders of Fula Town to discuss the need for a school in their community. It was decided that one would be built with the help of the administration up the hill at Ellebank Street, about fifty yards from the Jami-ul Salaam mosque.[48]

The enthusiasm of the community upon receiving the news of the administration's decision to open a school could hardly be contained. Such was their haste that, rather than wait for the colony government to commence construction on the location, the people mobilized the necessary labor force in July 1899 to begin construction of a temporary structure that would house what was to ultimately become Amaraia School, named for the local Imam masjid, Alfa Amara. The temporary structure was completed in two weeks! On 7 August 1899, Maj. Matthew Nathan, accompanied by the mayor of Freetown, Sir Samuel Lewis, and Dr. Blyden, among other dignitaries, officially opened the school amid much fanfare.[49] Alfa Amara formally welcomed the colony government officials and other invited guests to the community and offered prayers in Arabic and Yoruba. He then gave a brief lecture on the role and place of Muslims in Freetown society and the efforts of Muslim Krio to obtain a Western education. The Imam concluded his remarks by thanking the officials and others for their assistance in making the founding of the school possible and, perhaps as expected, pledged his community's loyalty to the British Crown.

Following Imam Amara, the government Arabic writer and interpreter, Mohammed Sanusie, gave a long and impassioned address; he drew attention to the bitter experience of Muslim Krio during an extended period of religious and political repression in the colony, when the presence of Muslims within the Liberated African society was fiercely contested by the colonial government as well as by the Christian clergy. Sanusie pointedly reminded the audience of the demolition by arson of the Fula Town mosque in 1839 as one of several dastardly acts of repression committed by "irresponsible and bigoted persons."[50] Sanusie's enthusiastic support for education in his community subsequently led him to accept the position of manager of the school.

APPOINTMENT OF BLYDEN AS DIRECTOR OF MOHAMMEDAN EDUCATION

The opening of Amaraia School was a historically important milestone for Muslims in Krio society. The fanfare that accompanied the formal opening of the school seemed to have galvanized the entire Muslim Krio population in the colony. In order not to be outdone, the people of Aberdeen became quite anxious about having a school of their own and soon commenced classes in the old mosque that was about to be replaced.[51]

In 1902, the colony administration enacted the so-called Mohammedan Education Ordinance, the express purpose of which was "the development and extension [of education] on western lines among the Mohammedans of the colony of Sierra Leone." The ordinance also required the creation of a curiously named Department of Mohammedan Education as part of the colony bureaucratic establishment. With a clear need for someone with the requisite experience, qualifications, and credibility to steer the development of Western education for Muslims in the colony, the administration formally appointed Dr. Blyden to the newly created position of director of Mohammedan education. Blyden was deemed the most appropriate person for the position because of his leading role in the education of Muslims and his long advocacy for the extension of Western education to Muslim Krio. His salary was fixed at £100.00 sterling per annum. However, support for Muslim education remained a low priority to the colony government; lack of trained teachers and limited financial aid from the administration created major challenges for Blyden in his new assignment.

Upon the assumption of his duties, Blyden became directly responsible for four existing schools within the Muslim Krio communities in the colony, in addition to another school in the Mandinka section of Freetown, off Magazine Cut. The two feuding factions at Fourah Bay each ran their own schools; the conservative Tamba, having demanded a school of its own and finding the space at the Harunia School (named for Imam Harun) inadequate, founded the Madrassa Sulaimania. The latter was formally opened on 7 January 1903 by Governor Sir Charles King-Harman, with the children singing "God Save the King" as the governor and his entourage entered the school compound.[52]

By the opening of the latest school at Fourah Bay, the madrassas were experiencing a slow but steady increase in student population. When Governor Cardew visited Amaraia School at Fula Town in August 1900, on the occasion of the first anniversary of the school's founding, the student population stood at 160, but with only 57 of the female gender.[53] Madrassa Sulaimania at Fourah Bay had 244 students, mostly boys; while its crosstown sister school, Harunia, had 113. In spite of the evident challenges, including gender inequity, Blyden had a very favorable assessment of the schools after his first year in office. According to him, the students were "most advanced in arithmetic, English, reading, grammar, writing from dictation, Arabic writing and grammar" and were quite "intelligent, zealous and energetic." However by 1903, the colony inspector of schools was unimpressed with the collective progress of the new schools. In reaction to a request from the headmaster of the Madrassa Harunia for increased financial assistance, the inspector of schools denied the request on grounds of the school's poor attendance record, noting that "during the quarter the attendance did not average sixty students."[54] The school's headmaster responded that "during the quarter in question the annual fast of Ramadan occurred," but that rationale was undermined by the fact that attendance at Amaraia School remained very high during the same quarter.

Blyden took issue with the inspector of schools' decision to deny financial aid to the Harunia school; he asserted that financial assistance need not be withheld on grounds of poor attendance, declaring that it is "not the number of pupils but the quality of the instruction imparted" that "should be the test in estimating results." He dismissed as ineffective the prevailing method wherein the number of students attending the school on a daily basis was emphasized. The director of Mohammedan education noted further that the school at Fula Town, at least, had made "great advancement since its opening," and he insisted that much progress might have been made by the schools "under a system better adapted to the [prevailing] conditions."[55] In his report to the governor in December 1903, Blyden emphasized that the managers and teachers in the madrassas were better qualified, and the students more disciplined, than was previously the case. He also observed that the schools no longer had an exclusively Muslim student body. By 1903, Christian parents were enrolling their children in what were by now desegregated schools.[56] As a result of the increasing enrollment of Christian students, the overall population of the madrassas grew significantly. Blyden, who had by this time obtained legendary status in the Muslim Krio communities, continued to harangue the colony government for increased grants-in-aid for the schools. But ill health and advanced age combined to slow him down. He was clearly no longer the vibrant and effervescent personality he once was.

On 31 December 1904, Blyden formally tendered his letter of resignation from his post as director of Mohammedan education.[57] He had earlier requested a six-month leave of absence without pay in order to receive medical attention. He was granted the leave of absence and subsequently left Freetown for London in order to receive the requisite medical attention. He finally officially vacated his position upon his return from the United Kingdom. In accepting Blyden's letter of resignation, Governor A. Lyttleton proposed that Blyden's position be abolished; however, he cautioned Whitehall that his proposal should not be construed as suggesting that "the creation of the office originally was unnecessary, but merely that I do not think that it would be practicable to appoint to the office any person possessing the special qualifications for the post that Dr. Blyden has and which he alone make [sic] the post of value to the government."[58]

Lyttleton's advice was accepted by Whitehall and he subsequently appointed a board of directors to oversee the Department of Mohammedan Education.

Obviously, the colony government had achieved a major feat in getting the Muslim Krio to accept Western education. After long resisting European cultural imperialism in the British colony, the Muslims of Freetown had finally accepted the very embodiment of that phenomenon, that is, Western education. While Lyttleton may have been disingenuous in stating that there was no other person with the requisite qualifications to replace Dr. Blyden, the governor was clearly delighted that the colonial establishment had succeeded in demonstrating that Western culture was the "locus of superiority/advancement."[59] No longer having to deal with Blyden, whom many in the colonial establishment may have construed as somewhat irascible and in many ways a thorn in the sides of colonial and evangelical officials, the colony administration would rather prefer a board of directors that could be replaced at will. And with the Muslim Krio by now virtually dependent on colony government support for the financial survival of the schools, the governor was by then in a position of strength vis-à-vis the former group.

But even if the Muslim Krio now had to depend on colony government largesse to maintain the schools, the inhabitants of Fourah Bay, Fula Town, and Aberdeen were certainly no longer in the tenuous position they had been in for much of the nineteenth century. They had clearly benefited from the intellectual and political dexterity of Blyden in their dealings with the colonial state. Also, the colony government had finally come to the realization that the Muslim Krio constituted an integral part of the colonial political economy, especially with regard to their important trade relations with the interior and the cultural life of the colony. It was now left to those who had obtained Western educations to assume leadership of the Muslim Krio communities and to seek a full integration into the colonial establishment. Blyden retained strong ties with the Muslim Krio and spent significant portions of his time at Fula Town, where he remained a legendary figure.

A larger-than-life personality in colonial Freetown following his relocation from Liberia, Blyden ultimately succeeded in brokering the colonial interactions between the emerging Muslim Krio communities and the state, and transformed the way in which education was perceived and utilized by the colonial and evangelical officials. Not only did he extend education beyond the constricted agenda of the church, but he also succeeded in secularizing the educational curriculum of the colony schools. The hitherto-limited Islamic education provided by the Muslim madrassas was modernized and transformed to include traditional subjects taught in Western educational institutions, including the social and natural sciences, without compromising the Islamic and African cultural aspects and values that had been part of the teachings of the Muslim Krio scholars.

In the end, Blyden's contribution to education in the Sierra Leone Colony and in West Africa, including Lagos Colony, where he served in a similar capacity, can be measured only by his triumph in moving education beyond the limited outlook of the European missionary community, which saw the schools as mere conduits for the conversion of the so-called natives to Christianity. In an even more profoundly immeasurable way, Blyden's efforts and scholarship debunked the long-held mistaken notion propagated by the likes of George Hegel and Hugh Trevor-Roper that Africans had not made any meaningful contribution to world history. He succeeded in transforming the school curriculum to reflect an African consciousness of history that predated the advent of the European in Africa. In the end, Blyden's major contribution to the discourse on social relations could be found in cross-cultural and religious encounters among Islam, Yoruba, and other indigenous African cultures, and Christianity. Perhaps an alternative exemplar of the concept of "triple heritage" of African, Islamic, and Christian religious and cultural values could be located in the Krio of Sierra Leone.

Postscript

BY THE END OF THE NINETEENTH CENTURY, Krio society, shaped by complex religious, social, and commercial forces, as explored in this book, was in full bloom. Just like their Christian counterparts, Muslim Krio in Sierra Leone asserted their cultural and social consciousness through religion, conflict, commerce, and education. Islam had been not only a shield for Muslims against the Christianizing efforts of the colonial state and missionaries, but also a source of internal strife within their communities. Commerce, on the other hand, provided a source of livelihood as well as new opportunities for the cross-cultural and transnational interactions that were the lifeblood of colonial Freetown. The various groups of Africans repatriated to the Sierra Leone Peninsula had been driven by necessity to engage in commerce after the fabled fertility of the colonial environment proved elusive. For Sierra Leone Muslims, the engagement in trade, apart from economic necessity, also reflected the almost symbiotic relations between their religion and commercial enterprise. As was the case with their prophet, Muhammad, who was exposed to new ideas and philosophies as a result of "cross-cultural interactions" with Jewish and Christian merchants in regional and long-distance trade outside his Bedouin Arab society, Muslim traders, male and female alike, ventured far afield to seek commercial opportunities in the hinterland of Sierra Leone and elsewhere in West Africa.

The decision of Muslim traders to venture away from the constricted space of colonial Sierra Leone to French and, sometimes, Portuguese- and Belgian-controlled territories, was not only aimed at resisting European efforts to "reconstruct" their lives, but it was clearly intended to "gain command over their means of producing social values and material wealth."[1] Many groups across the African continent adopted similar strategies in the face of British cultural and political hegemony. As the Sierra Leone Muslim traders traversed the West African landscape with their Christian counterparts, they forged a new kind of African cosmopolitanism as well as contributed to the creation of a Krio diaspora that stretched from Dakar to Lagos. Their creolizing/kriolizing influences, evident in linguistic practices, customary rituals, religious praxis, and kinship ties, permeated the various West African locations associated with this diaspora. Though deeply shaped by Yoruba customary practices, the Krio diaspora was dynamic and open enough to allow cultural contributions and accretions from other peoples. The Krio in the Gambia and Senegal, for example, were also capable of appreciating the contributions of Wolof culture to the growth of their society. The so-called Saro presence in the Bight of Benin subsequently transcended purely commercial relations; it laid the foundational basis for long-term social relations among the peoples of the West African subregion.

It is not surprising that the cross-cultural and religious encounters among Islam, Christianity, and Yoruba and indigenous African religions in Sierra Leone and across West Africa inspired the triple-heritage intellectual framework that permeated Blyden's magnum opus, *Islam, Christianity and the Negro Race*.[2] Though the work is regarded as one of the key texts of nascent Pan-Africanist thought in the late nineteenth century, it is also Blyden's attempt to highlight the dynamic cosmopolitanism of the people among whom he resided in the last decades of his life. Kwame Nkrumah would later reiterate Blyden's triple-heritage framework in his philosophical text *Consciencism*,[3] and Ali Mazrui deployed it with much effectiveness in analyzing Swahili culture of coastal East Africa.[4]

Following the publication of Blyden's work, the Sierra Leone press devoted much attention (between 24 November 1888 and 17 April 1889) to the interplay among Islam, Christianity, and African religious traditions and the resulting implications for Sierra Leone society. In private family gatherings, Muslims, Christians, and adherents of Sango and Ogun often confronted their religious differences without much acrimony. These debates, to be fair, were mostly held between Muslims and Christians, as Sango and Ogun worshippers were being increasingly marginalized. Nonetheless, the merits of the two monotheistic faiths were often voiced by their respective practitioners, cognizant of the continued influence of traditional religious customs in society at large.

Sango and Ogun worship may have waned by the end of the nineteenth century, but African cultural praxis remained resilient in Muslim and Christian Krio communities. The embracing of several African customary rituals, which transcended religious differences by the Krio in nineteenth-century colonial Freetown and West Africa, continues to this day. Indeed, by the turn of the twentieth century, a strong sense of cultural nationalism had emerged among the Krio, the vast majority of whom did not share the social and cultural outlooks of their leaders, who were substituting Victorian English middle-class values or Arab-Islamic cultural mores for traditional African (Yoruba) culture. Muslim Krio remained generally agreeable to the modernizing aspects of the colonial environment as well as to their Islamic faith, as long as neither sought to emasculate their way of living. It was within this context that many of the young people of the Muslim Krio communities of Fourah Bay, Fula Town, and Aberdeen, as well as a significant proportion of their Christian compatriots, embraced the efforts of Edward Blyden and others to celebrate African culture while simultaneously promoting the modernizing influences of Western education.

In January 1889, Muslim and Christian Krio leaders organized a meeting of all Krio of Yoruba heritage that was primarily geared toward facilitating a common ground and unity of Krio, for the shared purpose of ensuring the salvation of the African race. The participants in the meeting understood fully well that strong religious differences existed within Krio society, and among the members of the various Christian denominations and Muslim communities. All of the speakers at this event, including Rev. Abayomi Cole, a Christian, and Mohammed Sanusi, a Muslim, acknowledged the pivotal role of Islam and Christianity in forging their common society. The meeting was, however, more noteworthy for the racial and cultural solidarity between the participants than for their desire to resolve their religious differences. Unlike the colonial and church establishments, Christian attendees were not interested in facilitating the emergence of a Krio society that was exclusively Christian. Their Muslim counterparts similarly harbored no intentions of turning colonial Sierra Leone into a caliphate. Instead, the two communities focused on their shared racial and cultural heritage, their Yorubaness, as it were, and the ability of the larger society to absorb other cultures and adapt to their existential challenges. Their main concern was to create an environment in which Islam, Christianity, and African religious traditions could coexist without one of the two monotheistic faiths emasculating the other.

The growing awareness that Krio of all religious persuasions shared a common cultural heritage led to concrete expressions of solidarity across the religious divides and the creation of an organization to further their interests. The expressions of solidarity included providing support for the construction or reconstruction of Christian and Muslim places of worship that had been destroyed by subterfuge or natural disasters. Muslims lent their support to the repairing of Ebenezer Church, and Christians participated in the reconstruction of the Fula Town Mosque. In April 1889, the Krio Association was founded for the enhancement of the common socioeconomic and political interests of all Krio, Christians and Muslims. The foundation of the association also reflected a growing anxiety among the Krio about their marginalization by British colonial officials in an environment where European imperial competition to carve up the African continent had generated intense racism against Africans. April 1889 thus signaled a perceived need for the self-described descendants of "settlers" in the colony to organize in order to protect their collective socioeconomic and political interests.

The fin de siècle anxieties and actions at self-preservation by Muslim and Christian Krio were not entirely misplaced. In the late 1890s, the Krio suffered from both the capricious victimization of British colonial administrators and the violent resistance of African groups in the interior of Sierra Leone. Paradoxically, the victimization of the Krio started with their attempts to check British imperial excess and to defend the interests of their "native brethren." When the British declared a protectorate over the hinterland of Sierra Leone in 1896, the Krio, particularly those in control of the press, questioned colonial policies vis-à-vis the peoples of the newly conquered territory. Colony newspapers published by Krio were most critical of the imposition of a "hut tax" on the homes of the inhabitants of the protectorate. Krio opposition was based on the grounds that the tax was burdensome and represented an unreasonable economic imposition on an already financially challenged population. Many among the Krio intelligentsia were also by this time philosophically opposed to the "colonizing thrust" of Europeans in Africa. They also felt that colonial taxation would negatively affect trade between the Krio and the different peoples of the Sierra Leone hinterland.

When the people of the newly proclaimed protectorate took up arms against the "hut tax," the Freetown press loudly proclaimed their sympathy for the uprising. In particular, Krio support for the uprising in the northern region of the protectorate, led by Bai Bureh of Ksaaeh, alienated the administration of Governor Frederick Cardew.[5] Cardew decided to teach the Krio a lesson by systematically restricting their access to the colony's civil service. The deleterious impact of the governor's actions was compounded by the massacre of hundreds of Krio in the Mende uprisings in the eastern and southern regions of the protectorate in 1898. Paradoxically, it was the same British policy of *divide et impera*, which the Krio had been fighting against, that triggered the massacre of their kinsfolk. In the perceptions of the Mende, the Krio had become indentifiable with the British imperial state and "civilizing mission, their anti-colonial resistance notwithstanding."[6] The majority of those killed in 1898 were Christian traders and missionaries, but the killings led Krio of all creeds to circle the wagons in what they perceived as an attack on their identity. The massacre of Krio in the hinterland consequently instilled a deep distrust and antipathy toward the Mende among colony Krio.

The British colonial administration did punish some of the leaders who perpetuated the massacre of the Krio traders and missionaries, but did not relent in its efforts to marginalize the Krio in the colonial civil service. The backlash against the perceived arrogance of "an ungrateful people" resulted in the elimination of Krio personnel among the ranks of senior members of the colonial civil service. The colonial state further served notice to the "upstart" Krio intelligentsia by instituting residential segregation in 1905, when the Hill Station reservation was officially established, ostensibly to protect Europeans from falling victim to the anopheles mosquito.[7] In reality, the residential segregation was also a political move aimed at putting educated Krio on notice that theirs was a subordinate class vis-à-vis British colonial personnel. The point was not lost on educated Krio, who were quick to interpret the policy of residential segregation as a further manifestation of British racism and a harbinger of things to come.

The deterioration in Krio-British relations could not have come at a more inauspicious moment for the Muslim Krio. As discussed in chapter 6, by the beginning of the twentieth century, Muslims agreed to send their children to colonially funded Western-style schools tailored to their religious sensibilities. The different partners—Muslim leaders and colonial administrators—in the enterprise were much more confident that it would serve their own goals. The colonial state, even though unhappy with the assertiveness and antiracist nationalism of Krio, still believed in the effectiveness of Western-style schools to assimilate Africans into the colonial context. Sierra Leone Muslims, while calculating that these schools would deepen their solidarity with their Christian counterparts and enhance their citizenship within the colony, felt confident of their ability to resist European efforts at colonizing their minds.

Muslim confidence to resist European colonization derived from a number of considerations. The ethos of educational attainment from the colonial state or their Christian counterparts was not alien to Muslims. Islam enjoins them not only to "read," but also to seek knowledge for their spiritual enhancement. Furthermore, even as they dispatched their children to the colonially sponsored schools, Muslims retained the *ile kewu* (madrassa) as a countervailing influence to Western education. Paradoxically, both the Muslim and the Christian educational systems shared a common attribute of marginalizing local knowledge and languages. While Western education provided by mission schools privileged the English language and prohibited the speaking of patois on school grounds, and valorized Victorian English culture, the Islamic madrassa (*ile kewu*) laid equal emphasis on the importance, indeed, indispensability, of the Arabic language. The Qur'an had to be studied in the original Arabic and was prohibited from being translated into local languages. Islam thus came to serve as a creolizing influence, with Muslim children imbibing the cultural mores of Arab Islamic societies. This distinctive cultural experience of Muslims in Sierra Leone would add to the complicated layers of Krio society by the twentieth century.

In spite of the racism and machinations of British colonial administrators, Western education facilitated the inexorable assimilation of Krio into late nineteenth- and twentieth-century colonial society and economy. It led to the emergence of a class of Krio technocrats, who played a significant role within the colonial administration in Sierra Leone and across West Africa. For all Krio, Christian, and subsequently Muslim, obtaining a Western education became one of their enduring values. The 1931 Census in Sierra Leone, for example, reported that the literacy rate among the Krio was 57.5 percent.[8] On 20 October 1945, the magazine *West Africa*, inter alia, noted the contributions of the colony-educated elite to the political and economic landscapes of West Africa. According to this publication, Sierra Leone has "long been remarkable for a type of human export, the volume and character of which can hardly be realized in Britain. Its younger men, many trained at its Fourah Bay College, have gone forth into all the other West African colonies and far beyond to fill, in government and private employ, positions of trust and responsibility. It is surprising—to those who did not know the facts—how many men and women of light and leading throughout West Africa derive from Sierra Leone.[9]

At home, Muslim Krio who had obtained a Western education in mission schools ultimately came to play a significant part in the civic and professional lives of the colony by the 1930s and 1940s. While their numbers were still negligent relative to those of their Christian counterparts, Muslim personalities became prominent in colonial politics, particularly during the interwar and post–World War II period. Several became legal luminaries; none more so than Ahmed Alhadi, who rose to the position of master and registrar of the Colony Supreme Court. Alhadi would subsequently become a leading voice in conservative Krio politics in the postwar period; he would go on to advocate the "re-emancipation of the colony of Sierra Leone," in effect calling for a Krio homeland, separate from other groups in Sierra Leone.

Imams of Communities of Fourah Bay, Fula Town, and Aberdeen (1833–1908)

Fourah Bay
Alfa Yaddalieu Savage (1833–1849)
Alfa Alieu (1849–1875)
Alfa Uthman Cole (1875–1882)
Alfa Haruna George (1883–1892)
Alfa Mohammed Gheirawanieu George (1895–1903)
Alfa Sulaiman Johnson (1904–1905)
Alfa Alghali Savage (1905–1921)

Fula Town
Alfa Alieu / Alfa Adama (1833–1841)
Alfa Issa / Alfa Unusa (1841–1849)
Alfa Musa (1849–1875)
Alfa Amara (1875–1898)
Alfa Abu Bakarr (1898–1903)
Alfa Uthman (1903)

Aberdeen
Alfa Dowdu (1870–1893)
Alfa Uthman (1893–?)

Source: Barbara E. Harrell-Bond, Allen M. Howard, and David E. Skinner, *Community Leadership and the Transformation of Freetown, 1801–1976* (The Hague: Mouton, 1978).

Notes

INTRODUCTION

1. Scholars such as Arthur T. Porter, Christopher Fyfe, and Leo Spitzer, among others, were particularly responsible for the wider dissemination of this myth. It should be pointed out that John Peterson was a major exception among this generation of scholars, as he consistently sought to draw attention to the complexity of Krio society.

2. Christopher Fyfe, "Akintola Wyse: Creator of the Krio Myth," in *New Perspectives on the Sierra Leone Krio*, ed. Mac Dixon-Fyle and Gibril Cole (New York: Peter Lang, 2006), 27.

3. Akintola J. G. Wyse, *The Krio of Sierra Leone: An Interpretive History* (London: Hurst, 1989), 1.

4. Christopher Fyfe, A *History of Sierra Leone* (Oxford: Oxford University Press, 1962); Arthur T. Porter, *Creoledom: A Study of the Development of Freetown Society* (Oxford: Oxford University Press, 1963).

5. See Murray Last and Paul Richards, eds., *Sierra Leone, 1787–1987: Two Centuries of Intellectual Life* (Manchester: Manchester University Press, 1987); and Fyfe, "Akintola Wyse," 27. For a more detailed explication of the history of Krio society, see Fyfe, *History of Sierra Leone*; John Peterson, *Province of Freedom: A History of Sierra Leone, 1787–1870* (Evanston, IL: Northwestern University Press, 1969); Clifford N. Fyle, "Krio Ways of Thought and Expression," Africana Research Bulletin 3, no. 1 (1972); Leo Spitzer, *The Creoles of Sierra Leone: Responses to Colonialism, 1870–1945* (Madison: University of Wisconsin Press, 1974); Clifford N. Fyle and Eldred D. Jones, A *Krio-English Dictionary* (Oxford: Oxford University Press, 1980); Akintola J. G. Wyse, "On Misunderstandings Arising from the Use of the Term 'Creole' in the Literature on Sierra Leone: A Rejoinder," Africa 49, no. 4 (1979): 408–17; Wyse, "Kriodom: A Maligned Culture," *Journal of the Historical Society of Sierra Leone* 3 (1979): 37–48; Wyse, "Searchlight on the Krio of Sierra Leone: An Ethnographical Study of a West African People" (Occasional paper no. 3, Institute of African Studies, Fourah Bay College, Freetown, 1980); Wyse, "The Sierra Leone Krios: A Reappraisal from the Perspective of the African Diaspora," in *Global Dimension of the African Diaspora*, ed. Joseph E. Harris (Washington, DC: Howard University Press, 1982), 309–37; Wyse, "The Dissolution of Freetown City Council in 1926: A Negative Example of Political Apprenticeship in Colonial Sierra Leone," *Africa* 57, no. 4 (1987): 422–38; Wyse, *Krio of Sierra Leone*; Odile Goerg, "Sierra Leonais, Creoles, Krio: La Dialectique de L'Identite," *Africa* 65, no. 1 (1995): 114–32; Goerg, "Between Everyday Life and Exception: Celebrating Pope-Hennessy Day in Freetown, 1872–c1905," *Journal of African Cultural Studies* 15, no. 1 (2002): 119–31; James S. Thayer, "A Dissenting View

of Creole Culture in Sierra Leone," *Cahiers d'Études Africaines* 31 (1991): 215–30; E. Frances White, *Sierra Leone's Settler Women Traders: Women on the Afro-European Frontier* (Ann Arbor: University of Michigan Press, 1987); Martin Lynn, "Technology, Trade, and 'A Race of Native Capitalists': The Krio Diaspora of West Africa and the Steamship, 1852–95," *Journal of African History* 33 (1992): 421–40.

6. The exception to the masculinist formulation of nineteenth-century Krio society has been White, *Sierra Leone's Settler Women Traders*.

7. See Fyfe, *History of Sierra Leone*; and Peterson, *Province of Freedom*.

8. Samuel P. Huntington, *The Clash of Civilizations and the Remaking of World Order* (New York: Simon & Schuster, 1996); Laurie Goodstein, "Islam: Not in My Backyard?" *New York Times Upfront* 143 (September 2010); Goodstein, "Across Nation, Mosque Projects Meet Opposition," *New York Times*, 7 August 2010; John Alden Williams, "Misunderstanding Islam," *New York Times*, 22 September 2012.

9. For a look at the history of resistance to colonial domination in early Freetown, see James W. St. G. Walker, *The Black Loyalists: The Search for a Promised Land in Nova Scotia and Sierra Leone, 1783–1870* (Toronto: University of Toronto Press, 1992); see also Fyfe, *History of Sierra Leone*.

10. See Peterson, *Province of Freedom*; Fyfe, *History of Sierra Leone*; and Walker, *Black Loyalists*.

11. For a look at the impact of Islam on education in Sierra Leone between the mid-eighteenth and mid-twentieth centuries, see David E. Skinner, "Islam and Education in the Colony and Hinterland of Sierra Leone (1750–1914)," *Canadian Journal of African Studies* 10, no. 3 (1976): 449–520.

12. The Reverend Sigismund W. Koelle, who joined the faculty of Fourah Bay College in 1847, conducted research on the diversity of language groups, about two hundred in all, in the colony and subsequently published his *Polyglotta Africana* in 1854 (London: Church Missionary Society). Paul E. H. Hair noted that "half the languages of western African were still spoken" in Freetown in the mid-nineteenth century; see Hair, "Colonial Freetown and the Study of African Languages," in Last and Richards, *Sierra Leone*, 560–65.

13. See Tom Spencer-Walters, "Creolization and Kriodom: (Re)Visioning the 'Sierra Leone Experiment,'" in Dixon-Fyle and Cole, *New Perspectives*, 223–55.

14. Arthur Abraham also postulates that Mende "probably originated first as a language, a lingua franca," before the speakers of the language came to be identified as a distinct group; see Abraham, *An Introduction to the Pre-Colonial History of the Mende of Sierra Leone* (Lewiston, NY: Edwin Mellen Press, 2003), 2–3.

15. See J. D. Y. Peel, *Religious Encounter and the Making of the Yoruba* (Bloomington: Indiana University Press, 2003); see also J. Lorand Matory, *Black Atlantic Religion: Tradition, Transnationalism, and Matriarchy in the Afro-Brazilian Candomblé* (Princeton, NJ: Princeton University Press, 2005); and Solimar Otero, *Afro-Cuban Diasporas in the Atlantic World* (Rochester, NY: University of Rochester Press, 2010).

16. Peel, *Religious Encounter*, 8.

17. See Matory, *Black Atlantic Religion*.

18. Personal communication with Professor Ade Ajayi, to whom I am grateful for this information. The salutation of "Oku'o" is now exclusively used by members of esoteric institutions such as the Egugu, Gelede, Egunuko, and Odeh.

19. See Leroy Vail, ed., *The Creation of Tribalism in Southern Africa* (London: James Currey, 1989); Bruce Berman and John Lonsdale, *Unhappy Valley: Conflict*

in *Kenya and Africa*, bk. 2 (Athens: Ohio University Press, 1992); Archie Mafeje, "The Ideology of 'Tribalism,'" *Journal of Modern African Studies* 9, no. 2 (1971): 253–61.

20. Mahmood Mamdani, "Race and Ethnicity as Political Identities in the African Context," in *Keywords: Identity* (New York: Other Press, 2004), 3.

21. Mahmood Mamdani, *Saviors and Survivors: Darfur, Politics, and the War on Terror* (New York: Pantheon Books, 2009), 169.

22. Mamdani, "Race and Ethnicity." Mamdani further explores the effective use of ethnicity or tribalism in *Citizen and Subject: Contemporary Africa and the Legacy of Late Colonialism* (Princeton, NJ: Princeton University Press, 1996).

23. See Frederick Cooper and Rogers Brubaker, "Identity," in Frederick Cooper, *Colonialism in Question: Theory, Knowledge, History* (Berkeley: University of California Press, 2005), 72; see also Rogers Brubaker, *Ethnicity without Groups* (Cambridge, MA: Harvard University Press, 2004).

24. See Peel, *Religious Encounter*, 4.

25. V. Y. Mudimbe, *The Invention of Africa: Gnosis, Philosophy, and the Order of Knowledge* (Bloomington: Indiana University Press, 1998), 45–47, cited in Peel, *Religious Encounter*, 4.

26. Jean Comaroff and John L. Comaroff, *Of Revelation and Revolution*, vol. 1, *Christianity, Colonialism, and Consciousness in South Africa* (Chicago: University of Chicago Press, 1991), 11, cited in Peel, *Religious Encounter*, 4–5.

27. Peel, *Religious Encounter*, 5.

28. See David E. Skinner, "Sierra Leone Relations with the Northern Rivers and the Influence of Islam in the Colony," *International Journal of Sierra Leone Studies* 1, no. 1 (1988): 91–113; see also Michael Crowder, *West Africa under Colonial Rule* (London: Hutchinson, 1968), 93–94.

29. Skinner, "Sierra Leone Relations"; Sierra Leone Company officials, including Thomas and Matthew Winterbottom and James Watts, visited the interior in 1794.

30. Ibid., 4.

31. Ibid.

32. Ibid., 13; see also Fyfe, *History of Sierra Leone*, 81–83.

33. CO267/38 1814, enclosure no. 52, SLA.

34. CO267/91, Report of Commissioners Rowan and Wellington, 4 November 1827; also CO267/91, appendix 26, PRO.

35. See Allen M. Howard, "Trade and Islam in Sierra Leone, 18th–20th centuries," in *Islam and Trade in Sierra Leone*, ed. Alusine Jalloh and David E. Skinner (Trenton, NJ: Africa World Press, 1997), 21–63.

36. CO267/60, Hamilton to Bathurst, 21 April 1824, dispatch no. 6, PRO.

37. Ibid.

38. Ibid.

39. Hamilton to Kompa, 19 June 1824, Governor's Letter Book, SLA.

40. Fyfe, *History of Sierra Leone*, 303.

41. Dixon-Fyle and Cole, *New Perspectives*, 10–11; see also Barbara E. Harrell-Bond, Allen M. Howard, and David E. Skinner, *Community Leadership and the Transformation of Freetown, 1801–1976* (The Hague: Mouton, 1978), 42–48.

42. Dixon-Fyle and Cole, *New Perspectives*, 12.

43. See David Robinson, *Paths of Accommodation: Muslim Societies and French Colonial Authorities in Senegal and Mauritania, 1880-1920* (Athens: Ohio University Press, 2000).

44. For a more detailed examination of the colony-interior trade, see Allen M. Howard, "The Relevance of Spatial Analysis for African Economic History: The Sierra Leone-Guinea System," *Journal of African History* 17, no. 3 (1976): 365–88. For additional discussion of the Bambara Town community, see Harrell-Bond, Howard, and Skinner, *Community Leadership*.

45. Robinson, *Paths of Accommodation*, 2.

46. Ibid., 34.

47. Ibid., 5–6.

48. See John H. Lawrence, *Creole Houses: Traditional Homes of Old Louisiana* (New York: Abrams, 2007), 12.

49. Interview, Pa Babatunde Gabisi, Freetown, June 1978.

50. Thomas Decker, "The Krios of Sierra Leone," *African World* (July 1948): 9–10; Wyse, *Krio of Sierra Leone*, 6; also Wyse, "Sierra Leone Krios"; and Charles K. O. Nicol, "Origins and Orthography of the Kriyo Language," *West African Review* (August 1949).

51. Personal communication with Rowland Abiodun, John C. Newton Professor of Fine Arts and Black Studies, Amherst College, Massachusetts, for the translation of the original Yoruba.

52. Otero, *Afro-Cuban Diasporas*, 1..

53. Interview, Pa Babatunde Gabisi, Freetown, June 1978.

54. See Wyse, "Sierra Leone Krios"; Ibrahim Abdullah, in an online posting (Leonenet, 10 April 1997), suggests that the term may have been a pejorative used to poke fun at the peripatetic Liberated Africans in the rural villages in the nineteenth century, noting that it was only the poor who engaged in this practice.

55. The journals kept by mission officials consisted of "accounts of their experiences and activities, composed in the light of the great story which they wanted to write into the lives of the [people]." Peel, *Religious Encounter*, 2.

CHAPTER 1: CREOLIZATION AND (KRIO)LIZATION IN THE MAKING OF NINETEENTH-CENTURY SIERRA LEONE

1. See Ulf Hannerz, "The World in Creolisation," *Africa* 57, no. 4 (1987): 552.

2. Ibid., 549.

3. Ibid., 548.

4. Lamin O. Sanneh, *Piety and Power: Muslims and Christians in West Africa* (New York: Orbis Books, 1996), 68. In a chapter on "Christian-Muslim Encounter in Freetown in the Nineteenth Century," Sanneh discusses the "Implications for Interfaith Engagement" in a colonial environment wherein religious differences were assumed by the colonial authorities to constitute key factors in identity. Sanneh calls attention to the significance of the interfaith engagement, particularly to the "ecumenical solidarity" demonstrated by the people of an emergent Krio society.

5. Sanneh, *Piety and Power*, 69. This perspective was best, and consistently, articulated by Edward Wilmot Blyden in his many writings and lectures in Freetown and elsewhere.

6. Frederick Cooper and Rogers Brubaker, "Identity," in Frederick Cooper, *Colonialism in Question: Theory, Knowledge, History* (Berkeley: University of California Press, 2005), 62.

7. See Barbara E. Harrell-Bond, Allen M. Howard, and David E. Skinner, *Community Leadership and the Transformation of Freetown, 1801–1976* (The Hague: Mouton, 1978), 6.

8. See Cooper and Brubaker, "Identity," 65.

9. See Gibril R. Cole, "Re-thinking the Demographic Make-up of Krio Society," in *New Perspectives on the Sierra Leone Krio*, ed. Mac Dixon-Fyle and Gibril Cole (New York: Peter Lang, 2006), 33–51.

10. Akintola J. G. Wyse, *The Krio of Sierra Leone: An Interpretive History* (London: Hurst, 1987), 1.

11. Ibid., 1.

12. See Leo Spitzer, *The Creoles of Sierra Leone: Responses to Colonialism, 1870–1945* (Madison: University of Wisconsin Press, 1974); see also Spitzer, "The Sierra Leone Creoles, 1870–1900," in *Africa and the West: Intellectual Responses to European Culture*," ed. Philip D. Curtin (Madison: University of Wisconsin Press, 1972), 99–138.

13. See Cole, "Re-thinking the Demographic Make-up of Krio Society," 47. I have questioned the capacity of Spitzer and, for that matter, other scholars who share this perspective of the Krio, to recognize the nuanced nature of the group, and to recognize the subtleties in the cultural experiences of the society and the significant differences in the lived experiences of members of even a singular extended family.

14. David Eltis and David Richardson, eds., Voyages: The Trans-Atlantic Slave Trade Database (Atlanta, GA: Emory University, 2008, 2009), http://www.slavevoyages.org.

15. See Christopher Fyfe, *A History of Sierra Leone* (Oxford: Oxford University Press, 1962); and Arthur T. Porter, *Creoledom: A Study of the Development of Freetown Society* (Oxford: Oxford University Press, 1963).

16. John Peterson, *Province of Freedom: A History of Sierra Leone, 1787–1870* (London: Faber and Faber, 1969), 27. For other discussions of the early history of the colony of Freetown, see A. B. C. Sibthorpe, *The History of Sierra Leone* (London: Franc Cass, 1868); also Christopher Fyfe, *Sierra Leone Inheritance* (London: Oxford University Press, 1964); Porter, *Creoledom*; Christopher Fyfe and Eldred Jones, eds., *Freetown: A Symposium*, (Freetown: Sierra Leone University Press, 1968); Alexander P. Kup, *Sierra Leone: A Concise History* (London: David & Charles, 1975); and Steven J. Braidwood, *Black Poor and White Philanthropists: London's Blacks and the Foundation of the Sierra Leone Settlement: 1786–1791* (Liverpool: Liverpool University Press, 1994).

17. Akintola J. G. Wyse, "Searchlight on the Krio of Sierra Leone: An Ethnographical Study of a West African People" (Occasional Paper no. 3, Institute of African Studies, Fourah Bay College, Freetown, 1980).

18. Dixon-Fyle and Cole, *New Perspectives*, 3.

19. Linda M. Heywood and John K. Thornton , *Central Africans, Atlantic Creoles, and the Foundation of the Americas, 1585–1660* (Cambridge: Cambridge University Press, 2007), 236–93, have shown how enslaved Africans who lived in large communities in the New World were able to take advantage of "opportunities for networking" other enslaved Africans.

20. Ibid., 4.

21. For more substantive analyses of the making of the Yoruba, see J. D. Y. Peel, *Religious Encounter and the Making of the Yoruba* (Bloomington: Indiana University Press, 2003); see also J. Lorand Matory, *Black Atlantic Religion: Tradition, Transnationalism, and Matriarchy in the Afro-Brazilian Candomblé* (Princeton, NJ:

Princeton University Press, 2005); David Eltis, "The Diaspora of Yoruba Speakers, 1650–1865: Dimensions and Implications," in *The Yoruba Diaspora in the Atlantic World*, ed. Toyin Falola and Matt D. Childs (Bloomington: Indiana University Press, 2004). Others suggest an earlier date for the use of the term as a common name for all the children of the ancestral birthplace of Ife.

22. Eltis, "Diaspora of Yoruba Speakers," 18.

23. Robin Law, "Yoruba Liberated Slaves Who Returned to West Africa," in Falola and Childs, *Yoruba Diaspora in the Atlantic World*, 360. Law does not fully subscribe to this viewpoint regarding Yoruba ethnogenesis. He posits that a shared sense of common ethnic identity among the various Yoruba-speaking groups predated the founding of a post–slave trade settlement in West Africa, since this process was already under way in the Americas where "they first began to employ a common collective name for themselves."

24. Peel, *Religious Encounter*, 27.

25. Matory, *Black Atlantic Religion*, 52.

26. Ibid.

27. Ibid., 53.

28. Ibid., 54.

29. Peel, *Religious Encounter*, 284.

30. Rosalyn Howard, "Yoruba in the British Caribbean: A Comparative Perspective on Trinidad and the Bahamas," in Falola and Childs, *Yoruba Diaspora in the Atlantic World*, 158.

31. Ibid. See also Melville J. Herskovits, *The Myth of the Negro Past* (Boston: Beacon, 1958); and E. Franklin Frazier, *The Negro Family in the United States* (Chicago: University of Chicago Press, 1966).

32. Matory, *Black Atlantic Religion*, 61.

33. Luis Nicolau Parés, "The 'Nagôization' Process in Bahian Candomblé," in Falola and Childs, *Yoruba Diaspora in the Atlantic World*, 185. For a detailed and substantive treatment of the Candomblé in Brazil and its transnational import, see Matory, *Black Atlantic Religion*.

34. John W. Nunley, *Moving with the Face of the Devil: Art and Politics in Urban West Africa* (Chicago: University of Illinois Press, 1987), 20.

35. For a discussion of Ogun, see Sandra T. Barnes, ed., *Africa's Ogun: Old World and New* (Bloomington: Indiana University Press, 1997).

36. Rev. E. W. Fashole-Luke, "Religion in Freetown," in Fyfe and Jones, *Freetown*, 134–35.

37. Ibid.

38. Ibid.

39. Fyfe, *History of Sierra Leone*, 244.

40. Peterson, *Province of Freedom*, 250.

41. Ibid., 254; for further readings on Yoruba religion, see also Matory, *Black Atlantic Religion*; Babatunde Lawal, "Reclaiming the Past: Yoruba Elements in African American Arts," in Falola and Childs, *Yoruba Diaspora in the Atlantic World*, 291–324; Andrew Apter, *Black Critics and Kings: The Hermeneutics of Power in Yoruba Society* (Chicago: University of Chicago Press, 1992); Karin Barber, "How Man Makes God in West Africa: Yoruba Attitudes towards the Orisa," *Africa* 51, no. 3 (1981): 724–45; J. D. Y Peel, "A Comparative Analysis of Ogun in Precolonial Yorubaland," in Barnes, *Africa's Ogun*, 263–89.

42. Peterson, *Province of Freedom*, 254.

43. Ibid., 256.

44. Ibid., 257.

45. Interview with Marie Iscandari, Zanaibu Cole, and Tairatu Thomas, Fula Town, June 1978. In my fieldwork during this period, several of the inhabitants retold stories passed down from an earlier generation pertaining to the perceived supernatural capacity of the secret societies, including the Odeh, but especially the Ojeh and Egunuko. One such story alluded to the sounds of Egugu bata (drum) coming from an unoccupied igbaleh/ile late at night, which the locals and members of the Ojeh interpreted as instructions from the spirits to "play" (i.e., for the Ojeh to convene a public performance).

46. Lawal, "Reclaiming the Past," 297.

47. CA1/079, Journal of Reverend Crowther, June 1844, CMS.

48. Peterson, *Province of Freedom*, 265.

49. Interview with Alhaji Haroun O. Zubairu (Imam of Fula Town), May 1998, Freetown. It is common knowledge in Krio society that the Ojeh society in particular can inflict much harm through the use of a malignant concoction commonly known as "Allay."

50. See Wyse, *Krio of Sierra Leone*.

51. Peterson suggested that the Untin (Odeh) society was not an importation from the old country (*Province of Freedom*, 268); however, members of the Ojeh and Untin societies credit their Yoruba background for both societies. The titles of officeholders in the Untin society were and are directly related to those of traditional officeholders in Oyo and other Yoruba states (e.g., Balogun and Asipa).

52. Peterson, *Province of Freedom*, 268–69.

53. Personal communication with Abou Whyte (a Freetown float builder and cultural icon); Wyse, *Krio of Sierra Leone*, 53, credited "a pair of Muslim Nigerian twins, Hassani and Husseini," for the founding of the society.

54. For a detailed look at Gelede, see Henry John Drewal and Margaret Thompson Drewal, *Gelede: Art and Female Power among the Yoruba* (Bloomington: Indiana University Press, 1990).

55. Fyfe, *History of Sierra Leone*, 105–6; in *After Abolition: Britain and the Slave Trade Since 1807* (London: I. B. Tauris, 2007), Marika Sherwood indicts Britain for its complicity in perpetuating the trade in human beings even after the promulgation of the Abolition Act. Sherwood notes that "the British government was given plenty of evidence of British complicity in the slave trade by the British navy," as well as "by its own consuls ... to Brazil" (104). She asserts that the British government and prominent Britons directly engaged in the slave trade and slavery in the Caribbean and South America.

56. Wyse, "Searchlight on the Krio," 4.

57. Fyfe, *History of Sierra Leone*, 210.

58. CO267/65, Hamilton to Earl Bathurst, enclosure no. 3, 31 January 1825; Findlay to Hay, 23 March 1833, PRO.

59. CO267/11, Sierra Leone, 31 December 1808, PRO.

60. CO267/82, Campbell to Goderich, dispatch no. 72, 14 July 1827, PRO.

61. Eltis and Richardson, Voyages: The Trans-Atlantic Slave Trade Database (http://www.slavevoyages.org), contains evidence for the number of captives from a variety of points of embarkation along the West African coast who were relocated to Freetown beginning in 1819.

62. Fyfe, *History of Sierra Leone*, 77; See also, J. J. Crooks, *A History of the Colony of Sierra Leone, West Africa* (London: Browne and Nolan, 1903).

63. See Eltis and Richardson, Voyages.

64. *Liberated African Register*, vol. 3 (8589), SLA.

65. Register of Alien Children in the Colony (of Sierra Leone), 29 April 1865, SLA.

66. For a fascinating "review of ethnic and language identity formations" in Sierra Leone, see Joko Sengova, "Aborigines and Returnees: In Search of Linguistic and Historical Meaning in Delineations of Sierra Leone's Ethnicity and Heritage," in Dixon-Fyle and Cole, *New Perspectives*, , 167–99.

67. J. Berry, "The Origins of Krio Vocabulary," *Sierra Leone Studies*, n.s., no. 12 (December 1959): 298–307; Eldred D. Jones, "Some Aspects of the Sierra Leone Patois or Krio," *Sierra Leone Studies*, n.s., no. 6 (June 1956) 97–109.

68. For some sources on plant names, see F. C. Deighton, "Origins of Creole Plant Names," *Sierra Leone Studies*, o.s., no. 22 (September 1939): 29–32.

69. See Harrell-Bond, Howard, and Skinner, *Community Leadership*; also, Michael P. Banton, "The Origins of Tribal Administration in Freetown," *Sierra Leone Studies*, n.s., no. 2 (June 1954): 109–19; Banton, *West African City: A Study of Tribal Life in Freetown* (London: Oxford University Press, 1957); C. Magbaily Fyle, "XXX," Africana Research Bulletin 9, nos. 1–2 (October 1978): 100–104, has taken Harrell-Bond, Howard, and Skinner to task for their error in suggesting that the Christians in Krio society were ethnically or culturally distinct from the Muslims precisely because of religion. Like Banton, Harrell-Bond, Howard, and Skinner did not take into cognizance the fact that the referent "Oku" applied to all Liberated Africans of Yoruba provenance, regardless of creed. Hence, such Liberated Africans as Mohammed Shitta Bey, Bishop Samuel Adjai Crowther, Sir Samuel Lewis, and Mohammed Sanusie were all Oku, even though they were adherents of different religious faiths.

70. Peel, *Religious Encounter*, 190.

71. For a more substantive study of the concept of Creoles and creolization, see Charles Stewart, ed., *Creolization: History, Ethnography, Theory* (Walnut Creek, CA: Left Coast Press, 2007); Jean Bernabé, Patrick Chamoiseau, and Raphaël Confiant, Éloge de la Créolité (Paris: Gallimard, 1989); Edward Kamau Brathwaite, *The Development of Creole Society in Jamaica, 1770–1820* (Oxford: Clarendon Press, 1971); Robert Chaudenson, *Creolization of Language and Culture* (London: Routledge, 2001); Okwui Enwezor, Carlos Basualdo, Ute Meta Bauer, Susanne Ghez, Sarat Maharaj, Mark Nash, and Octavio Zaya, eds., *Créolité and Creolization, Documenta* 11, *Platform*3 (Ostfildern-Ruit: Hatje Cantz, 2002); Edouard Glissant, *Caribbean Discourse: Selected Essays*, trans. J. Michael Dash (Charlottesville: University of Virginia Press, 1999); Hannerz, "The World in Creolisation"; Jacqueline Knörr, "Towards Conceptualizing Creolization and Creoleness" (Working Paper, Max Planck Institute for Social Anthroplogy, Halle [Saale], Germany, 2008). For an analysis of the definition of *Creole* as applied to the Sierra Leone Krio, see John Peterson, "The Sierra Leone Creole: A Reappraisal," in Fyfe and Jones, *Freetown*, 100–117; see also David Skinner and Barbara E. Harrell-Bond, "Misunderstandings Arising from the Use of the Term 'Creole' in the Literature on Sierra Leone," *Africa* 47, no. 3 (1977): 305–20; and Akintola J. G. Wyse, "On Misunderstandings Arising from the Use of the Term 'Creole' in the Literature on Sierra Leone: A Rejoinder," *Africa* 49, no. 4 (1979): 408–17.

72. Dixon-Fyle and Cole, *New Perspectives*, 5.

73. Knörr, "Towards Conceptualizing Creolization and Creoleness," 3.

74. Ibid., 4; see also, Stewart, *Creolization*, 8. The so-called Black Poor included a few white women from England; however, they had virtually no demographic impact on the new society.

75. Peterson, "Sierra Leone Creole," 108.

76. Fashole-Luke, "Religion in Freetown," 127–42.

77. Muslim Krio parents who took in wards almost invariably refrained from changing the names of children adopted from interior communities; however, merchants from the Muslim Krio communities of Frobay, Fulatogn, and Aberdeen who took wives from the hinterland invariably changed the names of their new wives, and replaced the brides' "native" names with names of Yoruba origin.

78. Fyfe, *History of Sierra Leone*, 131.

79. Ibid., 172. The Register of the Annie Walsh Memorial School from its early years to the mid-twentieth century is illustrative of the (krio)lization process; a significant proportion of the girls enrolled in the school, from the turn of the century to later years, retained their "native" names, such as Fatmatta, Isatu, and so on.

80. Dixon-Fyle and Cole, *New Perspectives*, 13; Banton, *West African City*, 11–12; Fyfe, *History of Sierra Leone*, 480–87.

81. Dixon-Fyle and Cole, *New Perspectives*; Harrell-Bond, Howard, and Skinner, *Community Leadership*, 79–80.

82. Fyfe, *History of Sierra Leone*, 135.

83. Dixon-Fyle and Cole, *New Perspectives*, 13.

CHAPTER 2: ISLAM, CHRISTIANITY, AND THE STATE
IN COLONIAL FREETOWN

Epigraph: See T. G. O. Gbadamosi, *The Growth of Islam among the Yoruba, 1841–1908* (London: Longman, 1978).

1. David Robinson, in *Paths of Accommodation: Muslim Societies and French Colonial Authorities in Senegal and Mauritania, 1880–1920* (Athens: Ohio University Press, 2000), looks at the efforts of the French authorities to handle the Islamic presence in Saint Louis. Quite unlike the British, the French sought to develop an informed policy vis-à-vis its relations with the Muslim community in the city.

2. Ibid., 4.

3. Ibid., 6.

4. See Michael Crowder, *West Africa under Colonial Rule* (London: Hutchinson, 1968), 165–68.

5. Anglicized as *Aku* in Christopher Fyfe, *A History of Sierra Leone* (Oxford: Oxford University Press, 1962); John Peterson, *Province of Freedom: A History of Sierra Leone, 1787–1870* (London: Faber and Faber, 1969); and Akintola J. G. Wyse, *The Krio of Sierra Leone: An Interpretive History* (London: Hurst, 1989).

6. John S. Trimingham and Christopher H. Fyfe, "The Early Expansion of Islam in Sierra Leone," *Sierra Leone Bulletin of Religion* 2 (December 1960): 34. For a more detailed study of this episode in the history of Sierra Leone, see C. Magbaily Fyle, *The Solima Yalunka Kingdom: Pre-Colonial Politics, Economics, and Society* (Freetown: Nyakon, 1979).

7. See Fyle, *Solima Yalunka Kingdom*; and Fyfe, *History of Sierra Leone*, 5–6.

8. Fyfe, *History of Sierra Leone*, 65.

9. Ibid., 57–58.

10. Ibid., 89.

11. For a description of the evangelizing activities of Father Berreira among the Soso, see Christopher Fyfe, *Sierra Leone Inheritance* (London: Oxford University Press, 1964), 49–53 (hereafter cited in text as *SLI*).

12. It is probable that there were no Arabs in the region, as Europeans during this period had a tendency to describe the lighter-skinned Fula as "Arabs" or "Moors."

13. The journals of Watt and Winterbottom served to convince the colony government to approve the voyage of Dr. Edward Wilmot Blyden, eight decades later, to the same region.

14. Also see Alusine Jalloh and David E. Skinner, eds., *Islam and Trade in Sierra Leone* (Trenton, NJ: Africa World Press), 12.

15. Fyfe, *History of Sierra Leone*, 186; see also Jean H. Kopytoff, *A Preface to Modern Nigeria: The 'Sierra Leonians' in Yoruba, 1830–1890* (Madison: University of Wisconsin Press, 1965), 32–33; and Peterson, *Province of Freedom*, 215.

16. Kopytoff, *Preface to Modern Nigeria*, 32; and Jalloh and Skinner, *Islam and Trade*, 12.

17. CO 267/172 Madden Report, vol. 3, part 2, PRO.

18. For a discussion of efforts by church officials to undermine African traditional forms of religious worship, as well as Islam, see E. W. Fashole-Luke, "Christianity and Islam in Freetown," *Sierra Leone Bulletin of Religion* 9, no. 1 (June 1967): 1–16.

19. Christopher Fyfe, "Reform in West Africa: The Abolition of the Slave Trade," in *History of West Africa*, ed. J. F. Ade Ajayi and Michael Crowder (London: Longman, 1974), 2:33–34.

20. Ibid.

21. Peterson, *Province of Freedom*, 62–63.

22. See Arthur T. Porter, "Religious Affiliation in Freetown, Sierra Leone," *Africa* 23, no. 1 (1953): 7; and Kopytoff, *Preface to Modern Nigeria*, 5. The name Church Missionary Society was formally adopted in 1813.

23. CO 267/47, MacCarthy to Bathurst, 2 January 1818, PRO; Peterson, *Province of Freedom*, 65–66.

24. Fyfe, *History of Sierra Leone*, 140.

25. CO 267/65, Reffell to MacCarthy, enclosure no. 36, 19 December 1823, PRO.

26. Lamin Sanneh, *Abolitionists Abroad: American Blacks and the Making of Modern West Africa* (Cambridge, MA: Harvard University Press, 1999), 113.

27. CA1/04/22, Article 26, "Instructions to Managers of Liberated African Villages," CMS.

28. Fyfe, *History of Sierra Leone*, 129.

29. CO 267/42, MacCarthy to Colonial Office, dispatch no. 74, 31 May 1816, PRO.

30. Peterson, *Province of Freedom*, 97.

31. Fyfe, *History of Sierra Leone*, 131; see also Sanneh, *Abolitionists Abroad*, 116.

32. CA1/04/93, Lewis to Haensel, 10 April 1828, CMS; Fyfe, *History of Sierra Leone*, 131; the adage of "Spare the rod and spoil the child" was religiously adhered to in the mission schools, a practice that remained pervasive in Sierra Leone until recent times.

33. Peterson, *Province of Freedom*, 101.

34. CA1/0126B, Reverend Johnson's journal, 21 February 1820, CMS.

35. J. Lorand Matory, *Black Atlantic Religion: Tradition, Transnationalism, and*

Matriarchy in the Afro-Brazilian Candomblé (Princeton, NJ: Princeton University Press, 2005), 42–43.

36. CA1/079/1, Reverend Crowther to Reverend Jowett, Fourah Bay, 11 February 1837, CMS.

37. Ibid.

38. Ibid.

39. CA1/0126/2A, Reverend Johnson's journal, Regent, 25 March 1820, CMS.

40. Peterson, *Province of Freedom*, 163.

41. CO267/65, Hamilton to Bathurst (enclosure no. 3), 31 January 1825, PRO.

42. Ibid.

43. CO 267/47, MacCarthy to Bathurst (observations/explanation on minutes on Sierra Leone), 2 January 1818, PRO; Reffell to Raban, 13 December 1826, no. 8, CMS.

44. CA1/0105/33, Report of J. U. Graf, 25 June 1839, PRO.

45. CA1/0195/4b, Entry of J. U. Graf, 1 October 1844, CMS.

46. Linda M. Heywood and John K. Thornton, *Central Africans, Atlantic Creoles, and the Foundation of the Americas, 1585–1660* (Cambridge: Cambridge University Press, 2007), 65.

47. Ibid., 66–67.

48. CO 267/23, Council Chambers, Sierra Leone, 31 October 1849, PRO.

49. See Lamin O. Sanneh, "Historical Source Materials on Islam in Sierra Leone," *Journal of the Historical Society of Sierra Leone* 1, no. 2 (June 1977); see also Sanneh, *Islamic Consciousness and African Society: An Essay on Historical Interaction*, Sierra Leone Collection (Freetown: Fourah Bay College Library, n.d.), pamphlet.

50. Fyfe, *History of Sierra Leone*, 148–49.

51. Porter, "Religious Affiliation in Freetown," 7.

52. See Paul E. Lovejoy, "The Yoruba Factor in the Trans-Atlantic Slave Trade," in *Yoruba Diaspora in the Atlantic World*, ed. Toyin Falola and Matt D. Childs, 40–55; Fyfe, *History of Sierra Leone*, 156.

53. See J. F. Ade Ajayi, "The Aftermath of the Fall of Old Oyo," in Ajayi and Crowder, *History of West Africa*, 2:129–66; also see Saburi O. Biobaku, *The Egba and Their Neighbours, 1842–1872* (Ibadan, Nigeria: Ibadan University Press, 1991); and Gibril R. Cole, "Liberated Slaves and Islam in Nineteenth-Century West Africa," in Falola and Childs, *Yoruba Diaspora in the Atlantic World*, 383–403.

54. Biobaku, *Egba and Their Neighbours*, 13; see also J. F. Ade Ajayi, "Samuel Adjai Crowther of Oyo," in *Africa Remembered: Narratives by West Africans from the Era of the Slave Trade*, ed. Philip D. Curtin (Madison: University of Wisconsin Press, 1967); and Cole, "Liberated Slaves and Islam," 385.

55. See J. F. Ade Ajayi, *Christian Missions in Nigeria, 1841–1891: The Making of a New Elite* (London: Longman, 1965); Fyfe, *Sierra Leone Inheritance*, 149; and Cole, "Liberated Slaves and Islam."

56. Ajayi, "Aftermath of the Fall of Old Oyo," 142; and Cole, "Liberated Slaves and Islam."

57. CO 267/204, Report of Governor Pine, enclosed in dispatch no. 88, 27 October 1848, PRO.

58. CO 267/60, Turner to Bathurst, 20 September 1824, PRO.

59. CO 323/148, Denham to Hay, Freetown, 13 February 1827, PRO.

60. CO 267/118, Treason Indictment, J. W. Cole, Colonial Secretary, Freetown, 3 January 1833, PRO.

61. Peterson, *Province of Freedom*, 213.

62. *Liberated African Letter Book*, 1820–1826, J. Reffel to Superintendent, Government House, February 1826, SLA.

63. Fyfe, *History of Sierra Leone*, 188.

64. T. Cole to J. Auguin, Liberated African Department, Freetown, 1 April 1831, SLA.

65. Ibid.

66. Robinson, *Paths of Accommodation*, 79.

67. Ibid., 64–65.

68. CO 267/119, Order-in-Council Chamber, Executive Council Chamber, Freetown, Sierra Leone, 24 October 1832, PRO/SLA.

69. *Liberated African Letter Book*, 1830–1831, Liberated African Department, 11 September 1831, SLA.

70. *Liberated African Letter Book*, 1831, SLA.

71. *Liberated African letter Book*, 1831–1834, no. 5, F. Campbell to T. Caulker, 21 October 1832, Freetown, SLA.

72. *Liberated African Letter Book*, Findlay to Viscount Goderich, 15 May 1833, SLA.

73. Fyfe, *History of Sierra Leone*, 190.

74. *Liberated African Letter Book*, 1831–1834, C. B. Jones to J. Dougherty, 12 November 1832, SLA.

75. CO 267/118, Enclosure no. 4, Findlay to R.W. Hay, 14 January 1833, PRO.

76. CO 267/118. One of the injured militia troops suffered from "a blow from a cutlass [machete] on the head, the other with an arrow in the cheek."

77. *Liberated African Letter Book*, Findlay to Goderich, 15 May 1833, SLA.

78. Peterson, *Province of Freedom*, 215.

79. Fyfe, *History of Sierra Leone*, 187.

80. Cole, "Liberated Africans and Islam," 389.

81. Findlay to Goderich, 15 May 1833, PRO; Peterson, *Province of Freedom*, 215.

82. Findlay to R. W. Hay (Report on Cobolo, no. 69), 5 December 1832, SLA.

83. CO 267/118, Findlay to Hay, 15 May 1833, PRO.

84. Findlay to Hay, May 1833, PRO.

85. Findlay to Hay (Examination of Ackoo Rebels, enclosure no. 4), 14 January 1833, PRO.

86. Findlay to Hay, January 1833, PRO.

87. CO323/15, W. H. Savage to Hay, personal letter dated 11 July 1828, PRO.

88. Savage to Hay, 1828, PRO.

89. Peterson, *Province of Freedom*, 216–17.

90. Ibid.; Fyfe, *History of Sierra Leone*, 187.

91. Peterson, *Province of* Freedom, 216.

92. Quoted in Fyfe, *History of Sierra Leone*, 187.

93. CO 267/119, Findlay to Hay, 2 March 1833 (Proclamation dated 1 March 1833, enclosure no. 1), PRO.

94. CO 267/119, Findlay to Hay, PRO.

95. Howard Temperley, "Anti-Slavery as a Form of Cultural Imperialism," in *Anti-Slavery, Religion, and Reform: Essays in Memory of Roger Anstey*, ed. Christine Bolt and Seymour Drescher (Folkestone, Kent: Dawson, 1980), 335–50.

96. CO 267/119, Proclamation, 1 March 1833, PRO.

97. Ibid.

98. Ibid.

99. Ibid.

100. M. S. D. Alharazim, "The Origins and Progress of Islam in Sierra Leone," *Sierra Leone Studies*, o.s., no. 21 (January 1939): 13–26.

101. Peterson, *Province of Freedom*, 218.

102. B. B. Ibrahim, *Fourah Bay: The First Hundred Years 1836–1936*. A pamphlet presented at the launching of the Fourah Bay Community Foundation, 11 April 1993. Mohammed Badamasie may have added the surname of Savage as a tribute to the benefactor of the Muslim community.

103. Interview with Pa Babatunde Deen-Gabisie, Fourah Bay, June 1978.

104. Peterson, *Province of Freedom*, 164.

105. CA1/0195/48b, Rev, J. F. Schon, Report of 3rd Quarter, 19 August 1836, CMS.

106. Ibid.

107. CO 267/154, Doherty to Lord John Russell, enclosure no. 1 (in dispatch no. 77), 4 December 1839, PRO.

108. Ibid.

109. CO 267/154, Doherty to Russell, enclosure no. 2, 4 December 1839, PRO.

110. Ibid. "Lass-mamy" refers to holy water used by local Muslims, which the Christian clergy equated with superstition.

111. Ibid.

112. Ibid.; see also Cole, "Liberated Africans and Islam," 391.

113. CO 267/154, Doherty to Russell.

114. CO 267/154, Doherty to Russell, dispatch no. 77, PRO.

115. Ibid.

116. CO 267/154, Doherty to Russell, PRO.

117. Ibid.; Cole, "Liberated Africans and Islam," 392.

118. Cole, "Liberated Africans and Islam," 392.

119. CO 267/154, enclosure no. 4, PRO.

120. Ibid.

121. CO 267/154, Russell to H. M. Advocate Attorney and Solicitor General, 19 March 1840, PRO.

122. CO 267/154, Russell to Doherty, no. 41, 3April 1840, PRO.

123. Fyfe, *History of Sierra Leone*, 218.

124. CO 267/172, Madden Report, part 3, 1841, PRO.

125. Fyfe, *History of Sierra Leone*, 223.

126. CO 267/193, Macdonald to Gladstone, dispatch no. 119, 13 July 1846, PRO.

127. Ibid.

128. Lamin Sanneh, *Piety and Power: Muslims and Christians in West Africa* (New York: Orbis Books, 1996), 10.

129. See Jean Herskovits, "The Sierra Leoneans of Yorubaland," in *Africa and the West: Intellectual Responses to European Culture*, ed. Philip D. Curtin (Madison: University of Wisconsin Press, 1972), 75–98.

130. For a detailed study of the life and work of Rev. (later Bishop) Samuel Adjai Crowther, see Ajayi, *Christian Missions*; Ajayi, "Samuel Crowther of Oyo"; and E. A.Ayandele, *The Missionary Impact on Modern Nigeria, 1842–1914: A Political and Social Analysis* (London; Longman, 1966).

131. Ajayi, *Christian Missions*, 26. Reverend Crowther ultimately combined his "Christian" and Yoruba names, as did many Krio.

132. CA1/079/o, Reverend Crowther's journal, 11 December 1843, CMS.

133. CA1/079/o, Reverend Crowther's journal, CMS.

134. CA1/079/11a, Reverend Crowther's journal, 25 March 1844, CMS.

135. CA1/079/11a, Reverend Crowther's journal. CMS; also Cole, "Liberated Africans and Islam," 394.

136. Cole, "Liberated Africans and Islam."

137. Ibid.

138. Robinson, *Paths of Accommodation*, 80.

CHAPTER 3: TRADE, RELIGION, AND THE COLONIAL STATE

1. Nehemia Levtzion, "Islam in the Bilad al-Sudan to 1800," in *The History of Islam in Africa*, ed. Nehemiah Levtzion and Randall L. Pouwels (Athens: Ohio University Press, 2000), 63–91. See also Philip D. Curtin, *Economic Change in Pre-colonial Africa: Senegambia in the Era of the Slave Trade* (Madison: University of Wisconsin Press, 1975); Boubacar Barry, *Senegambia and the Atlantic Slave Trade* (Cambridge: Cambridge University Press, 1988); Yves Person, *Samori: Une Revolution Dyula*, 3 vols. (Dakar, Senegal: IFAN, 1968–75); Richard Roberts, "Long-Distance Trade and Production: Sinsani in the Nineteenth Century," *Journal of African History* 21, no. 2 (1980): 169–88.

2. Governor's Letter Book, Local Letters, 1854, SLA.

3. R. Dougan to Calle Modu, Freetown, 30 May 1855, Governor's Letter Book (local letters 1854–59), SLA.

4. David Robinson, *Paths of Accommodation: Muslim Societies and French Colonial Authorities in Senegal and Mauritania*, 1880–1920 (Athens: Ohio University Press, 2000), 80.

5. Sierra Leone Blue Book, 1879, SLA.

6. Edward W. Blyden, *Christianity, Islam and the Negro Race*, 2nd ed. (London: Whittingham, 1887; Baltimore: Black Classic Press, 1994), 263.

7. Christopher Fyfe, *A History of Sierra Leone* (Oxford: Oxford University Press, 1962), 368.

8. Interview with Mrs. Tairatu Deen, Freetown, June 1978.

9. Miscellaneous, Aborigines no. 54, Caravans from Interior, 2 April 1879, SLA.

10. Ibid.

11. T. G. Lawson to Government House, Miscellaneous, 7 April 1879, SLA.

12. Lawson to Parkes, Memorandum, A107/86, 13 October 1886, SLA.

13. Momodu Wakka, miscellaneous, no. 110/86, Re. Complaint for Charges on Canoe Hire, Freetown, 13 October 1886, no. 551, SLA.

14. For a discussion of the role of caravans in long-distance commerce in nineteenth-century West Africa, see Roberts, "Long-Distance Trade and Production."

15. Miscellaneous, no. A42/8G, Lawson to Parkes, 10 November 1886, SLA; see also David Skinner, "Sierra Leone Relations with the Northern Rivers and the Influence of Islam in the Colony," *International Journal of Sierra Leone Studies* 1, no. 1 (1989): 91–113.

16. Lawson to Parkes, 20 December 1888, SLA.

17. Lawson to Parkes, 29 December 1886, SLA.

18. Fyfe, *History of Sierra Leone*, 448.

19. See M'baye Gueye and A. Adu Boahen, "African Initiatives and Resistance in West Africa, 1880–1914," in *Africa Under Colonial Domination, 1880–1935*, ed. A. Adu Boahen, vol. 3 of *General History of Africa* (Berkeley: University of California Press, 1985), 114–48.

20. Ibid., 125–26.

21. Ibid., 236.

22. Blyden, *Christianity, Islam and the Negro Race*, 268.

23. Allen M. Howard, "Trade and Islam in Sierra Leone, 18th–20th Centuries," in *Islam and Trade in Sierra Leone*, ed. Alusine Jalloh and David E. Skinner (Trenton, NJ: Africa World Press, 1997), 22–27.

24. Howard uses the example of Aberdeen traders to illustrate the role of Muslim Krio in the kola and cattle trade between the interior and the colony. However, the involvement of the Muslim Krio transcended the trade in these items; the Aberdeen, Fula Town, and Fourah Bay merchants often pooled their resources in order to procure large quantities of diverse trade items for resale in Freetown (interview with Mrs. Ajola Deen, Freetown, June 1978); see also Robinson, *Paths of Accommodation*, for similar developments in Senegal.

25. Interview with Baba Tounkara, Krojimi sub-division of Fourah Bay, Freetown, July 1998.

26. Trade diaspora groups, such as the Tounkara at Fourah Bay, were part of a "highly-inter-related network of communities which maintain ethnic and cultural consciousness through common ethnic identity (and) function(ed) through concerted maintenance of ethnic exclusivity."

27. Howard, "Trade and Islam in Sierra Leone," 29. I am grateful to Professor Howard for graciously providing me with a transcript of personal interviews conducted in Aberdeen village in September 1968.

28. Interviews with Alhaji Mohammed Mahdi (Fourah Bay) and Tairatu Thomas (Fula Town), Freetown, June 1978.

29. Walter Rodney, *A History of the Upper Guinea Coast, 1545–1800* (Oxford: Clarendon Press, 1970), 206.

30. Ibid.

31. Howard interview with Pa Liwali Cole, Aberdeen. See also C. Magbaily Fyle, *The History of Sierra Leone: A Concise Introduction* (London: Evans, 1981), 87–88.

32. Howard interview with Pa Liwali Cole.

33. Muslim Krio farmers had been engaged in small-scale agricultural production for decades before their displacement in interior trade, and their farm production was often recorded in official outlets. CO267/204, Report on Blue Book for 1847 (enclosed in Pine to Grey, 27 October 1848, no. 88), PRO. See also Muctarr J. A. Lewally-Taylor, "The Aku Muslim Communities of East Freetown in the Nineteenth and Twentieth Centuries" (MLitt thesis, University of Edinburgh, 1976).

34. Report on Blue Book, 1847, PRO.

35. Howard interview with Pa Liwali Cole.

36. *Sierra Leone Gazette*, April 1875 (Boat and Canoe Licenses), Sierra Leone Collection, Fourah Bay College Library, Freetown.

37. For a discussion of the fishing techniques of the Fante community and its use

of the drift net, see Emmanuel K. Akyeampong, *Between the Sea and the Lagoon: An Eco-Social History of the Anlo of Southeastern Ghana, c. 1850 to Recent Times* (Athens: Ohio University Press, 2001).

38. *Sierra Leone Gazette*, April 1875.

39. Jones Brothers, "Early History of the Trade of Sierra Leone before the Advent of the Railway System in 1896" (Sierra Leone Collection, Fourah Bay College, Freetown, n.d.), pamphlet.

40. E. Frances White, *Sierra Leone's Settler Women Traders: Women on the Afro-European Frontier* (Ann Arbor: University of Michigan Press, 1987), 27–28; see also her article on "Creole Women Traders in the Nineteenth Century" (working Paper no. 27, African Studies Center, Boston University, 1980), in which White depicts the role of Krio women in colony and interior trade. She traces their ability to excel in trade to an early socialization of girls in the commerce of Yoruba society. See also Mac Dixon-Fyle and Gibril Cole, eds., *New Perspectives on the Sierra Leone Krio* (New York: Peter Lang, 2006), 9–10.

41. *Sierra Leone Weekly News* (SLWN), 28 April 1888, British Library (Newspaper Annex), Colindale, England.

42. *SLWN*, 22 August 1885.

43. Ibid.

44. Ibid.

45. *SLWN*, 1 May 1886, British Library (Newspaper Annex), Colindale, England.

46. Fyfe, *History of Sierra Leone*, 444.

47. Ibid., 383.

48. For an informative and nuanced analysis of the history and role and place of Syrian (and Lebanese, after World War II) merchants in the colonial and postcolonial political economy of Sierra Leone, see Farid R. Anthony, *Sawpit Boy* (Freetown: published by author, 1980).

49. Fyfe, *History of Sierra Leone*, 427–28; see also Michael Crowder, *West Africa under Colonial Rule* (London: Hutchinson, 1968), 93–94. For an analysis of the economic factors accounting for the quest for land appropriation by the imperial powers in West Africa, see J. E. Flint, "Economic Change in West Africa in the Nineteenth Century," in *History of West Africa*, ed. J. F. Ade Ajayi and Michael Crowder, vol. 2 (London: Longman, 1974).

50. Fyfe, *History of Sierra Leone*, 488.

51. Ibid.

52. For a detailed look at the Hut Tax War, see LaRay Denzer and Michael Crowder, "Bai Bureh and the Sierra Léone Hut Tax War of 1898," in *Protest and Power in Black Africa*, ed. Robert I. Rothberg and Ali A. Mazrui (New York: Oxford University Press, 1970), 169–212. See also Arthur Abraham, *An Introduction to the Pre-Colonial History of the Mende of Sierra Leone* (Lewiston, NY: Edwin Mellen Press, 2003), for a substantive discussion of the *Puu Goi* (Hut Tax War).

53. White, *Sierra Leone's Settler Women Traders*, 42–43.

54. Fyfe, *History of Sierra Leone*, 318.

55. Ibid., 460.

56. John D. Hargreaves, "Another Creole Frontier: The Upper Senegal, 1889," *Journal of the Historical Society of Sierra Leone* 1, no. 2 (June 1977). The French colonial administration in Senegal would become concerned subsequently, due to the increased involvement of Muslim and Christian Krio in the activities of Marcus Garvey's Universal Negro Improvement Association in the Senegambia valley.

57. Interview with Alhaji Haroun O. Zubairu, Imam of Fula Town, May 1998. (Alhaji Zubairu was the son of Yazid Fadlu-Deen.)

58. Howard interview with Pa Liwali Cole.

59. Sierra Leone Blue book, 1900, SLA.

60. Interview with Mrs. Tairatu Thomas and Alhaji Mohammed Mahdi, Freetown, June 1978. By the 1900s, the holder of the office of Alkali was restricted to hearing minor cases involving family disputes and issues involving the internal affairs of the jamaat, due to the primacy of the British common law system in the colony.

61. Interview, Alhaji Mohammed Mahdi.

62. Martin Lynn, "Technology, Trade and 'A Race of Native Capitalists': The Krio Diaspora of West Africa and the Steamship, 1852–95," *Journal of African History* 33 (1992): 421–40.

63. Ibid., 422.

64. White, *Sierra Leone's Settler Women Traders*, 43.

65. Interview, Mrs. Tairatu Thomas, June 1978.

66. Ramatoulie O. Othman has cataloged some of the activities of the Muslim Krio community in Banjul (formerly Bathurst) in a pamphlet titled *A Cherished Heritage: Tracing the Roots of the Oku-Marabou—Early 19th to Mid-20th Century*, released amid much fanfare in the Muslim community of Banjul, the Gambia, in 1999.

67. J. Lorand Matory, *Black Atlantic Religion: Tradition, Transnationalism, and Matriarchy in the Afro-Brazilian Candomblé* (Princeton, NJ: Princeton University Press, 2005), 91–92.

68. Interview with Alhaji Mohammed Madhi, July 1978.

CHAPTER 4: THE KRIO DIASPORA IN NIGERIA

1. Hakeem B. Harunah, "Lagos-Abeokuta Relations in Nineteenth Century Yorubaland," in *History of the Peoples of Lagos State*, ed. Ade Adefuye, Babatunde Agiri, and Akinjide Osuntokun (Lagos: Lantern Books, 1987), 194.

2. Christopher Fyfe, *A History of Sierra Leone* (Oxford: Oxford University Press, 1964), 212.

3. Ibid., 213.

4. CA2/031b, Crowther, Extracts for Quarter Ending 25 March 1845, CMS; see also Saburi O. Biobaku, *The Egba and Their Neighbours, 1842–1872* (Ibadan, Nigeria: Ibadan University Press, 1991).

5. Fyfe, *History of Sierra Leone*, 228.

6. CO267/184, N. W. MacDonald, Colonial Secretary (Government Notice), Freetown, 12 June 1844; also, CO267/172, Notice For Emigrants to Demerara and Jamaica, Freetown, 1844, PRO. For a discussion of the recruitment and "transportation" of Liberated Africans to the West Indies, see Monica Schuler, *"Alas, Alas, Kongo": A Social History of Indentured African Immigration into Jamaica 1841–1865* (Baltimore: Johns Hopkins University Press, 1980).

7. CA1/097/7, Crowther, Extracts for Quarter Ending 25 June 1841, CMS.

8. T. G. O. Gbadamosi, *The Growth of Islam among the Yoruba, 1841–1908* (London: Longman, 1978), 27–28.

9. Ibid., 4; Gbadamosi notes that the Lander brothers witnessed a "colourful celebration of the Id al-Fitr" by the local Muslim community on 27 March 1830, as reported

in the published journal of their expedition to trace the course of the Niger during the nineteenth century.

10. L. C. Dioka, *Lagos and Its Environs* (Lagos: First Academic Publishers, 2001), 7–11. For a discussion of Badagry's place in the Atlantic system, see Philip D. Curtin, "The Atlantic Slave Trade, 1600–1800," in *History of West Africa*, ed. J. F. Ade Ajayi and Michael Crowder (London: Longman, 1974), 1:240–68; for relations between Oyo and Dahomey, see I. A. Akinjogbin, "The Expansion of Oyo and the Rise of Dahomey, 1600–1800," in Ajayi and Crowder, *History of West Africa*, 1:305–43.

11. Ade Adefuye, "Oba Akinsemoyin and the Emergence of Modern Lagos," in Adefuye, Agiri, and Osuntokun, *History of the Peoples of Lagos State*, 33–46.

12. For a discussion of this proposition, which was rejected by the British, see Fyfe, *History of Sierra Leone*, 212; see also Jean H. Kopytoff, *A Preface to Modern Nigeria: "The Sierra Leonians" in Yoruba, 1830–1890* (Madison: University of Wisconsin Press, 1965); and Jean Herskovits, "The Sierra Leoneans of Yorubaland," in Curtin, *Africa and the West*, 75–98.

13. For a discussion of the origins of Islam in Yoruba society, see Gbadamosi, *Growth of Islam*, 4–5.

14. Robin Law, "Yoruba Liberated Slaves Who Returned to West Africa," in *The Yoruba Diaspora in the Atlantic World*, ed. Toyin Falola and Matt D. Childs (Bloomington: Indiana University Press, 2004), 350.

15. For a detailed discussion of this episode of the Yoruba experience in Brazil, see Joao José Reis, *Slave Rebellion in Brazil: The Muslim Uprising of 1835 in Bahia*, trans. Arthur Brakel (Baltimore: Johns Hopkins University Press, 1993); see also Joao José Reis and Beatriz Gallotti Mamigonian, "Nagô and Mina: The Yoruba Diaspora in Brazil," in Falola and Childs, *Yoruba Diaspora in the Atlantic World*, 77–110.

16. Law, "Yoruba Liberated Slaves," 356.

17. Gbadamosi, *Growth of Islam*, 28.

18. Solimar Otero, *Afro-Cuban Diasporas in the Atlantic World* (Rochester, NY: University of Rochester Press, 2010), 60.

19. Ibid., 30.

20. Akijide Osuntokun, "Introduction of Christianity and Islam in Lagos State," in Adefuye, Agiri, and Osuntokun, *History of the Peoples of Lagos State*, 126–38.

21. Gbadamosi, *Growth of Islam*, 124–25.

22. Ibid., 126–27. The efforts of Muslims were thwarted by Ifa divination, which granted permission to the CMS to preach in the town.

23. CA2/056, Johnson to CMS, 29 April 1875; also quoted in Gbadamosi, *Growth of Islam*, 124–25.

24. Titilola Euba, "Shitta Bey and the Lagos Muslim Community, 1850–1895," pt. 2, *Nigerian Journal of Islam* 2, no. 2 (June 1972–June 1974): 7–18.

25. Ibid., 15.

26. The term *Oyimbo* was a referent for Europeans in Yoruba society.

27. For a look at the role of women in Lagos markets, see Nina Mba, "Women in Lagos Political History," in Adefuye, Agiri, and Osuntokun, *History of the Peoples of Lagos State*, 233–45. It can be surmised that Saro women may have been involved in supporting the political activities of their fellow Saro, Herbert Macauley, during the early twentieth century.

28. See Gbadamosi, *Growth of Islam*, 31; see also Euba, "Shitta Bey," 7; Lord John Russell to the Duke of Newcastle, recommending the annexation of Lagos, 7 February

1861, in William H. Worger, Nancy L. Clarke, and Edward A. Alpers, *Africa and the West: A Documentary History from the Slave Trade to Independence* (Phoenix, AZ: Oryx Press, 2001), 161.

29. Gbadamosi, *Growth of Islam*, 31–32.

30. See Gibril Cole, "Liberated Slaves and Islam in Nineteenth Century West Africa," in Falola and Childs, *Yoruba Diaspora in the Atlantic World*, 398.

31. Gbadamosi, *Growth of Islam*, 30.

32. Cole, "Liberated Slaves and Islam," 398.

33. Euba explains that the title of Seriki Musulumi is derived from the Hausa Sarkin Musulumi, which is itself a derivative of the Arabic *Amir al- Mu'minin* (Commander of the Faithful). While the title was usually invested in a singular individual serving as both secular and spiritual leader, it appears that the position was split in the Yoruba context.

34. Euba, "Shitta Bey," 8.

35. Ibid., 11.

36. Gbadamosi, *Growth of Islam*, 137.

37. Ibid., 138.

38. Euba, "Shitta Bey," 12; Gbadamosi, *Growth of Islam*, 167.

39. Euba, "Shitta Bey," 13.

40. Ibid. Memories of Quilliam's visit and the opening of the Shitta Bey mosque remain important in the history of Islam in Nigeria, particularly in Lagos. A British barrister, Quilliam was converted to Islam in 1888 and subsequently gained recognition as the Sheikh-ul Islam of the British Isles in 1894, largely due to his counseling and legal work for and on behalf of the Turkish and Persian sovereigns. The conferring of the Order of the Medjidiye on Shitta was appreciated, particularly because it was "the highest distinction that can be bestowed on a civilian."

41. Ibid., 14.

42. Ibid.

CHAPTER 5: PIETY AND PRAXIS:
RELIGION IN DAILY LIFE

1. David Robinson, *Muslim Societies in African History* (Cambridge: Cambridge University Press, 2004), 43.

2. See T. G. O. Gbadamosi, *The Growth of Islam among the Yoruba, 1841–1908* (London: Longman, 1978), for a description of the administrative structure of the mosque in nineteenth-century Lagos. While there existed some similarities between the mosques in Freetown and Lagos, there was a striking dissimilarity between the two regarding the integration of traditional Yoruba titles. The Freetown Oku Muslim communities did not incorporate such traditional Yoruba titles as *Oba Imale* (king of the Muslims), and secular titles like Balogun, Asipa, and Otun into the administrative structure of the mosque. Titles like Balogun and Asipa were incorporated into the leadership structure of esoteric societies such as the Odeh (Untin Society).

3. John Renard, *101 Questions and Answers on Islam* (New York: Gramercy Books, 1998), 33. For more detailed studies of the religious teachings of Islam, and Islam in African societies, see *The Cambridge History of Islam*, ed. Peter M. Holt, Ann K. S. Lambton, and Bernard Lewis, 4 vols. (Cambridge: Cambridge University Press, 1977);

The New Cambridge History of Islam, vol. 1, *The Formation of the Islamic World, Sixth to Eleventh Centuries*, ed. Chase F. Robinson (Cambridge: Cambridge University Press, 2009); Marshall G. S. Hodgson, *The Venture of Islam*, vol. 1, *The Classical Age of Islam* (Chicago: University of Chicago Press, 1974); Ira M. Lapidus, *A History of Islamic Societies* (Cambridge: Cambridge University Press, 1988); Ahmed Ali, *Al-Qur'an: A Contemporary Translation* (Princeton, NJ: Princeton University Press, 2001); John L. Esposito, ed., *The Oxford History of Islam* (Oxford: Oxford University Press, 2000); Seyyed Hussein Nasr, *Islam: Religion, History, and Civilization* (New York: HarperCollins, 2002).

4. For a detailed examination of the office of Imam, see M. el Farsi and I. Hrbek, "The Coming of Islam and the Expansion of the Muslim Empire," in *Africa from the Seventh to the Eleventh Century*, ed. M. El Fasi and I. Hrbek, vol. 3 of *General History of Africa* (Berkeley: University of California Press, 1988), 16–30; see also Murray Last, "The Sokoto Caliphate and Borno," in *Africa in the Nineteenth Century Until the 1880s*, ed. J. F. Ade Ajayi, vol. 6 of *General History of Africa* (Berkeley: University of California Press, 1985), 545–59; and M. A. Haleem Eliasii, *The Holy Quran: Transliteration in Roman Script* (New Delhi: Kitab Bhavan, 1978), x–xi.

5. Eliasii, *Holy Quran*, x.

6. Imam Yadalieu adopted the surname of Savage in tribute to the benefactor of the Fourah Bay community, William Savage, who had served, pro bono, as counsel for the Liberated African Muslims in Sierra Leone's first treason trial in 1839.

7. M. S. D. Alharazim, "The Origins and Progress of Islam in Sierra Leone," *Sierra Leone Studies*, o.s., no. 21 (January 1939): 13–26.

8. Imam Yadalieu's compound, which came to be known as Yadie, served as the spiritual center of the Fourah Bay community and still remains a prominent spot. Yadie was in essence the first place of community worship for the jamaat, a fact that partly accounts for the mosque dispute at Fourah Bay.

9. Barbara E. Harrell-Bond, Allen M. Howard, and David E. Skinner, *Community Leadership and the Transformation of Freetown, 1801–1976* (The Hague: Mouton, 1978), 108.

10. For a substantive analysis of early Islamic education in the colony, see David E. Skinner, "Islam and Education in the Colony and Hinterland of Sierra Leone (1750–1914)," *Canadian Journal of African Studies* 10, no. 3 (1976): 449–529; see also John Peterson, *Province of Freedom: A History of Sierra Leone, 1787–1870* (London: Faber and Faber, 1969), 243.

11. Alharazim, "Origins and Progress of Islam," 16.

12. Ibid.

13. Imam Yadalieu and some of his fellow clerics from Fourah Bay attempted a second trip to Dinguiraye following the successful jihad of Al-Hajj Umar; however, on a stopover visit at Forekaria and Melakhori, the Fourah Bay Imam took ill and eventually died in Forekaria in 1849.

14. See Michael Crowder, *West Africa Under Colonial Rule* (London: Hutchinson, 1968).

15. Gbadamosi, *Growth of Islam*, 60.

16. Peterson, *Province of Freedom*, 243.

17. Ibid.

18. Muslim Krio demonstrated a preference for the Mende form of Bondo, perhaps due to physical proximity and social space shared by the Liberated Africans of Yoruba,

Hausa, and Igbo origins and Liberated Africans of Mende origins in the rural villages outside the colony, particularly at Waterloo , with its exclusive Kossoh (Mende) Town, so named because of its demographic makeup.

19. See Peterson, *Province of Freedom*, 267–68.

20. Ibid., 268.

21. John S. Mbiti, *African Religions and Philosophy* (London: Heinemann, 1969), 121. The issue of clitoridectomy has become a source of serious conflict within contemporary Sierra Leone society, as it is elsewhere in Africa and especially the West, where the circumcision process has acquired the inflammatory epithet of female genital mutilation (FGM), a term that is rejected and much resented by Bondo practitioners in African societies.

22. Olumbe Bassir, "Marriage Rites Among the Aku (Yoruba) of Freetown," *Africa* 24, no. 3 (July 1954): 251–56.

23. Interview, Alhaji Sheku Othman, Imam of Foulah Town, June 1978.

24. Mbiti, *African Religions and Philosophy*, 25.

25. Akintola J. G. Wyse, *The Krio of Sierra Leone: An Interpretive History* (London: Hurst, 1989), 11. While *awujoh* generally refers to the ritual ceremony, the word *sara* was exclusively used by the Muslim Krio; however, both refer to the same ritual.

26. Abdul K. Ghazali, "Sierra Leone Muslims and Sacrificial Rituals," *Sierra Leone Bulletin of Religion* 2, no. 1 (June 1960): 27–32. The Fida'u refers to prayers of redemption in Arabic.

27. Eliassi, *Holy Quran*, ix.

28. *Sierra Leone Church Times* 2, no. 10 (16 September 1885).

29. *Methodist Herald*, 23 September 1885.

30. See John W. Nunley, *Moving with the Face of the Devil: Art and Politics in Urban West Africa* (Chicago: University of Illinois Press, 1987), for an interesting study of the "art, lifestyle, organization, and social function" of cultural masquerade groups in contemporary Freetown. Hunley's work looks at the Odelay societies from the perspective of an art historian, and seeks to throw light on "the vigorously creative traditions of Yoruba art in Freetown and shows how the city's secret societies have made these traditions an integral part of life in urban West Africa."

31. Gbadamosi, *Growth of Islam*, 197.

32. Christopher Fyfe, *A History of Sierra Leone* (Oxford: Oxford University Press, 1962), 234; also, Peterson, *Province of Freedom*, 264; Nunley, *Moving with the Face of the Devil*, 24–26.

33. Nunley, *Moving with the Face of the Devil*, 26.

34. CA 1/079/12a, Bishop Crowther's journal, for the quarter ending 25 June 1844, CMS. For a discussion of the Egungun (as the group is known in Yorubaland) in the Nigerian context, see Wole Soyinka, *Aké: The Years of Childhood* (New York: Vintage, 1989). Chinua Achebe's *Things Fall Apart* (London: Heinemann, 1962) also discusses the society in Igbo culture.

35. CA1/097/12a, Bishop Crowther's journal.

36. Ibid.

37. Peterson, *Province of Freedom*, 264.

38. Muctarr J. A. Lewally-Taylor, "The Aku Muslim Communities of East Freetown in the Nineteenth and Twentieth Centuries" (MLitt thesis, University of Edinburgh, 1976). Lewally-Taylor posits that the Alkali's incapacity to resolve the communal dispute led to the abolishing of the office. It will be more accurate to note, however, that

the office suffered a reduction in social significance, due to the primacy of the colonial magistrate court system. The communities of Fourah Bay, Fula Town, and Aberdeen continued to elect Alkali to preside over civil matters, albeit on a limited basis, till recent times.

39. *Sierra Leone Weekly News (SLWN)*, 1 and 8 April 1899, SLA.

40. Fyfe, *History of Sierra Leone*, 609.

41. *SLWN*, 1 April 1899, SLA.

42. Ibid.

43. Interviews with Alhaji Sheku Othman, Imam of Fula Town, and Pa Babatunde Gabisi of Fourah Bay, June 1978, Freetown.

44. Alharazim, "Origins and Progress of Islam," 15–16; Harrell-Bond, Howard, and Skinner, *Community Leadership*, 109; see also Lewally-Taylor, "Aku Muslim Communities."

45. Alharazim, "Origins and Progress of Islam," 15–16.

46. Lewally-Taylor, "Aku Muslim Communities," 116.

47. Alharazim, "Origins and Progress of Islam," 16.

48. Lewlly-Taylor, "Aku Muslim Communities," 116.

49. *SLWN*, 1 April 1899, 2–3, SLA. The editor cited an "Arabic document dated February 1, 1836," which was tendered, as evidence in the case, as Yadalieu's proof of ownership of the land.

50. Ibid. It appears that even though he had several children, William Savage did not leave a will upon his death, thereby creating a situation that led to intrafamily disputes over his vast real-estate holdings.

51. Ibid. See also *Trust Deed of the Fourah Bay Mosque*, Sierra Leone Collection (Freetown: Fourah Bay College Library, n.d.). The fluid transfer of ownership of the land in Fourah Bay was complicated by the acquisitive capacity of British merchants such as T. A. Rosenbush, who, with his brother, started a "loan bank" in Freetown, and "even issued their own banknotes." (See Fyfe, *History of Sierra Leone*, 346.)

52. *Division at Fourah Bay*, Sierra Leone Collection (Freetown: Fourah Bay College Library, n.d.). The authenticity of this document is also a source of controversy, with questions raised as to who actually wrote it, when it was written, and whose version of the land dispute is represented therein.

53. The land was purchased for the sum of £48.5s.

54. *SLWN*, 1 April 1898, p. 3, SLA.

55. Ibid.

56. Ibid.

57. Ibid.

58. Fyfe, *History of Sierra Leone*, 498. Like almost all Muslim Krio in the colony, George had Christian as well as Muslim names and so was able to secure admission into Christian institutions such as the CMS Grammar School and Fourah Bay College.

59. Ibid.

60. Lewally-Taylor, "Aku Muslim Communities," 128–29.

61. *SLWN*, 27 December 1902, SLA.

62. Robinson, *Muslim Societies*, 42–43.

63. Secret society masquerade groups, including the Egugu, were, and still are, cognizant of the need to refrain from performing adjacent to the mosque in the Muslim Krio communities.

64. Lewally-Taylor, "Aku Muslim Communities," 179.

65. Gbadamosi, *Growth of Islam*, 199.

66. The liberal wing of the jamaat, led by Gheirawanieu George, ultimately won the lawsuit in 1901; however, the conservative Tamba remained unreconciled, leading to further legal tussles between the two groups in subsequent years during the twentieth century. The Tamba faction still retains control of the central mosque.

67. C. Magbaily Fyle, "Popular Islam and Political Expression in Sierra Leone," in *Islam and Trade in Sierra Leone*, ed. Alusine Jalloh and David E. Skinner (Trenton, NJ: Africa World Press, 1997), 161–77; see also Nunley, *Moving with the Face of the Devil*. The lantern celebration has grown to unanticipated proportions in present-day Freetown and is identified with, and has become known more for, "debauchery" than for the piety reflected in the nineteenth century. Consequently, Freetown Muslim leaders have sought to prevail on the local government to discontinue the practice at the end of the Ramadan fasting period.

68. Fyfe, *History of Sierra Leone*, 228.

69. The tradition of using songs to parody social conditions in the nation, and the use of the lantern parades as vehicles for political expression, continue to this day, as shown by C. Magbaily Fyle, cited above. The inhabitants of the Freetown Muslim communities likewise used the occasion of lantern parades to lampoon colony government policy and community officials in the late nineteenth and early twentieth centuries.

70. Nunley, *Moving with the Face of the Devil*, 161–62.

71. Personal communication with Abou Whyte, a leading float builder and Freetown cultural icon, June 2009.

72. Wyse, *Krio of Sierra Leone*, 9–10.

73. Ibid., 10.

74. *SLWN*, 22 April 1893, SLA.

75. *SLWN*, 27 December 1902, SLA.

76. Ibid.

77. Gibril R. Cole, "Embracing Islam and African Traditions in a British Colony: The Muslim Krios of Sierra Leone, 1787–1910" (PhD diss., University of California, Los Angeles, 2000), 198.

78. Alharazim, "Origins and Progress of Islam," 16; Fyfe, *History of Sierra Leone*, 414–15.

CHAPTER 6: EDUCATION AND EDUCATIONAL REFORM WITHIN THE MUSLIM COMMUNITY

1. E. A. Ayandele, *The Missionary Impact on Modern Nigeria, 1842–1914: A Political and Social Analysis* (London: Longman, 1966), 206. See also Jean Herskovits, "The Sierra Leoneans of Yorubaland," in *Africa and the West: Intellectual Responses to European Culture*, ed. Philip D. Curtin (Madison: University of Wisconsin Press, 1972), 88–89.

2. Jean Herskovits, "Sierra Leoneans of Yorubaland."

3. See also Curtin, "African Reactions in Perspective," in *Africa and the West*, 231–44.

4. *SLWN*, 27 May 1893, SLA; *Sierra Leone Times*, 27 May 1893; see also Peter O. Esedebe, *Pan-Africanism: The Idea and Movement, 1776–1963* (Washington, DC:

Howard University Press, 1982); and Hollis R. Lynch, ed., *Black Spokesman: Selected Published Writings of Edward Wilmot Blyden* (London: Frank Cass, 1971), 200–201.

5. Lynch, *Black Spokesman*.

6. Harry Sawyerr, "The Development of Theology at Fourah Bay College," in *One Hundred Years of University Education in Sierra Leone, 1876–1976* (Freetown: Celebrations Committee, 1976), 1–7.

7. CO323/148, Liberated African Department, Order of the General Superintendent of Schools, 25 March 1827, PRO; Findlay to Goderich, 7 April 1832, Liberated African Letter Book, 1831–1834; Lamb to Wright, 6 July 1877, CMS; see also John Peterson, *Province of Freedom: A History of Sierra Leone, 1787–1870* (Evanston, IL: Northwestern University Press, 1969), 164–65.

8. CO323/148.

9. CO267/204, Report on Blue Book for 1847, enclosed in Pine to Grey, 27 October 1848, no. 88, PRO.

10. Ibid.

11. CO267/182, Campbell to Bathurst, dispatch no. 51, 22 April 1827, PRO.

12. Interview, Alhaji Sheikh Othman, June 1978; for a scholarly analysis of Islamic education in Sierra Leone, see David E. Skinner, "Islam and Education in the Colony and Hinterland of Sierra Leone (1750–1914)," *Canadian Journal of African Studies* 10, no. 3 (1976): 499–520; and Skinner, "Mande Settlement and the Development of Islamic Institutions in Sierra Leone," *International Journal of African Historical Studies* 11 (1978): 32–62.

13. Edward W. Blyden, *Christianity, Islam and the Negro Race*, 2nd ed. (London: Whittingham, 1887; Baltimore: Black Classic Press, 1994), xiii (hereafter cited in text as *CIN*).

14. Pfander (1803–1865) served in the CMS mission in Agra, northern India, and later in Peshawar, and after 1837 aroused great controversy by what many Muslims perceived as his unflattering scholarly representation of the Islamic faith compared to his own Christian religion.

15. Skinner, "Islam and Education."

16. Barbara A. Harrell-Bond, Allen M. Howard, and David E. Skinner, *Community Leadership and the Transformation of Freetown, 1801–1976* (The Hague: Mouton, 1978), 114.

17. Peterson, *Province of Freedom*, 245. Alfa Amara emerged subsequently as a prominent and influential leader in the colony's Muslim community and was quite pivotal in creating a relationship of mutual accommodation and cooperation between the colony government and Muslims.

18. Interviews: Nasiru Dahnya, June 1978; and Alieu Muctarr, Foulah Town, June 1978. Fieldwork done at Foulah Town reflected a deep-seated affection for Dr. Blyden and his son, Edward Blyden II, in the community the elder Blyden called home for much of his life. In many ways, the Blyden family is considered an integral part of the community up to the present.

19. J. Isawa Elaigwu and Ali A. Mazrui, "Nation-Building and Changing Political Structures," in *Africa Since 1935*, ed. Ali A. Mazrui, vol. 8 of *General History of Africa* (Berkeley: University of California Press, 1999), 477; see also Christopher Fyfe, A *History of Sierra Leone* (Oxford: Oxford University Press, 1962), 385.

20. CA1/047, Blyden to Venn, 6 September 1871, CMS.

21. Ibid.

22. Ibid.

23. Peterson, *Province of Freedom*, 244.

24. David Robinson, *Paths of Accommodation: Muslim Societies and French Colonial Authorities in Senegal and Mauritania, 1880–1920* (Athens: Ohio University Press, 2000), 80.

25. Peterson, *Province of Freedom*, 244.

26. Fyfe, *History of Sierra Leone*, 389.

27. For a detailed biography of Blyden, see Edith Holden, *Blyden of Liberia: An Account of the Life and Labors of Edward Wilmot Blyden, LL.D.* (New York: Vantage Press, 1967); and also Hollis R. Lynch, *Edward Wilmot Blyden, Pan-Negro Patriot, 1832–1912* (London: Oxford University Press, 1967),

28. Robert W. July, *A History of the African People*, 4th ed. (New York: Scribner, 1964), 297.

29. Fyfe, *History of Sierra Leone*, 385.

30. CA1/047, Blyden to Venn, 24 August 1871, CMS.

31. Ibid.

32. Fyfe, *History of Sierra Leone*, 385.

33. Thomas W. Livingston, *Education and Race: A Biography of Edward Wilmot Blyden* (San Francisco: Glendessary Press, 1975), 212.

34. Livingston, *Education and Race*, 160.

35. CA1/047, Blyden to Venn, 6 September 1871, CMS.

36. Ibid. Blyden had already been given the sobriquet of Abdul Kareem by the scholars of the interior states.

37. Livingston, *Education and Race*, 212.

38. CA1/047, Blyden to Venn, 6 September 1871, CMS .

39. CA1/047/8, Blyden's Journal, 27 December 1871, Sierra Leone, CMS.

40. CA1/047/20A, Blyden to Venn, Freetown, 27 April 1871, CMS.

41. Fyfe, *History of Sierra Leone*, 389.

42. Lynch, *Black Spokesman*.

43. Harrell-Bond, Howard, and Skinner, *Community Leadership*, 123.

44. Livingston, *Education and Race*, 161.

45. B. B. Ibrahim, *Fourah Bay: The First Hundred Years, 1836–1936*, a pamphlet presented at the launching of the Fourah Bay Community Foundation, Freetown, 11 April 1993, 20.

46. *Sierra Leone Weekly News* (SLWN), 29 April 1899, SLA.

47. Fyfe, History of Sierra Leone, 498.

48. *SLWN*, 3 January 1899, SLA.

49. *SLWN*, 29 August 1899, SLA.

50. Ibid.

51. Livingston, *Education and Race*, 170.

52. *SLWN*, 10 January 1903, SLA; see also Muctarr J. A. Lewally-Taylor, "The Aku Muslim Communities of East Freetown in the Nineteenth and Twentieth Centuries" (MLitt thesis, University of Edinburgh, 1976), 264.

53. Governor's Letter Book, Blyden to King-Harman, 29 April 1901, Freetown, SLA.

54. Ibid.

55. Ibid.

56. Livingston, *Education and Race*, 181.

57. Letter of Resignation of E. W. Blyden, 31 December 1904, SLA.

58. Ibid., no. 53, SLA.

59. Barbara Bair, "Pan-Africanism as Process: Adelaide Casely Hayford, Garveyism, and the Cultural Roots of Nationalism," in *Imagining Home: Class, Culture and Nationalism in the African Diaspora*, ed. Sidney E. Lemelle and Robin D. G. Kelley (New York: Verso, 1994), 122.

POSTSCRIPT

1. Jean Comaroff and John L. Comaroff, *Of Revelation and Revolution*, vol. 1, *Christianity, Colonialism, and Consciousness in South Africa* (Chicago: University of Chicago Press, 1991), 310.

2. Edward W. Blyden, *Christianity, Islam and the Negro Race*, 2nd ed. (London: Whittingham, 1887; Baltimore: Black Classic Press, 1994).

3. Kwame Nkrumah, *Consciencism: Philosophy and Ideology for De-Colonization* (London: Heinemann, 1964).

4. Ali A. Mazrui, *The Africans: A Triple Heritage* (New York: Little, Brown, 1987).

5. Arthur Abraham. "Bai Bureh, the British, and the Hut Tax War," *International Journal of African Historical Studies* 7, no. 1 (1974): 99–106.

6. See John D. Hargreaves, "The Establishment of the Sierra Leone Protectorate and the Insurrection of 1898," *Cambridge Historical Journal* 12, no. 1 (January 1956): 56–80.

7. Stephen Frenkel and John Western, "Pretext or Prophylaxis? Racial Segregation and Malarial Mosquitos in a British Tropical Colony: Sierra Leone," *Annals of the Association of American Geographers* 78, no. 2 (June 1988): 211–28.

8. See John R. Cartwright, *Politics in Sierra Leone, 1947–67* (Toronto: University of Toronto Press, 1970).

9. *West Africa*, 20 October 1945.

Bibliography

UNPUBLISHED ARCHIVAL SOURCES

Sierra Leone Archives (Fourah Bay College, University of Sierra Leone):
   Annie Walsh Memorial School Register, 1849–1995
   CMS Grammar School Register 1849–1995
Colonial Secretary's Letter Book
Department of Mohammedan Education Minute Papers
Government Interpreter's Letter Books
Governor's Letter Book
Liberated Africans Letter Book
Liberated Africans Register
Local Letters Received
Local Minute Papers
Register of Alien Children
Sierra Leone Blue Book
Sierra Leone Government Gazette

NEWSPAPERS

(copies found in the Sierra Leone Archives are also available at the British Library
Newspaper Annex in Colindale, England):
Artisan
Methodist Herald
Negro
Saturday Ho!
Sierra Leone Church Times
Sierra Leone Watchman
Sierra Leone Weekly News
Sierra Leone Weekly Times
Trader
West Africa

PUBLIC RECORD OFFICE

(London, England):
CO267 1787–1900: Dispatches from the Colony of Sierra Leone, including letters and

other documents sent by governors and other colonial officials in Sierra Leone to
the Colonial Office in London, England

CO268: Entry books, correspondence, and warrants
CO269: Colonial government decrees
CO270: Sessional papers, Sierra Leone
CO271: Sierra Leone Government Gazette
CO272: Sierra Leone Government Blue Book
CO323: Private papers of R. W. Hay
CO806: Confidential prints
FO804: Courts of mixed commission

CHURCH MISSIONARY SOCIETY (CMS)

Archives (University of Birmingham, UK):

CA1/E 0105–95: These documents include records of the CMS West African mission,
1808–1934; journals of CMS clergymen; and letters and reports from missionaries in
Freetown and the rural villages of the colony to the Central Committee in London.

BOOKS, ARTICLES, AND PAMPHLETS

Abraham, Arthur. "Bai Bureh, the British, and the Hut Tax War." *International Journal
of African Historical Studies* 7, no. 1 (1974): 99–106.

———. *An Introduction to the Pre-Colonial History of the Mende of Sierra Leone.*
Lewiston, NY: Edwin Mellen Press, 2003.

———. *Mende Government and Politics under Colonial Rule: A Historical Study of Political
Change in Sierra Leone, 1890–1937.* Freetown: Sierra Leone University Press, 1978.

———, ed. *Topics in Sierra Leone History: A Counter-Colonial Interpretation.* Freetown:
Sierra Leone Publishers, 1976.

Achebe, Chinua. *Things Fall Apart.* London: Heinemann, 1962.

Adefuye, Ade. "Oba Akinsemoyin and the Emergence of Modern Lagos." In Adefuye,
Agiri, and Osuntokun, *History of the Peoples of Lagos State*, 33–46.

Adefuye, Ade, Babatunde Agiri, and Akinjide Osuntokun, eds. *History of the Peoples of
Lagos State.* Lagos: Lantern Books, 1987.

Ajayi, J. F. Ade, ed. *Africa in the Nineteenth Century until the 1880s.* Vol. 6 of *General
History of Africa.* Berkeley: University of California Press, 1985.

———. "The Aftermath of the Fall of Old Oyo." In Ajayi and Crowder, *History of West
Africa*, 2:129–66.

———. *Christian Missions in Nigeria, 1841–1891: The Making of a New Elite.* London:
Longman, 1965.

———. "Samuel Adjai Crowther of Oyo." In *Africa Remembered: Narratives by West
Africans from the Era of the Slave Trade*, edited by Philip D. Curtin (Madison:
University of Wisconsin Press, 1967): 289–316.

Ajayi, J. F. Ade, and Michael Crowder, eds. *History of West Africa.* 2 vols. London:
Longman, 1974.

Ajayi, J. F. Ade, and Robert Smith. *Yoruba Warfare in the Nineteenth Century.* Ibadan,
Nigeria: Ibadan University Press, 1971.

Akinjogbin, I. A. "The Expansion of Oyo and the Rise of Dahomey, 1600–1800." In Ajayi and Crowder, *History of West Africa*, 1:305–43.

Akyeampong, Emmanuel K. *Between the Sea and the Lagoon: An Eco-Social History of the Anlo of Southeastern Ghana, c. 1850 to Recent Times*. Athens: Ohio University Press, 2001.

Alharazim, M. S. D. "The Origins and Progress of Islam in Sierra Leone." *Sierra Leone Studies*, o.s., no. 21 (January 1939): 13–26.

Ali, Ahmed. *Al-Qur'an: A Contemporary Translation*. Princeton, NJ: Princeton University Press, 2001.

Anthony, Farid R. *Sawpit Boy*. Freetown: published by author, 1980.

Apter, Andrew. *Black Critics and Kings: The Hermeneutics of Power in Yoruba Society*. Chicago: University of Chicago Press, 1992.

Asiegbu, Johnson U. J. *Slavery and the Politics of Liberation, 1787–1861: A Study of Liberated African Emigration and British Anti-Slavery Policy*. New York: Africana Publishing, 1969.

Ayandele, E. A. *The Missionary Impact on Modern Nigeria, 1842–1914: A Political and Social Analysis*. London: Longman, 1966.

Bair, Barbara. "Pan-Africanism as Process: Adelaide Casely Hayford, Garveyism, and the Cultural Roots of Nationalism." In *Imagining Home: Class, Culture and Nationalism in the African Diaspora*, edited by Sidney E. Lemelle and Robin D. G. Kelley, 121–44. New York: Verso, 1994.

Banton, Michael P. "The Origins of Tribal Administration in Freetown." *Sierra Leone Studies*, n.s., no. 2 (June 1954): 109–19.

——. *West African City: A Study of Tribal Life in Freetown*. London: Oxford University Press, 1957.

Barber, Karin. "How Man Makes God in West Africa: Yoruba Attitudes towards the Orisa." *Africa* 51, no. 3 (1981): 724–45.

Barnes, Sandra T., ed. *Africa's Ogun: Old World and New*. Bloomington: Indiana University Press, 1997.

Barry, Boubacar. *Senegambia and the Atlantic Slave Trade*. Cambridge: Cambridge University Press, 1988.

Bassir, Olumbe. "Marriage Rites Among the Aku (Yoruba) of Freetown." *Africa* 24, no. 3 (July 1954): 251–56.

Batran, A. A. "The Nineteenth-Century Islamic Revolutions in West Africa." In Ajayi, *Africa in the Nineteenth Century Until the 1880s*, 537–54.

Berman, Bruce, and John Lonsdale. *Unhappy Valley: Conflict in Kenya and Africa*. Bk. 2. (Athens: Ohio University Press, 1992).

Bernabé, Jean, Patrick Chamoiseau, and Raphaël Confiant. Éloge de la Créolité. Paris: Gallimard, 1989.

Berry, J. "The Origins of Krio Vocabulary." *Sierra Leone Studies*, n.s., no. 12 (December 1959): 298–307.

Biobaku, Saburi O. *The Egba and Their Neighbours, 1842–1872*. Ibadan, Nigeria: Ibadan University Press, 1991.

Blyden, Edward W. *Christianity, Islam and the Negro Race*. 2nd ed. London: Whittingham, 1887; Baltimore: Black Classic Press, 1994.

Bolt, Christine, and Seymour Drescher, eds. *Anti-Slavery, Religion, and Reform: Essays in Memory of Roger Anstey*. Folkestone, Kent: Dawson, 1980.

Bradshaw, A. T. Von S. "A List of Yoruba words in Krio." *Sierra Leone Studies* 5 (November 1966): 61–71.

Braidwood, Stephen J. *Black Poor and White Philanthropists: London's Blacks and the Foundation of the Sierra Leone Settlement: 1786–1791*. Liverpool: Liverpool University Press, 1994.

———. "Initiatives and Organization of the Black Poor, 1786–1787." *Slavery and Abolition* 3, no. 3 (December 1982).

Brathwaite, Edward Kamau. *The Development of Creole Society in Jamaica, 1770–1820*. Oxford: Clarendon Press, 1971.

Brooks, George E. *Eurafricans in Western Africa: Commerce, Social Status, Gender, and Religious Observance from the Sixteenth to the Eighteenth Century*. Athens: Ohio University Press, 2003.

Brubaker, Rogers. *Ethnicity without Groups*. Cambridge, MA: Harvard University Press, 2004.

Campbell, Mavis C. *Back to Africa: George Ross and the Maroons, from Nova Scotia to Sierra Leone*. Trenton, NJ: Africa World Press, 1993.

Cartwright, John R. *Politics in Sierra Leone, 1947–67*. Toronto: University of Toronto Press, 1970.

Chaudenson, Robert. *Creolization of Language and Culture*. London: Routledge, 2001.

Cole, Gibril R. "Embracing Islam and African Traditions in a British Colony: The Muslim Krios of Sierra Leone, 1787–1910." PhD diss., University of California, Los Angeles, 2000.

———. "Liberated Slaves and Islam in Nineteenth-Century West Africa." In Falola and Childs, *The Yoruba Diaspora in the Atlantic World*, 383–403.

———. "Re-thinking the Demographic Make-up of Krio Society." In Dixon-Fyle and Cole, *New Perspectives*, 33–51.

Cole, Robert Wellesley. *Kossoh Town Boy*. Cambridge: Cambridge University Press, 1960.

Comaroff, Jean, and John L. Comaroff. *Of Revelation and Revolution*. Vol. 1, *Christianity, Colonialism, and Consciousness in South Africa*. Chicago: University of Chicago Press, 1991.

Cooper, Frederick. *Colonialism in Question: Theory, Knowledge, History*. Berkeley: University of California Press, 2005.

———, and Rogers Brubaker. "Identity." In *Colonialism in Question*, 59–90.

Cox-George, N. A. "Direct Taxation in the Early History of Sierra Leone." *Sierra Leone Studies*, n.s., no. 5 (1955): 20–35.

Crooks, J. J. A *History of the Colony of Sierra Leone, West Africa*. London: Browne and Nolan, 1903.

Crowder, Michael. *West Africa under Colonial Rule*. London: Hutchinson, 1968.

Crowther, Samuel A. *Vocabulary of the Yoruba Language*. London: Church Missionary Society, 1843.

Curtin, Philip D., ed. *Africa and the West: Intellectual Responses to European Culture*. Madison: University of Wisconsin Press, 1972.

———. "African Reactions in Perspective." In *Africa and the West*, 231–44.

———. "The Atlantic Slave Trade, 1600–1800." In Ajayi and Crowder, *History of West Africa*, 1:240–68.

———. *Economic Change in Pre-Colonial Africa: Senegambia in the Era of the Slave Trade.* Madison: University of Wisconsin Press, 1975.

Davidson, J. "Creole or Sierra Leonean: Some Evidence from 1898." *Sierra Leone Studies* (1985): 5–13.

Decker, Thomas. "The Krios of Sierra Leone." *African World* (July 1948): 9–10.

Deighton, F. C. "Origins of Creole Plant Names." *Sierra Leone Studies*, o.s., no. 22 (September 1939): 29–32.

Denzer, LaRay, and Michael Crowder. "Bai Bureh and the Sierra Léone Hut Tax War of 1898." In *Protest and Power in Black Africa*, edited by Robert I. Rotberg and Ali A. Mazrui, 169–212. New York: Oxford University Press, 1970.

Dike, Kenneth O. *Trade and Politics in the Niger Delta, 1830–1885.* Oxford: Clarendon, 1956.

Dioka, L. C. *Lagos and Its Environs.* Lagos: First Academic Publishers, 2001.

Division at Fourah Bay. Sierra Leone Collection. Freetown: Fourah Bay College, n.d. Pamphlet.

Dixon-Fyle, Mac. *A Saro Community in the Niger Delta, 1912–1984: The Potts-Johnsons of Port Harcourt and Their Heirs.* Rochester, NY: Rochester University Press, 1999.

Dixon-Fyle, Mac, and Gibril Cole, eds. *New Perspectives on the Sierra Leone Krio.* New York: Peter Lang, 2006.

Drewal, Henry John, and Margaret Thompson Drewal. *Gelede: Art and Female Power among the Yoruba.* Bloomington: Indiana University Press, 1990.

Elaigwu, J. Isawa, and Ali A. Mazrui, "Nation-Building and Changing Political Structures." In *Africa since 1935*, edited by Ali A. Mazrui, 435–67. Vol. 8 of *General History of Africa*. Berkeley: University of California Press, 1999.

El Fasi, M., and I. Hrbek. "The Coming of Islam and the Expansion of the Muslim Empire." In *Africa from the Seventh to the Eleventh Century*, edited by M. El Fasi and I. Hrbek, 16–30. Vol. 3 of *General History of Africa*. Berkeley: University of California Press, 1988.

Eliasii, M. A. Haleem. *The Holy Quran: Transliteration in Roman Script.* New Delhi: Kitab Bhavan, 1978.

Eltis, David. "The Diaspora of Yoruba Speakers, 1650–1865: Dimensions and Implications." In Falola and Childs, *The Yoruba Diaspora in the Atlantic World*, 17–39.

Eltis, David, and David Richardson, eds. Voyages: The Trans-Atlantic Slave Trade Database. Atlanta, GA: Emory University, 2008, 2009. http://www.slavevoyages.org.

Eltis, David, and James Walvin, eds. *The Abolition of the Slave Trade: Origins and Effects in Europe, Africa, and the Americas.* Madison: University of Wisconsin Press, 1981.

Enwezor, Okwui, Carlos Basualdo, Ute Meta Bauer, Susanne Ghez, Sarat Maharaj, Mark Nash, and Octavio Zaya, eds. *Créolité and Creolization, Documenta 11, Platform 3.* Osterfildern-Ruit: Hotje Cantz, 2002.

Esedebe, Peter O. *Pan-Africanism: The Idea and Movement, 1776–1963.* Washington, DC: Howard University Press, 1982.

Esposito, John L., ed. *The Oxford History of Islam.* Oxford: Oxford University Press, 2000.

Euba, Titilola. "Shitta Bey and the Lagos Muslim Community, 1850–1895." Pt. 2. *Nigerian Journal of Islam* 2, no. 2 (June 1972–June 1974): 7–18.

Falola, Toyin, and Matt D. Childs, eds. *The Yoruba Diaspora in the Atlantic World.* Bloomington: Indiana University Press, 2004.

Fashole-Luke, E. W. "Christianity and Islam in Freetown." *Sierra Leone Bulletin of Religion* 9, no. 1 (June 1967): 1–16.

——. "Religion in Freetown." In Fyfe and Jones, *Freetown*, 127–42.

Flint, J. E. "Economic Change in West Africa in the Nineteenth Century". In Ajayi and Crowder, *History of West Africa*, 2:380–401.

Fox, William. *A Brief History of the Wesleyan Missions on the Western Coast of Africa.* London: Aylott and Jones, 1851.

Frazier, E. Franklin. *The Negro Family in the United States.* Chicago: University of Chicago Press, 1966.

Frenkel, Stephen, and John Western, "Pretext or Prophylaxis? Racial Segregation and Malarial Mosquitos in a British Tropical Colony: Sierra Leone." *Annals of the Association of American Geographers* 78, no. 2 (June 1988): 211–28.

Fyfe, Christopher. "Akintola Wyse: Creator of the Krio Myth." In Dixon-Fyle and Cole, *New Perspectives*, 25–32.

——. "European and Creole Influence in the Hinterland of Sierra Leone before 1896." *Sierra Leone Studies* 6 (June 1956): 77–85.

——. *A History of Sierra Leone.* Oxford: Oxford University Press, 1962.

——. "Reform in West Africa: The Abolition of the Slave Trade". In Ajayi and Crowder, *History of West Africa*, 2:30–56.

——. *A Short History of Sierra Leone.* London: Longman, 1962.

——. *Sierra Leone Inheritance.* London: Oxford University Press, 1964.

——. "Thomas Peters: History and Legend." *Sierra Leone Studies* 1 (December 1953): 4–13.

Fyfe, Christopher, and Eldred Jones, eds. *Freetown: A Symposium.* Freetown: Sierra Leone University Press, 1968.

Fyle, Clifford N. "Krio Ways of Thought and Expression." *Africana Research Bulletin* 3, no. 1 (1972).

Fyle, Clifford N., and Eldred D. Jones. *A Krio-English Dictionary.* Oxford: Oxford University Press, 1980.

Fyle, C. Magbaily. *The History of Sierra Leone: A Concise Introduction.* London: Evans, 1981.

——. "The Kabala-Complex: Koranko-Limba Relationship in Nineteenth-Century Sierra Leone." In Abraham, *Topics in Sierra Leone History*, 104–19.

——. "Popular Islam and Political Expression in Sierra Leone." In Jalloh and Skinner, *Islam and Trade in Sierra Leone*, 161–77.

——. *The Solima Yalunka Kingdom: Pre-Colonial Politics, Economics, and Society.* Freetown: Nyakon, 1979.

Gbadamosi, T. G. O. *The Growth of Islam among the Yoruba, 1841–1908.* London: Longman, 1978.

Ghazali, Abdul K. "Sierra Leone Muslims and Sacrificial Rituals." *Sierra Leone Bulletin of Religion* 2, no. 1 (June 1960): 27–32.

Glissant, Edouard. *Caribbean Discourse: Selected Essays.* Translated by J. Michael Dash. Charlottesville: University of Virginia Press, 1999.

Goerg, Odile. "Between Everyday Life and Exception: Celebrating Pope-Hennessy Day in Freetown, 1872–c1905." *Journal of African Cultural Studies* 15, no. 1 (2002): 119–31.

———. "Sierra Leonais, Creoles, Krio: La Dialectique de L'Identite." *Africa* 65, no. 1 (1995): 114–32.

Goodstein, Laurie. "Across Nation, Mosque Projects Meet Opposition." *New York Times*, August 7, 2010.

———. "Islam: Not in My Backyard?" *New York Times Upfront* 143 (September 2010).

Gueye, M'baye, and A. Adu Boahen. "African Initiatives and Resistance in West Africa, 1880–1914." In *Africa Under Colonial Domination, 1880–1935*, edited by A. Adu Boahen, 114–48. Vol. 3 of *General History of Africa*. Berkeley: University of California Press, 1985.

Hair, Paul E. H. "An Analysis of the Register of Fourah Bay College, 1827–1950." *Sierra Leone Studies* 7 (1956): 155–60.

———. "Colonial Freetown and the Study of African Languages." In Last and Richards, *Sierra Leone*, 560–65.

Hall, Gwendolyn Midlo. *Africans in Colonial Louisiana: The Development of Afro-Creole Culture in the Eighteenth Century*. Baton Rouge: Louisiana State University Press, 1992.

Hannerz, Ulf. "The World in Creolisation." *Africa* 57, no. 4 (1987): 546–59.

Hargreaves, John D. "Another Creole Frontier: The Upper Senegal, 1889." *Journal of the Historical Society of Sierra Leone* 1, no. 2 (June 1977).

———. "The Establishment of the Sierra Leone Protectorate and the Insurrection of 1898." *Cambridge Historical Journal* 12, no. 1 (January 1956): 56–80.

———. *A Life of Sir Samuel Lewis*. London: Oxford University Press, 1958.

Harrell-Bond, Barbara E., Allen M. Howard, and David E. Skinner. *Community Leadership and the Transformation of Freetown, 1801–1976*. The Hague: Mouton, 1978.

Harris, John M. *Annexations to Sierra Leone, and Their Influence on British Trade with West Africa*. London: Berridge, 1883.

Harunah, Hakeem B. "Lagos-Abeokuta Relations in Nineteenth Century Yorubaland." In Adefuye, Agiri, and Osuntokun, *History of the Peoples of Lagos State*.

Herskovits, Jean. "The Sierra Leoneans of Yorubaland." In Curtin, *Africa and the West*, 75–98.

Herskovits, Melville J. *The Myth of the Negro Past*. Boston: Beacon, 1958.

Heywood, Linda M., and John K. Thornton. *Central Africans, Atlantic Creoles, and the Foundation of the Americas, 1585–1660*. Cambridge: Cambridge University Press, 2007.

Hodgson, Marshall G. S. *The Venture of Islam*. Vol. 1, *The Classical Age of Islam*. Chicago: University of Chicago Press, 1974.

Holden, Edith. *Blyden of Liberia: An Account of the Life and Labors of Edward Wilmot Blyden, LL.D.* New York: Vantage Press, 1967.

Holt, Peter M., Ann K. S. Lambton, and Bernard Lewis, eds. *The Cambridge History of Islam*. 4 vols. Cambridge: Cambridge University Press, 1977.

Howard, Allen M. "Contesting Commercial Space in Freetown, 1860–1930: Traders, Merchants, and Officials." *Canadian Journal of African Studies* 37 (2003): 236–68.

———. "The Relevance of Spatial Analysis for African Economic History: The Sierra Leone–Guinea System." *Journal of African History* 17, no. 3 (1976): 365–88.

———. "Trade and Islam in Sierra Leone, 18th–20th Centuries." In Jalloh and Skinner, *Islam and Trade*, 21–63.

Howard, Rosalyn. "Yoruba in the British Caribbean: A Comparative Perspective on

Trinidad and the Bahamas." In Falola and Childs, *The Yoruba Diaspora in the Atlantic World*, 157–76.

Huntington, Samuel P. *The Clash of Civilizations and the Remaking of World Order.* New York: Simon & Schuster, 1996.

Ibrahim, B. B. *Fourah Bay: The First Hundred Years, 1836–1936.* April 11, 1993. Pamphlet.

Jalloh, Alusine, and David E. Skinner, eds. *Islam and Trade in Sierra Leone.* Trenton, NJ: Africa World Press, 1997.

Jones, Eldred D. "Some Aspects of the Sierra Leone Patois or Krio." *Sierra Leone Studies*, n.s., 6 (June 1956): 97–109.

Jones Brothers. *Early History of the Trade of Sierra Leone before the Advent of the Railway System in 1896.* Sierra Leone Collection. Freetown: Fourah Bay College Library, n.d. Pamphlet.

July, Robert W. *A History of the African People.* 4th ed. New York: Scribner, 1964.

Knörr, Jacqueline. "Towards Conceptualizing Creolization and Creoleness." Working Paper, Max Planck Institute for Social Anthropology, Halle (Saale), Germany, 2008.

Koelle, Sigismund W. *Polyglotta Africana.* London: Church Missionary Society, 1854.

Kopytoff, Jean H. *A Preface to Modern Nigeria: The "Sierra Leonians" in Yoruba, 1830–1890.* Madison: University of Wisconsin Press, 1965.

Kup, Alexander P. *Sierra Leone: A Concise History.* London: David & Charles, 1975.

Lapidus, Ira M. *A History of Islamic Societies.* Cambridge: Cambridge University Press, 1988.

Last, Murray. "The Sokoto Caliphate and Borno." In Ajayi, *Africa in the Nineteenth Century Until the 1880s*, 545–59.

Last, Murray, and Paul Richards, eds. *Sierra Leone, 1787–1987: Two Centuries of Intellectual Life.* Manchester: Manchester University Press, 1987.

Law, Robin. "Ethnicity and the Slave Trade: 'Lucumi' and 'Nago' as Ethnonyms in West Africa." *History in Africa* 24 (1997): 205–19.

———. "Yoruba Liberated Slaves Who Returned to West Africa." In Falola and Childs, *The Yoruba Diaspora in the Atlantic World*, 349–65.

Lawal, Babatunde. "Reclaiming the Past: Yoruba Elements in African American Arts." In Falola and Childs, *The Yoruba Diaspora in the Atlantic World*, 291–324.

Lawrence, John H. *Creole Houses: Traditional Homes of Old Louisiana.* New York: Abrams, 2007.

Levtzion, Nehemiah. "Islam in the Bilad al-Sudan to 1800." In *The History of Islam in Africa*, edited by Nehemiah Levtzion and Randall L. Pouwels, 63–91. Athens: Ohio University Press, 2000.

Lewally-Taylor, Muctarr J. A. "The Aku Muslim Communities of East Freetown in the Nineteenth and Twentieth Centuries." MLitt thesis, University of Edinburgh, 1976.

Little, Kenneth. *The Mende of Sierra Leone: A West African People in Transition.* London: Routledge and Kegan Paul, 1967.

Livingston, Thomas W. *Education and Race: A Biography of Edward Wilmot Blyden.* San Francisco: Glendessary Press, 1975.

Lovejoy, Paul E. "The Yoruba Factor in the Trans-Atlantic Slave Trade." In Falola and Childs, *The Yoruba Diaspora in the Atlantic World*, 40–55.

Lynch, Hollis R. *Edward Wilmot Blyden, Pan-Negro Patriot, 1832–1912.* London: Oxford University Press, 1967.

————, ed. *Black Spokesman: Selected Published Writings of Edward Wilmot Blyden.* London: Frank Cass, 1971.

Lynn, Martin. "Technology, Trade and 'A Race of Native Capitalists': The Krio Diaspora of West Africa and the Steamship, 1852–95." *Journal of African History* 33 (1992): 421–40.

Mafeje, Archie. "The Ideology of 'Tribalism,'" *Journal of Modern African Studies* 9, no. 2 (1971): 253–61.

Mamdani, Mahmood. *Citizen and Subject: Contemporary Africa and the Legacy of Late Colonialism.* Princeton, NJ: Princeton University Press, 1996.

————. "Race and Ethnicity as Political Identities in the African Context." In *Keywords: Identity*, edited by Nadia Tazi, New York: Other Press, 2004; 1-23.

————. *Saviors and Survivors: Darfur, Politics, and the War on Terror.* New York: Pantheon Books, 2009.

Matory, J. Lorand. *Black Atlantic Religion: Tradition, Transnationalism, and Matriarchy in the Afro-Brazilian Candomblé.* Princeton, NJ: Princeton University Press, 2005.

Mazrui, Ali A. *The Africans: A Triple Heritage.* (New York: Little, Brown, 1987).

Mba, Nina. "Women in Lagos Political History." In Adefuye, Agiri, and Osuntokun, *History of the Peoples of Lagos State,* 233–45.

Mbiti, John S. *African Religions and Philosophy.* London: Heinemann, 1969.

Mudimbe, V. Y. *The Invention of Africa: Gnosis, Philosophy, and the Order of Knowledge.* Bloomington: Indiana University Press, 1988.

Nasr, Seyyed Hussein. *Islam: Religion, History, and Civilization.* New York: HarperCollins, 2002.

Newland, H. Osman. *Sierra Leone: Its People, Products, and Secret Societies.* London: John Bale, Sons & Danielsson,, 1916.

Nicol, Charles K. O. "Origins and Orthography of the Kriyo Language." *West African Review* (August 1949).

Nkrumah, Kwame. *Consciencism: Philosophy and Ideology for De-Colonization.* London: Heinemann, 1964.

Nunley, John W. *Moving with the Face of the Devil: Art and Politics in Urban West Africa.* Chicago: University of Illinois Press, 1987.

Osuntokun, Akijide. "Introduction of Christianity and Islam in Lagos State." In Adefuye, Agiri, and Osuntokun, *History of the Peoples of Lagos State,* 126–38.

Otero, Solimar. *Afro-Cuban Diasporas in the Atlantic World.* Rochester, NY: University of Rochester Press, 2010.

Othman, Ramatoulie O. *A Cherished Heritage: Tracing the Roots of the Oku-Marabou—Early 19th to Mid-20th Century.* Banjul, Gambia: Edward Francis Small, 1999. Pamphlet.

Parés, Luis Nicolau. "The 'Nagôization' Process in Bahian Candomblé." In Falola and Childs, *The Yoruba Diaspora in the Atlantic World,* 185–208.

Peel, J. D. Y. "A Comparative Analysis of Ogun in Precolonial Yorubaland." In Barnes, *Africa's Ogun,* 263–89.

————. *Religious Encounter and the Making of the Yoruba.* Bloomington: Indiana University Press, 2003.

Person, Yves. *Samori: Une Revolution Dyula.* 3 vols. Dakar, Senegal: IFAN, 1968–75.

Peterson, John. *Province of Freedom: A History of Sierra Leone, 1787–1870.* Evanston, IL: Northwestern University Press, 1969.

——. "The Sierra Leone Creole: A Reappraisal." In Fyfe and Jones, *Freetown*, 100–117.

Porter, Arthur T. *Creoledom: A Study of the Development of Freetown Society*. Oxford: Oxford University Press, 1963.

——. "Religious Affiliation in Freetown, Sierra Leone." *Africa* 23, no. 1 (1953): 3–14.

Proudfoot, Leslie. "The Fourah Bay Dispute. An Aku Faction Fight in East Freetown." *Sierra Leone Bulletin of Religion* 4 (December 1962): 75–88.

——. "Mosque Building and Tribal Separatism in Freetown East." *Africa* 29, no. 4 (1959): 405–16.

——. *Towards Muslim Solidarity in Freetown*. Sierra Leone Collection. Freetown: Fourah Bay College Library, n.d. Pamphlet. Also published in *Africa* 31 (1961).

Ranger, Terrence O. "The Moral Economy of Identity in Northern Matabeleland." In *Ethnicity in Africa: Roots, Meaning and Implications*, edited by Louise de la Gorgendiere, Kenneth King, and Sarah Vaughan, 213–35. Edinburgh: University of Edinburgh Press, 1996.

Reis, Joao José. *Slave Rebellion in Brazil: The Muslim Uprising of 1835 in Bahia*. Translated by Arthur Brakel. Baltimore: Johns Hopkins University Press, 1993.

Reis, Joao José, and Beatriz Gallotti Mamigonian. "Nagô and Mina: The Yoruba Diaspora in Brazil." In Falola and Childs, *The Yoruba Diaspora in the Atlantic World*, 77–110.

Renard, John. 101 *Questions and Answers on Islam*. New York: Gramercy Books, 1998.

Roberts, Richard. "Long Distance Trade and Production: Sinsani in the Nineteenth Century." *Journal of African History* 21, no. 2 (1980): 169–88.

Robinson, Chase F., ed. *The New Cambridge History of Islam*. Vol. 1, *The Formation of the Islamic World, Sixth to Eleventh Centuries*. Cambridge: Cambridge University Press, 2009.

Robinson, David. *Muslim Societies in African History*. Cambridge: Cambridge University Press, 2004.

——. *Paths of Accommodation: Muslim Societies and French Colonial Authorities in Senegal and Mauritania, 1880–1920*. Athens: Ohio University Press, 2000.

Rodney, Walter. *A History of the Upper Guinea Coast, 1545–1800*. Oxford: Clarendon Press, 1970.

Sanneh, Lamin O. *Abolitionists Abroad: American Blacks and the Making of Modern West Africa*. Cambridge, MA: Harvard University Press, 1999.

——. "Historical Source Materials on Islam in Sierra Leone." *Journal of the Historical Society of Sierra Leone* 1, no. 2 (June 1977).

——. *Islamic Consciousness and African Society: An Essay on Historical Interaction*. Sierra Leone Collection. Freetown: Fourah Bay College Library, n.d. Pamphlet.

——. *Piety and Power: Muslims and Christians in West Africa*. New York: Orbis Books, 1996.

Sawyerr, Harry. "The Development of Theology at Fourah Bay College." In *One Hundred Years of University Education in Sierra Leone, 1876–1976*, 1–7. Freetown: Celebrations Committee, 1976.

Schuler, Monica. *"Alas, Alas Kongo": A Social History of Indentured African Immigration into Jamaica, 1841–1865*. Baltimore: Johns Hopkins University Press, 1980.

Sengova, Joko. "Aborigines and Returnees: In Search of Linguistic and Historical Meaning in Delineations of Sierra Leone's Ethnicity and Heritage." In Dixon-Fyle and Cole, *New Perspectives*, 167–99.

Sherwood, Marika. *After Abolition: Britain and the Slave Trade Since 1807*. London: I. B. Tauris, 2007.

Sibthorpe, A. B. C. *The History of Sierra Leone*. London: Frank Cass, 1868.

Skinner, David E. "Islam and Education in the Colony and Hinterland of Sierra Leone (1750–1914)." *Canadian Journal of African Studies* 10, no. 3 (1976): 449–520.

———. "Islam and Trade in Sierra Leone in the Nineteenth Century." PhD diss., University of California, Berkeley, 1971.

———. "Mande Settlement and the Development of Islamic Institutions in Sierra Leone." *International Journal of African Historical Studies* 11 (1978): 32–62.

———. "Sierra Leone Relations with the Northern Rivers and the Influence of Islam in the Colony." *International Journal of Sierra Leone Studies* 1, no. 1 (1988): 91–113.

Skinner, David E., and Barbara E. Harrell-Bond. "Misunderstandings Arising from the Use of the Term 'Creole' in the Literature on Sierra Leone." *Africa* 47, no. 3 (1977): 305–20.

Soyinka, Wole. *Aké: The Years of Childhood*. New York: Vintage, 1989.

Spencer-Walters, Tom. "Creolization and Kriodom: (Re)Visioning the 'Sierra Leone Experiment.'" In Dixon-Fyle and Cole, *New Perspectives*, 223–55.

Spitzer, Leo. *The Creoles of Sierra Leone: Responses to Colonialism, 1870–1945*. Madison: University of Wisconsin Press, 1974.

———. "The Sierra Leone Creoles, 1870–1900." In Curtin, *Africa and the* West, 99–138.

Stewart, Charles, ed. *Creolization: History, Ethnography, Theory*. Walnut Creek, CA: Left Coast Press, 2007.

Temperley, Howard. "Anti-Slavery as a Form of Cultural Imperialism." In Bolt and Drescher, *Anti-Slavery, Religion, and* Reform, 335–50.

Thayer, James S. "A Dissenting View of Creole Culture in Sierra Leone." *Cahiers d'Études Africaines* 31 (1991): 215–30.

Thomas, Ola. *Freetown Muslims in the Nineteenth Century*. Sierra Leone Collection. Freetown: Fourah Bay College Library, n.d.

Trimingham, John S., and Christopher H. Fyfe. "The Early Expansion of Islam in Sierra Leone." *Sierra Leone Bulletin of Religion* 2 (December 1960).

Trust Deed of the Fourah Bay Mosque. Sierra Leone Collection. Freetown: Fourah Bay College Library, n.d. Pamphlet.

Vail, Leroy, ed. *The Creation of Tribalism in Southern Africa*. London: James Currey, 1989.

Walker, James W. St. G. *The Black Loyalists: The Search for a Promised Land in Nova Scotia and Sierra Leone, 1783–1870*. Toronto: University of Toronto Press, 1992.

Webster, James B., and A. Adu Boahen. *The Revolutionary Years: West Africa since 1800*. London: Longman, 1980.

White, E. Frances. "Creole Women Traders in the Nineteenth Century." Working Paper no. 27, African Studies Center, Boston University, 1980.

———. *Sierra Leone's Settler Women Traders: Women on the Afro-European Frontier*. Ann Arbor: University of Michigan Press, 1987.

Williams, John Alden. "Misunderstanding Islam." *New York Times*, September 22, 2012.

Wilson, Ellen G. *The Loyal Blacks*. New York: Putnam, 1976.

Winterbottom, Thomas. *An Account of the Native Africans in the Neighbourhood of Sierra Leone*. London: Whittingham, 1803. Reprint, London: Frank Cass, 1969.

Worger, William H., Nancy L. Clarke, and Edward A. Alpers. *Africa and the West:*

A Documentary History from the Slave Trade to Independence. Phoenix, AZ: Oryx Press, 2001.

Wylie, Kenneth C. *The Political Kingdoms of the Temne: Temne Government in Sierra Leone, 1825–1910.* New York: Africana Publishing, 1977.

Wyse, Akintola J. G. "The Dissolution of Freetown City Council in 1926: A Negative Example of Political Apprenticeship in Colonial Sierra Leone." *Africa* 57, no. 4 (1987): 422–38.

———. "Kriodom: A Maligned Culture." *Journal of the Historical Society of Sierra Leone* 3 (1979): 37–48.

———. *The Krio of Sierra Leone: An Interpretive History.* London: Hurst, 1989.

———. "On Misunderstandings Arising from the Use of the Term 'Creole' in the Literature on Sierra Leone: A Rejoinder." *Africa* 49, no. 4 (1979): 408–17.

———. "Searchlight on the Krio of Sierra Leone: An Ethnographical Study of a West African People." Occasional Paper no. 3, Institute of African Studies, Fourah Bay College, Freetown, 1980.

———. "The Sierra Leone Krios: A Reappraisal from the Perspective of the African Diaspora." In *Global Dimensions of the African Diaspora,* edited by Joseph E. Harris, 309–37. Washington, DC: Howard University Press, 1982.

Young, Robert J. C. "Ethnicity as Otherness in British Identity Politics." In *Beyond Dichotomies: Histories, Identities, Cultures, and the Challenges of Globalization,* edited by Elisabeth Mudimbe-Boyi, 153–67. Albany: State University of New York Press.

Index